M000288632

SFO Personal Investor Series:
PSYCHOLOGY OF TRADING

INTRODUCTION BY:
RUSSELL R. WASENDORF, SR.

EDITED BY:
LAURA SETHER

PUBLISHING

P.O. Box 849, Cedar Falls, Iowa 50613
www.w-apublishing.com

Library of Congress Control Number: 2007929167
ISBN: 978-1-934354-02-5
ISBN-10: 1-934354-02-3

Printed in the United States of America.

10 9 8 7 6 5 4 3 2 1

CONTENTS

INTRODUCTION

BY RUSSELL R. WASENDORF, SR.

"If you don't know who you are, the stock market is an expensive place to find out."

--George Goodman (1959)

Success in trading is a learned activity. Traders who seek success in the markets spend preparatory hours reading, doing homework, studying strategies and methods. Once a trader has honed in on a specific market, time frame, and method that he or she wishes to trade, paper trading and journaling is advised as a way to further refine technique and to avoid unnecessary financial losses. There are myriad strategies and methods that one can employ to profit in the financial market arena. The strategies run the gamut from fundamental to technical and could include a moving average crossover approach, overbought/oversold buy and sell signals, trading off of unexpected economic news and dozens of more methods. The bottom line is that there are many ways to successfully profit within the financial arena. So, then what is the key stumbling block for many?

The answer lies within. Often the difference between a winning trade and a losing trade may not ultimately be the system or method that the trader is employing, but instead one's self. Mental, psychological, and emotional roadblocks can create obstacles that traders must overcome in order to achieve success. Perhaps you've heard the saying that genius is five percent inspiration and ninety-five percent perspiration. When it comes to trading success, a similar analogy could be made with five percent relating to your strategy (once you've done your homework on it) and ninety-five percent to your mental and emotional approach.

> "*Knowing others is intelligence; knowing yourself is true wisdom. Mastering others is strength; mastering yourself is true power.*"
> --Lau Tzu (Shaolin monk, founder of Taoism)

I have found in my thirty years of trading that one of the best things about trading is that it forces one to learn more about one's self. After all what is it that drives markets to bottoms and tops? Fear and greed. Taking profits and taking losses can be intricately tied in with one's emotions, one's method of market discipline, and the mental resolve of sticking with one's pre-planned system of trade entry and exit.

Readers of Jack D. Schwager's *Market Wizards* (Collins, 1993)) may remember the quote from top trader Ed Seykota, "Win or lose, everybody gets what they want out of the market. Some people seem to like to lose, so they win by losing money." At first I know that may seem to be a non-sequitur, as many are drawn to the trading world by the prospects of limitless financial gain and the freedom to trade from anywhere, at any time. But, in order to realize those dreams and goals, there is quite a bit of serious hard work that needs to be accomplished and that includes work on one's own mental and emotional state.

> *Selling a soybean contract is worth two years at Harvard Business School.*
> -Robert Stovall (managing director, Wood Asset Management)

We've all experienced it. The thrill of having a profitable trade on. Do you remember the euphoria, the magnetic pull of the trading screen as you are glued to the market's every uptick and downtick. I once heard someone say that trades are like relationships. It is easy to get into them, but hard to get out. Even taking profits can pose a challenge. If you take them too soon you kick yourself as the market continues to trend in your favor. Or, perhaps the market turns against your position and you convince yourself that it will come back. Many of these problems can solved by doing your homework and creating a trading plan, which includes specific money management rules for profit and loss exit points. From there, however, the individual must feel comfortable and confident enough with the method in order to follow through. Some of the hurdles to success that emerge from there could be psychological or emotional.

Trading is the worst place to express passion, fear, and greed, joy, hope, or for that matter any kind of emotion. Some of the best traders have said they don't get a thrill or jolt of excitement from the completion of a successful trade. Instead, these successful traders seek excitement, thrill, and euphoria in other ways. Trading is a job and it must be treated in that fashion.

As W&A Publishing launches our latest book, a compendium of the best trading psychology articles from *SFO* magazine, we are proud to offer you material that provides practical solutions to real trading problems. All traders confront cognitive and/or emotional habits or tendencies, which can block attempts at successful implementation of a strategy or method. We present you with our best articles that feature cutting-edge information from the field of behavioral finance and the science of the brain, which ultimately can significantly affect one's actions and reactions. Good luck with your study and trading.

Russell R. Wasendorf, Sr., is chairman and CEO of Peregrine Financial Group, Inc., publisher of *SFO,* and author of *The Complete Guide to Single Stock Futures* (McGraw-Hill, 2003) and *All About Futures* (McGraw-Hill, 2000).

SECTION ONE
Types of Trading: What's Right For You?

Many traders believe the key to achieving the top level of success involves mastering technical indicators and important fundamental reports. They spend countless hours and dollars studying advanced wave theory, stochastic indicators, or crop reports. But even if you're a technical or fundamental wizard, you still need to be able to pull the trigger on a trade, execute a stop, and pull out of a losing trade. What's going on in your head is at least as important as the charts—if not more so.

The first step is making sure your trading practice is right for you. Your trading style is as individual as your fingerprints. Your personality, daily schedule, and comfort with risk will say a lot about where you should be investing. What motivates you to trade? Are you a natural day trader or a long-term mutual fund investor? Are you best suited for the forex markets or pork belly futures?

And what makes a great trader? Qualities like smarts, attitude, persistence, and determination are important, but it also requires plenty of practice and hard work. Learning to trade is no different from learning any other high-level activity in life. People learn by doing, and experts are made by immersing themselves in an activity, with structured, hands-on, repetitive practice.

Psychology has made significant strides in understanding how we acquire information and build skills. It's eye-opening for traders in a hurry to achieve. Slow down.

We have also included a trader's self-test to see if you have the personal attributes and potential to become a successful trader. Van Tharp has fashioned his extensive research on the qualities of great traders and investors into an inventory to predict success in the markets. Check it out and see how you measure up.

1

WHAT'S IN YOUR HEAD?

BY BRETT N. STEENBARGER, PhD, AND DOUG FOSTER II

Before we describe the training program that we coordinate at our propri-
etary trading firm, a disclaimer is in order. All too many articles that appear
in trading publications are thinly veiled promotions for the authors' products
or services. Such infomercials must be read with more than the normal grain
of salt. In describing our training program, we are not soliciting applications
from would-be traders, nor are we trying to convince readers to abandon
their day jobs and pursue trading as a full-time occupation. Indeed, as you
will see, we have numerous reasons—based on our experience—for dissuad-
ing people from such courses of action. Instead, we use our training program
to illustrate the learning process involved in the development of trading talent
and the ways in which psychology can facilitate that learning curve.

The field of trading psychology is generally associated with techniques to help traders manage their emotions, improve discipline,
and sharpen decision making. Forgotten, however, is that the science
of psychology began as an experimental discipline to identify principles of learning. Since those pioneering 19th century investigations,
psychology has made significant strides in understanding how we
acquire information and skills. In this first chapter, we will explore
some of these advances and illustrate their implications for the development of trading prowess, drawing upon our experience of coordi-
nating a training program for professional traders.

When we began the training program, we drew upon Brett's experience as a faculty member of a medical school and divided the cur-

riculum into introductory ("internship") and advanced ("residency") phases. A popular phrase that captures the philosophy of medical education is "see one, do one, teach one." The idea is that people learn first by observing, then by supervised doing, and finally by instructing others. It's not that didactics are unimportant—book learning and lectures make up the lion's share of a medical student's first years of education—but when it comes to application, nothing substitutes for the hands-on experience of seeing and doing.

Research in the psychology of learning strongly supports this educational approach. Studies conducted and reviewed by K. Anders Ericsson, PhD, find that the acquisition of expertise in most fields (art, sports, and games of skill such as chess) is a function of deliberative practice. Experts, such as Olympic performers and chess masters, tend to spend far more time than non-experts in structured, goal-oriented practice with feedback. Indeed, University of California, Santa Cruz, researcher Dean Keith Simonton, PhD, cites a wealth of evidence that suggests it takes ten years of such immersion in a discipline before greatness can be achieved. Given this reality, it is clear that no amount of lecture time or reading, in and of itself, can produce a skillful surgeon, artist or trader. One learns surgery by observing surgeons, assisting them, practicing techniques on models, conducting simple procedures, and finally graduating to more challenging ones. Similarly, we find that developing trading proficiency begins with observation and repetitive practice.

The introductory phase of the training program consists of intensive exposure to different trading markets. Although much briefer, it is similar to the educational experience that medical students receive during their initial four years of training. It combines didactic instruction with observation of successful traders and structured hands-on trading experience. Each practice trading session is preceded by a set of objectives for the group to work on, such as limiting the size of losing trades. The feedback at the end of the session then focuses on the traders' ability to meet the objectives.

Master the Elements

Structuring the practice with goals and rapid feedback is essential to the learning process. Research in sports psychology finds that athletes gain significantly more from practice if it includes specific

Having a Mentor

Several factors have convinced us that mentorship is an essential element in the development of trading prowess.

Preparation for unforeseen events: Distributions of price changes in financial markets display fat tails. These unusual events occur much more often than one would expect under conditions of normality. Such events—large swings that occur in the face of news events or out-of-line economic reports—are difficult to prepare for because they occur so infrequently. Experienced mentors can help new traders identify markets that are trading unusually and adjust trading accordingly. Just as attending physicians help medical students identify diseases that don't conform to textbook presentations, senior traders can orient new traders to markets that are moving atypically.

Creation of a constructive learning environment: Traders are by nature competitive and often are unwilling to voice uncertainty, doubt, or discouragement. Mentors provide traders with an open forum to voice ideas about what they may or may not be seeing in the marketplace. They also provide a safe and private setting for constructive criticism in which new traders need not feel threatened or harshly judged.

Support: As trading has increasingly moved from the pit—a very close interpersonal medium—to the screen, it has become difficult for professional traders to benefit from the accumulated wisdom of peer traders. Mentorship was frequently built into the process of becoming a pit trader, as experienced traders would oversee—and even stake—their protégés. This provided substantial support in an environment that was otherwise harsh and competitive. Traders learning their craft on the screen frequently lack this support, yet compete in an environment that is no less challenging.

goals and prompt feedback regarding the meeting of these goals. An interesting set of studies reviewed by Ericsson found that championship chess players rarely played for fun. When they played, it was to study openings, hone their end game, etc. Similarly, passively following markets is unlikely to have the same benefits as directed practice focusing on concrete guidelines for entering and exiting trades.

There may be a second reason why chess masters avoid leisure play. Research summarized by Singer, Hausenblas, and Janelle in their excellent text, *Handbook of Sport Psychology*, 2nd ed. (Wiley,

1991), shows that learning is enhanced by breaking tasks down into component pieces and working systematically upon each. For example, a beginning chess player would not start his or her training by exclusively playing entire games. Rather, there would be a concentrated focus on learning opening moves and strategies, followed by dedicated attention to the middle game, defenses, and endings. Training in the martial arts is similar, where intensive practice of individual movements precedes practice and tournament matches.

Our experience is that beginning traders too often want to learn trading by actually trading. This is similar to the martial arts novice starting with tournament competition. Segmentation of the trading process into component elements, such as pattern recognition, order execution, and trade management—combined with intensive rehearsal of the segments—is far more likely to yield long-term skill acquisition.

It's All about Practice

Research in the *Handbook of Sport Psychology* also notes that simulations are valuable in skill development. A number of trading software programs, such as eSignal, offer simulation modules that allow traders to rehearse strategies in real-time. While such simulation cannot fully capture the pressures of trading with real money on the line, it is an effective bridge between casual paper trading and going live. More importantly, it permits repetitive practice on the aforementioned components of trading—with built-in profit/loss (P/L) feedback.

Lee and colleagues also note that mental rehearsal has been found to produce effective training results in the sports world, especially with respect to the cognitive elements of performance. A trader, for example, can effectively rehearse the mindset he would like to adopt during trading (and his self-instructions during trading) by structuring guided-imagery sessions that simulate a segment of a trading day. Over the course of such practice, new traders learn many things about themselves—how they handle risk and frustration, how they perform under scrutiny, and how well they can stick to basic trading rules. Most important, like medical students, they learn the answers to two questions:

• Do I really want to do this for a living?
• If so, which area of trading would I choose for a specialty?

Finding a Niche

The importance of this latter question cannot be overstated. One sometimes hears that there is no difference between trading one market and
trading another: "trading is trading." Our experience is quite different.
Traders who are successful in one market segment (such as equity indexes) do not necessarily find success tackling another segment (such as
forex). Just as the specialties of medicine involve different combinations
of interests and aptitudes, the various types of trading (scalping, spread
trading, position trading, discretionary trading, systems trading) call
upon unique skill sets. There is no better way to discover the fit between
a trader, trading style, and market than to actually observe one's own
enthusiasm, frustration, and progress across different situations.

The importance of finding a fit between traders and trading styles
and markets also is supported by psychological research. Studies reported by Simonton find that highly successful performers are characterized by an early aptitude and passion for their fields. Traders are
most likely to succeed at trading when they find a niche that piques
their interest and motivation. We find that traders are most likely to
progress in their training if they feel a special affinity for the market
they are trading and the way they trade in it.

Advanced Learning

Once a medical student finishes the initial four years of training, he is not
qualified to practice and, indeed, cannot even obtain a license. Practice
normally begins only after another several years of residency training in
which the new doctor develops proficiency in a specialty.

Just as resident physicians assume greater responsibility as their
training progresses, advanced students of trading start with very small
positions and gradually grow their position sizes. The medical dictum,
"above all else, do no harm," applies equally to new traders. The goal at
the start is to survive one's learning curve. A worthwhile philosophy
for new traders is that a rise in position size must always be justified by
recent trading results. You must earn the right to trade two lots before
abandoning a one-lot default; you must show profitability in simulation
mode before going live. The goal is not to trade, but to trade successfully.

Earlier we mentioned that two questions are answered during
the initial weeks of learning: the desire to be a trader and the area
of trading to be selected as a specialty. One question that is not ad-

Personality Characteristics of Success

Listed below are several of the personality characteristics that researchers have found to be correlated with high degrees of success in a chosen field:

A high degree of belief in oneself D. W. MacKinnon concludes, "The truly creative individual has an image of himself as a responsible person with a sense of destiny about himself as a human being."

Capacity for sustained effort An early investigation by Catharine Cox found that, "youths who achieve eminence are characterized not only by high intellectual traits, but also by persistence of motive and effort, confidence in their abilities, and great strength or force of character."

Aggressiveness Dean Keith Simonton has observed, "Attainment of distinction in any endeavor is a function of both cognitive and motivational traits of character. For both creators and leaders, eminence is a positive function of intelligence and aggressiveness."

Passion for their pursuits Simonton further finds that, "geniuses cannot spend so many hours without an inherent passion for what they do. Therefore, we might do better to say that all the motives that can stimulate the energies of the (creative) human being all converge on a single activity, a monomaniacal preoccupation."

dressed is whether or not aspiring traders actually possess the skills needed to be financially self-supporting as a trader. There is a good reason for this, once again grounded in psychological research. If the development of competence and expertise requires sustained deliberative practice, it is unlikely that students will have enough exposure in a brief time to see a meaningful emergence of skills— especially if the practice is scattered among different skill components and trading specialties. A research program conducted by Dr. Arthur Reber at Brooklyn College found that it took thousands of trial-and-error sequences with immediate feedback before people could learn to recognize and anticipate complex patterns within data. To amass those trials under realistic trading conditions—and to observe the emergence of skill—requires months, not weeks.

Trading is not unique in the length of its learning curve. Studies of young chess masters have found that the single most important predictor of a player's rating is the number of hours spent in serious study and practice. Janet Starkes at McMaster University in Ontario, Canada, and her research colleagues examined the facets of such practice across such domains as figure skating and musical performance. She found that practice was most predictive of success when the practice was associated with high levels of effort and concentration. It is thus the quality of rehearsal—and not just the quantity—that appears to be important in advanced training. One can practice for months under less-than-optimal conditions of a challenge and fail to see meaningful skill development.

Coaching is particularly important in such fields as sports, musical training, and the martial arts. It is very difficult for students to gauge the level of challenge that is sufficient to build skills and yet not so difficult as to generate undue frustration and discouragement. A useful analogy is bodybuilding: setting a weight machine at a setting that is too low will not build strength; setting it too high can promote harm. The most helpful training is often at levels of difficulty that lie just beyond the student's comfort level—a level that can be set and monitored by a coach.

For this reason, formal instruction and supervision is a common feature of advanced learning processes across performance domains. In the trading world, we have similarly found that sitting traders in front of a screen and expecting that they will pick up trading simply by observing markets and trying to trade is not realistic. (Would we sit a new chess player in front of a board and say, "Go at ...it"?) Successful training requires mentorship, which entails a one-to-one relationship that adapts the learning process to the skills and progress of individual traders.

Keeping Records

Traders also can benefit from the collection of data regarding their trading. Such data include basic P/L, but might also incorporate detailed information on trading patterns under varying market conditions. For example, a journal might include not only a summary of trades made during the day, but a description of the market conditions accompanying each of those trades (morning or afternoon, trending or non-trending, high or low volatility). This allows traders to review how successfully they've traded various markets, highlighting both strengths and weaknesses that can form the basis for future learning goals.

There is another subtle benefit to the collection of trading data that is grounded in learning research. The progress that is made by traders is first visible by examining their patterns of trading; only later does it show up as distinct improvements in P/L. To the casual observer, it may look like new traders have made a sudden leap—as if a light bulb went on in their heads—when P/L finally goes green. In fact, however, this is likely the last step in a learning process that first manifests itself in cognitive and behavioral change. This is precisely the same change process that we observe in counseling and psychotherapy. Before depressed people exhibit functional improvement (i.e., gains in their work and relationship functioning) in cognitive therapy, for example, they first change how they process information (monitoring cognitive distortions), and then alter how they respond to life situations (challenging negative assumptions by testing them out in reality). These changes are not immediately observable, but establish an important foundation for visible, behavioral changes at home and in the workplace.

Traders, too, make important internal changes that eventually show up on the bottom line. A trader who loses money during weeks with large wins and large losses has made a valuable change when the size of those oscillations decreases – even if overall weekly P/L remains relatively constant. The reason for this is that the large oscillations are frequently due to expanded holding times that reflect stubbornness in getting out of winning and losing trades. Occasionally, the refusal to take winners will produce large gains, but over time it also produces outsized losses. If the trader makes progress in containing the perfectionism and frustration underlying this stubbornness, those oscillations will dampen.

Lessons for Aspiring Traders

Earlier in the chapter, we explained that we were not trying to recruit traders or encourage people to enter the trading field. There are several reasons for this:

- The learning process does not appear to be any shorter for traders than it is for successful musicians, athletes, or chess players. It is not unusual for significant P/L improvements to take several months to occur, with consistent profitability requiring even more time. Significant effort and plenty of patience are needed to undertake such an effort. Most traders fail at trading for the same reason that dieters fail to lose weight. It is much easier to initiate a directed effort than to sustain it.

• If a professional trading firm with advanced technology and in-house mentors needs significant time to facilitate trader profitability, the odds of traders achieving similar results on their own can be slim indeed. Expecting to develop a high level of competency from a part-time home experience is no more realistic than expecting to become a world-class athlete or musician under similar conditions. It is difficult to identify a single successful athlete, scientist, or artist who accomplished great things without full-time effort and ongoing coaching or instruction.

• The duration of the learning curve means that traders must have unusually deep pockets to sustain the educational process. A significant number of individual traders are poorly capitalized and, indeed, look to trading as a way to make large sums of money relatively quickly. On the contrary, students of the markets can expect a sustained period of time to elapse before they earn a paycheck large enough to cover their living costs and trading expenses. Failure to account for this business reality is a major reason why individual traders experience a low success rate.

• Our experience is that the learning process in trading is not one of a distinct beginning and end. In this sense, it is much like medicine, which requires ongoing education to keep up with ever-changing technological and pharmaceutical advances. Traders whose learning takes place in a bull market find themselves challenged in bear markets; those who grew up with volatility suddenly find themselves trading like rookies in bracketing markets. Success at trading is not just a matter of making oneself successful; it is a continual challenge to remake oneself as markets change. Only an unusual commitment to lifelong development—and a true love of the learning process—can sustain such an effort.

Do You Have What It Takes?

Research conducted by Dr. Arnold Ludwig and reported in his book, *The Price of Greatness* (The Guilford Press, 1996), offers a summary of the factors that account for high levels of achievement in different fields. Among the factors he cites are "special ability, unique talents, and a drive for supremacy" where one is willing to tackle seemingly insurmountable obstacles. This is also what we have detected in our training efforts. Persistence, yoked to specific cognitive and behavioral talents, distinguishes those who progress from those who do not. Training cannot supply talent where there is none, nor can it provide an abiding drive for success. What it can do is channel these forces and mold them into a sustained learning curve. Psychological research suggests that structured practice, prompt feedback, and continuous mentorship catalyze this learning curve across performance fields. These factors cannot guarantee success, but their absence almost surely will result in failure.

Brett N. Steenbarger, PhD, is associate clinical professor of psychiatry and behavioral sciences at SUNY Upstate Medical University in Syracuse, NY. As director of trader development for Kingstree Trading, LLC, in Chicago, he mentors professional traders and coordinates a trader training program. An active trader of the stock indexes, Steenbarger uses statistically based pattern recognition for intra-day trading. The author of *Enhancing Trader Performance: Proven Strategies from the Cutting Edge of Trading Psychology* (Wiley Trading, 2006) and *The Psychology of Trading: Tools and Techniques for Minding the Markets* (Wiley, 2002), Steenbarger maintains a trading archive and blog at www.brettsteenbarger.com and a blog of market analytics at www.traderfeed.blogspot.com.

Doug Foster II is an independent consultant in electronic trading and co-owner of Zoo Trading Group in Chicago, which specializes in technology and new markets. Foster began his career as a fixed income trader at the Chicago Board of Trade. He was one of the early pioneers of electronic trading and assisted in the redesign of the front-end system. Foster previously worked in software technology at EasyScreen, PLC, and at Kingstree Trading, where he created trading tools, managed market vendor services, and managed and trained new traders. Foster studied economics at Loyola University in Chicago. This article originally appeared in *SFO* in July 2005.

SHARPEN YOUR PENCILS:
Take the Trader's Test

BY VAN K. THARP, PhD

Test yourself to see if you have the skills and qualities necessary to become a successful trader. Will you pass with flying colors or fail miserably? Entering into the trading world is very easy. There are no tests to pass. You don't have to demonstrate any special knowledge. All you have to do is have some money and sign some forms to convince your broker that you won't lose so much money that they could have a problem covering your losses. Once you've passed these easy criteria, you can start competing with the many professionals who make their living in the market. The net result, for most people, is usually a very expensive lesson.

By 1982, I'd had three such lessons. In 1962 I purchased my first stock, watching it go from $8 to $20 and then down to zero. Little did I realize that I'd violated almost every fundamental concept that I coach traders and investors on today. About twelve years later, I watched a $20,000 trading account disappear in six months. And in 1982, I discovered that you could lose more than you had accumulated, through margin.

By 1982, I had a PhD in psychology. Perhaps that's what it took for me to realize that there was a pattern to my trading. I'd jump into the markets and my money would disappear quickly. Furthermore, most of my trades were losing trades. Perhaps the results I was getting had something to do with me!

Investment Psychology Inventory

As a result, I began extensive research to determine the qualities that great traders and investors had, qualities that I seemed to lack. By the end of 1982, I had developed a test to measure those qualities in people, a test I called the investment psychology inventory. Over the years, it's proven to be a great predictor of success in the markets.

The complete test has 176 questions, with a number of questions in the ten areas that my research shows is important to investment and trading success. This chapter includes a mini-test to give you a rough idea of where you might stand. Before we discuss the qualities of great traders and investors, it might be helpful for you to do the self-assessment at the end of the chapter.

This mini-test will give you a rough idea of where you stand compared to more than five thousand traders who have taken the full investment psychology inventory. When you finish, use the scoring key in the box on the last page.

Though taking this test provides a measure of your market skills, you are probably interested in a lot more than that. What are your strengths and weaknesses, and how do you compare with some of the best traders in the world?

Qualities of Top Traders and Investors

So what makes a top trader? When I work with people, I start by looking for two qualities: personal responsibility and commitment. People who have these qualities are easy to coach to greatness.

Personal Responsibility. Personal responsibility is probably the most important quality that a top trader or investor can have. It's the core of everything, because as you move through life you can assume either that you create your own results or that things happen to you depending on luck or what others do.

People who assume that they create their own results turn trading into a learning process. They constantly ask themselves, "How did I create that result?" They pinpoint patterns in their behavior that lead to undesirable results. The markets become a university where they can learn how to correct mistakes and improve themselves.

In contrast, people who assume that success is due to luck or other external factors tend to repeat the same mistakes over and over again. For example, during my early trading disasters I felt as if my broker would send signals to Wall Street whenever I did anything so that everyone else could do the opposite. And, of course, I continued to repeat the same mistakes until I decided that my results might in some way be due to my actions. This is a very difficult step for many people to take, but when you take the step, it pays huge dividends.

Commitment. Success in the markets comes when you treat investing and trading like a business. This means you are willing to do the work necessary to develop a business plan and a foundation that will guarantee your success. Building a foundation requires work and study, and it's typically only accomplished by those who are totally committed to doing whatever it takes to be successful. Warren Buffett once said that to become an investor you should know a lot about every listed company. And when someone responded that there were over eight thousand listed companies, Buffett replied, "Start with the A's."

We find that people who are not committed do not do the work necessary for success. They get sidetracked by every little obstacle. And the bottom line for them is usually a lot of trading losses. Think about it. If you are a doctor, an engineer, an IT professional, or any sort of professional, then you had to prove yourself worthy before you could get a job in that profession. While there are no such standards for trading the markets, there are strict standards for success in the markets. Generally the only people who manage to reach success in the markets are very committed people.

When a potential trader has the first two qualities, he can easily learn and adopt the other qualities necessary for success. Each of these depends upon how you think and look at the world (your psychological makeup). Psychology and trading are a lot more related than most people think. So let's look at each quality and why it might predict success:

Low stress and high stress protection. When you are stressed, the body pumps adrenaline into the bloodstream, diverting blood flow from the brain and toward the major muscles. You are now prepared to run from or fight with a predator, but not very prepared to face the market. Since the blood flows away from the brain, your capacity for dealing with complex market information is minimal. When a bevy of stressors bear down and you have little stress protection, the markets can overwhelm you. But with stress protection and few stressors, you can be a master of the markets.

A positive outlook. You don't trade the market. You simply trade your beliefs about the market. For example, if you believe that trend following works in the market, then you will look for trends and figure out how to participate in them. If you believe that value trading works, then you would have trouble with a strong momentum stock simply because you'd think it was overvalued. Instead, you would be looking for undervalued stocks. So whatever you believe tends to shape your trading behavior.

Now what if you had a negative view about the future and your potential for success? People who have that sort of outlook allow that negativity to darken everything they do in trading. If you believe you are going to lose money, then you probably will.

Lack of internal conflict. Lack of conflict is related to the quality of commitment. If you are totally focused on trading success, without any conflict, then you are fully committed. However, each element of conflict that you have will tend to take away from that commitment. So what is conflict? Suppose you want trading success, but don't believe that traders contribute anything to society. Or you feel that by making money in the markets you'll hurt others, and you don't want to hurt others. Or perhaps you want to make a lot of money in the markets, but also believe that money is the root of all evil. Those are all examples of conflicts. The more focused you are on trading success and the fewer conflicts you have, the more likely you are to achieve that success.

Independent thinking. Good traders and investors tend to be independent thinkers. They are not influenced by what their neighbors say, what some guru says on television, or even something that might distract them from their method of trading. Instead, top professionals will have a method that generates low-risk ideas, manages the trade to cut losses short and let profits run, and have a position-sizing algorithm to help them meet their objectives. What someone else says about the market or their positions will not influence them at all.

Efficient decision making. Over the last twenty years psychologists have done extensive research on how people make decisions. Most people, it seems, have numerous decision-making short-cuts that cause them to be very inefficient decision makers. In fact, a new area of economics has sprung up, called behavioral finance, which studies inefficient decision making in financial markets. Psychologist Daniel Kahnemann and economist Amos Tversky won the Nobel prize in economics in 2002 for prospect theory, which, grossly simplified, means that people tend to be risky with losses and conservative with profits. This means that they have trouble following the golden rule of trading, "cut your losses short and let your profits run."

Thus, another quality of top traders and investors is that they hone their decision-making and overcome natural biases to be inefficient decision makers. For example, if you have a strong need to be right on every position or you have a strong need to control the market, you are probably an inefficient decision maker.

Intuitive ability. Most good traders and investors have a great feel for the markets. They spend years studying the markets to develop one or more methods that work well for them. And from that background, they also develop a sixth sense about when something is wrong or different. Does this mean that the best traders and investors are intuitive? No, that's not the case at all. Instead, it means that they have developed a sufficient base of knowledge and skill to effectively manage positions even when something unusual happens.

Impulsive action. Is there a part of you that thinks playing the markets is exciting? You enjoy day trading, getting in the market quickly with the idea of making a quick profit, even though it might turn into a quick loss. There is just something about you that is drawn to the excitement of trading.

Mini-Test of Trading Ability

Answer each question by indicating whether you believe it to be true or false. Think about what typically characterizes your behavior or your beliefs with respect to the market, and use that as the basis for your answers. Be honest!

1. I sell on bad news. ☐ T ☑ F
2. I seldom change my mind about a trade once it is made. ☑ T ☐ F
3. Sometimes I buy just to be active in the markets. ☑ T ☐ F
4. I worry about things more than I should. ☑ T ☐ F
5. My trading rules are written down and reviewed often. ☐ T ☑ F
6. Business always comes before pleasure for me. ☑ T ☐ F
7. A falling stock with a price earnings ratio of 7 is probably a better long-term investment than a rapidly rising stock with a price earnings ratio of 27. ☐ T ☑ F
8. When I get up, I eagerly look forward to the day. ☑ T ☐ F

How did you Score?

If you answered any of the questions with the same answer as below, then circle that answer. In the space at the bottom of this box, enter the number of answers you circled. If you circled question four or eight, score two points for each of those questions.

1. T	3. T	5. F	7. F
2. F	4. T**	6. T	8. F**

**Number of circled questions (counting questions 4 and 8 as two each)_____

Mini-Test of Trading Ability

Answer each question by indicating whether you believe it to be true or false. Think about what typically characterizes your behavior or your beliefs with respect to the market, and use that as the basis for your answers. Be honest!

1. I sell on bad news. ☐ T ☐ F
2. I seldom change my mind about a trade once it is made. ☐ T ☐ F
3. Sometimes I buy just to be active in the markets. ☐ T ☐ F
4. I worry about things more than I should. ☐ T ☐ F
5. My trading rules are written down and reviewed often. ☐ T ☐ F
6. Business always comes before pleasure for me. ☐ T ☐ F
7. A falling stock with a price earnings ratio of 7 is probably a better long-term investment than a rapidly rising stock with a price earnings ratio of 27. ☐ T ☐ F
8. When I get up, I eagerly look forward to the day. ☐ T ☐ F

How did you Score?

If you answered any of the questions with the same answer as below, then circle that answer. In the space at the bottom of this box, enter the number of answers you circled. If you circled question four or eight, score two points for each of those questions.

| 1. T | 3. T | 5. F | 7. F |
| 2. F | 4. T** | 6. T | 8. F** |

**Number of circled questions (counting questions 4 and 8 as two each)_____

If this statement describes you, then I have bad news for you. Great traders and investors avoid those impulses. They consider such impulsive action to be a mistake that typically costs them money. In fact, what's really true about good trading is that it can be very boring. Traders must constantly follow their rules, get out of losing positions, tolerate drawdowns, and avoid behaviors that produce a feeling of excitement at all costs.

Organizational skills. Great traders tend to have superb organizational skills. These skills allow them to assess the big picture (i.e., macroeconomics) to determine the types of markets and trading they should focus on. These skills also help them develop a business plan to guide their trading.

Most importantly, good organizational skills enable traders to develop a trading system that fits them. To do that you have to find a system that fits your beliefs about who you are, what your objectives are, how markets work, how to select the right markets to trade, how to enter the market (or re-enter if you somehow exit prematurely), how to exit, how to take profits, and how to position size to meet your objectives.

Good traders and investors have strong beliefs about each of these topics. Consequently, they are able to map out their beliefs and then develop a system that fits those beliefs. Furthermore, they know their personal criteria for being comfortable with a system and then successfully trade that system.

Do You Have What It Takes?		So What's Your Score?
Personal Responsibility	3	If it's above 25, you probably have the
Commitment	3	makings of a great trader/investor.
Stress Protection	✓	If it's above 15, you are probably
Positive Outlook	✓	above average, but you have a lot of
Lack of Conflict	✓	work to do.
Independent Thinking	3	And if it's below 15, ask yourself how
Efficient Decision Making	✓	serious you are about wanting to
Strong Base for Intuition	1	make profits in the market.
Not Impulsive	1	
Strong Organization	✓	
Total Score	21	

Where Do You Stand?

So where do you think you stand? First, take the mini-test on the previous page. That will give you a starting point. If you score high, give some serious consideration to doing some work before you lose more money.

Next, honestly evaluate yourself on each of the traits in the table above on a one-to-three scale. Give yourself a rating of three if you think you excel in that particular trait or quality. If you think you've done significant work in that area, give yourself a rating of two. If you've at least thought about that area and done a little work on it, give yourself a rating of one. And if you think you've totally neglected the area, congratulate yourself for the insight, but give yourself a zero for that area.

How did you do? If you have five or more points, then the markets are probably a very dangerous place for you if you do not do a lot of work on yourself.

If you have two to five points, you are probably better than average, but you still could have difficulty with the markets. And if you have less than two points, then you probably do very well in the markets—or you really know how to take tests well.

Your answers that tend to predict the areas where you might have a problem being a successful trader or investor.

Van K. Tharp, PhD, is the founder of the International Institue of Trading Mastery. He has been coaching traders and investors since 1982 and was featured in Jack Schwager's book *Market Wizards* (Collins, 1993). He is the author of *Trade Your Way to Financial Freedom* (McGraw-Hill, 1998), *Financial Freedom through Electronic Day Trading* (McGraw-Hill, 2000) and *Safe Strategies for Financial Freedom* (McGraw-Hill, 2004). For more information on the investment psychology inventory visit www.iitm.com. This article originally appeared in *SFO* in July 2006.

WHAT'S YOUR TRADING BLOOD TYPE?

BY ILAN LEVY-MAYER

Perhaps the greatest luxury I have in this business is the ability to observe the experiences of many traders with different personalities, life schedules, and risk capital levels, each trading in a variety of markets. What most astute brokers realize is that, over time, as some individuals prematurely exit winners while others desperately cling to losers, it becomes quite possible to match different "blood types" of those traders with their correct "trading diets." Clearly, we're not talking the medical blood type here, but in the figurative sense it makes the right point. With practice, it's not too hard to determine blood types (type of trading best suited to the individual) based on the personality of the trader, and then prescribe a diet based on that individual trader's capital, experience, risk profile, and schedule.

Just like a diet, where there is no right plan for everyone, in trading there is no single plan for all traders. Before deciding whether to cut out the carbs, add more fiber, or simply avoid certain markets, do some self-assessment, starting with personality. For example, are you hesitant or impulsive? Patient or short-tempered? Identify strengths and weaknesses, and then let someone close to you help pinpoint those personality pros and cons. Have a tough skin; it's for your own good.

To further understand your personality, keep a trading journal to help zone in on specific traits and how they affect your trading. Remember, understanding your personality is one thing; understanding it when you're trading is another. While patience with children is good, patience with a losing trade is not. A journal enables traders to review winning and losing trades and identify factors that aided in success or contributed to failure.

After reviewing inner traits, don't forget to review the outer ones—your schedule and risk capital. Think long and hard about how much you have available in terms of time and risk capital when it comes to trading, and don't delude yourself. In addition, look at how you are using your time and risk capital. Go over the market(s) you are trading, the style of trading and time frames you are using. Is this market, this style and this time frame suitable to your risk capital and personal schedule? Are they suitable to your personality?

Doing some self-assessment is absolutely essential to determining what type of trading diet you should be on, as the examples later will make clear. But first let's define the trading blood types and their respective diets.

Blood Types and Trading Diets

No A-positive or universal donor types are necessary here. Instead, for our purposes, let's classify types by using NT, PT, DT, and ST.

NT (No Trading). Is futures trading suitable for you at all? That is the first question to ask yourself. Futures require a desire to take risks and, of course, the ability to afford to take them. These simple suitability questions must be firmly answered in the affirmative before anyone can consider taking the futures plunge. Those who have little desire for risk, have little risk capital to spare (and completely disposable income at that), and little time to devote to this very challenging exploit are classified as blood type NT. The right diet is no trading at all. No carbs, no cals, no fiber, no fat. Nada.

PT (Position Trading). Those who are either gun-shy or trigger-happy would be classified as blood type PT. With what kind of regime, you ask? Clearly this type requires a rule-based diet. Developing those rules, first and foremost, means doing some homework after market hours. Once these rules are in place, test any possible trade idea against those guidelines because each trade must pass this test before Mr. or Ms. PT enters the trade. This is the time to plan a trade from start to finish, visualizing a few different scenarios with a possible action plan. It may also be the time to employ the assistance of a full-service broker. His or her job should be to help implement the rules that will keep the trigger-happy trader from going nuts or help the trader with a fear of pulling the trigger to take the right kinds of actions.

DT (Day Trading). Some traders simply cannot take any positions home with them. It hurts the quality of their after-trading-hours life and makes them uncomfortable. Most are impatient by nature and tend to over-trade. They feel a need to be in the market at all times because they are scared of missing a good trade and scared of losing too much. This blood type is classified as DT.

Patience, discipline and strategy are the main diet ingredients for this group, but certainly not exclusive to it. Setting daily loss limits is a must, and a daily trading journal will help them quite a bit. The correct training cycle for successful day trading involves education, planning, routine, survival, and getting to the point where a trader finds the set-ups with which he is both most comfortable and can produce high success rates. A note here: more often than not, the biggest obstacle DTs face is the patience for such a set-up; they feel they are not working if they are not trading, because they are day traders. This is one mentally crippling thought they must get over to survive. Being a day trader does not mean that the individual must be in the market with frequency—only that he must be flat at the end of the session so as not to take his position(s) home with him.

ST (Swing Trading). Then there are traders who try to go with the flow of the market and take small to medium bites out of market ranges or, perhaps, trade ranging markets between different support and resistance levels. Many will do it well for a period of time until they are almost married to it and get stuck with a loser. Let's classify this group as blood type ST.

The biggest problem most swing traders have is the ability to take losses. One too many traders—even those who are generally good, consistent traders—fail by carrying one big loser one too many times. Is this stubbornness, the inability to admit making a wrong move(s), simply a case of hoping instead of trading? Those who have walked in these shoes know who they are and should be ready for the ST diet—placing stops and understanding that even the best of traders have more losers than winners. The math is simple. Because many markets will trade sideways, there are times when both longs and shorts will come out losers. Some trades simply don't work. The bottom line is that the total of a person's winning trades should outnumber losing trades.

How Two Traders Changed Their Diets

The following two examples, which combine traits of various clients with whom I've worked over the years, point out some of the considerations of which traders must be mindful as they try to figure out what trading diet is most appropriate. The names have been changed to protect both the innocent and the guilty.

Karen was one of my first clients. A smart and outgoing woman, she worked in the human resources department of a large company. During her first two years, she had some winning trades but, overall, her account was down.

Karen juggled a busy schedule every day. She had numerous meetings and often traveled, yet she insisted on day trading stock index futures. I tried to direct her into a different approach, but she resisted.

My advice did not sink in until she hit a period during which all of her trades were going against her, and she was facing a margin call. When I spoke with Karen, her normally self-assured demeanor had changed. She was scared. She was no longer looking forward to the next trading day. After losing most of her money, Karen struggled to make a trading decision. The once confident, outgoing, and independent trader was now grasping for outside advice from a variety of newsletters and other resources. She was desperate.

On the morning after a long holiday weekend, Karen called me and with a steady, confident voice, placed orders to get herself out of all of her positions. Over the weekend, she had read a book or two and had some conversations with her husband. It's hard to determine which of these produced the "epiphany," but she now wanted to try a different approach—one of a longer-term nature (PT). After careful reflection, Karen recognized that she was at times impulsive, stubborn, and simply not realistic (not good for a DT).

27

Even though she clearly could not devote the time necessary to be a day trader with her current work schedule and mentality, she realized that her routine and dedication must change completely no matter what the trading time frame. She was now dedicating thirty minutes during the day and/or evening to go over the markets. She adjusted her trading size to fit a longer-term approach but, most importantly, she had a plan, and that plan fit her schedule. She no longer had to make decisions in the heat of the moment. She started looking for longer-term trends that did not require hour-to-hour decision making.

Karen finally understood how to successfully incorporate trading into her life while having another demanding career. Her account has grown over the last two years through the changes she implemented in her routine, behavior, and trading style.

John started trading about four years ago. He seemed an agreeable enough person, but very business-like with no time for chit-chat. He wanted to trade online from the start because he had plenty of stock trading experience. John lived on the West Coast and was a real estate agent who did pretty well in the dot-com bull market trading stocks until the market met its maker. Confident, willing to learn, and fairly disciplined, he was trading with $25,000 of pure-risk capital, adequate for a first-time futures trader.

Days went by and every morning as I was going over my clients' daily statements, I noticed that John was trading coffee. Not only was he trading coffee, but he was sometimes day trading coffee. I let him know that I would be pleased to talk with him about various markets if he wanted. He would call once in a while checking on fills and asking about different reports.

A few weeks down the road, John called and mentioned he would be in the L.A. area and would like to meet for lunch. During lunch, he mentioned his frustration over recent losses when trading futures. At this point, his account was down to about $14,000 over a six-month period. I asked him why he was attempting to day trade coffee, and he said his brother-in-law was a coffee importer/exporter, and he thought that it would help him. The coffee market was open from 6:15 a.m. to 9:30 a.m. PST, which perfectly suited his work schedule, but as I found out later, not his personality.

I asked him to start writing a trading journal, which allowed him to look back objectively and find patterns in behavior that both helped him and hindered him. John's journal revealed that he was frustrated with the slow fills of the open-outcry coffee market, and so he was quick to get out of winning trades and too slow getting out of his losers. He was trigger happy and at times traded larger positions than he should have.

I suggested that we change his trading diet around a bit and introduced him to the U.S. Treasury bond and the E-mini stock index futures—both trade electronically and provide instant fills. These markets were perfect both for his schedule and personality. I felt that these were good markets for both day trading and swing trading and recommended a few concepts in money management and trade management. The first was the maximum daily loss that he should set and place in a visible way as a reminder. The second was the setting of a daily profit target. Though it was somewhat hard to implement, if he could walk away when he was down to his maximum daily loss or when he reached his daily profit target, he would last much longer as a trader. It also would give him a better chance of succeeding down the road—in other words, smaller steps down that longer road.

John is still down in his account, but he is making progress. Here are a few tips that have helped him: instead of buying and selling five contracts at a time and starting and finishing the trade this way, he now gets into his trades in multiples of three. In the past, John simply would buy five contracts when he thought he needed to go long and sell five when he felt he needed to take profits or cut his losses.

When John gets into a trade these days (let's say in a long position), he will buy six contracts and place a stop loss on all six. Initially, he looks for a small profit on the first two contracts. (It helps him mentally to know "I took a profit on this trade.") He then raises his stop loss and changes it to a four lot. He looks for a second profit target for two more contracts based on his support and resistance levels. If that profit level is reached, he can get greedy with the last two contracts. In essence, he now knows how to manage his trades in a way that increases his profitability. And, further, and perhaps as importantly (based on his personality), he does not feel like he is missing out on big moves if they happen, and he still locks in small profits when they present themselves by using the first and second targets.

Be Realistic

Succeeding in futures trading takes hard work and time, and new traders need to be realistic and introspective right from the start. This is no time to devote anything but risk capital. Beginners should start small, allowing periodic checks to learn from mistakes...and from successes.

Just like anything else in life, from diet and exercise to business and career choice, one size does not fit all. Before anyone can succeed in trading, he or she must spend time doing homework, as well as ascertain personal strengths and weaknesses, schedule, risk capital, trading experience, and knowledge. Only with those in place, can traders choose the trading diet that will work for their blood type.

A commodity broker since 1998, Ilan Levy-Mayer is the vice president of Cannon Trading Co., Inc., E-futures.com, and E-mini.com. Ilan Levy-Mayer is also the chief investment strategist of LEVEX Capital Management Inc., a commodity trading advisor specializing in short-term, diversified, momentum trading. He can be reached at ilan@cannoncapital.com. This article originally appeared in *SFO* in July 2004.

DEFINE YOUR TRADING GAME

BY CHRISTOPHER TERRY

We all attempt to play the trading game "correctly," either from buying breakouts, pullbacks, or shorting the rallies, fading the gaps, or using our stochastic or MACD indicators and moving averages. That's all fine and good, but the real question we need to ask ourselves is, do we play the RIGHT game? Does the style we use in our trading really fit our particular profile or personality?

I recently had a pretty frank conversation with one of my close trader friends, Mary. This article is built around her game. Mary is quite an intelligent person, but she was really having difficulties making a profit in the markets, buying every gap down, shorting gap ups, taking swing trades, buying bull flags and shorting bear flags, counter trend trading and, also, trading breakouts. She traded anything and everything that she could find, but wasn't having much luck. She explained to me her criteria for trading, specific trade ideas, why she pulled the trigger to enter, how she placed her stop losses and profit targets, and it all seemed logical to a point. So, how could she lose doing the right thing? Everything sounded right and, yet, it turned out to be wrong in her case. Was she overtrading or not trading enough or...?

Of course, there are many others like Mary who want to become good traders and have a rewarding career in this field. And, like her, they do not have a set game plan, a clearly defined roadmap of what's right for them and what will help them on their journey toward being a successful trader.

Initially, I thought that perhaps there were some very obvious trading errors that I could identify for Mary. I asked myself if it might be possible that Mary was trading NYSE stocks on a 60-minute chart when she should be using a 5-minute chart, and so on. Each question I asked her led to a series of new questions and, finally, I began to understand what made her tick, what her profile was, and what the right game for her was.

Then the light bulb went on—I thought of all the people with whom I have come into contact over the years, and the same identical thread seemed to run through the middle of each of them—that is, they clearly did not know what questions to ask themselves in a very introspective manner to determine what their particular style or game was. Without that, they continued to make errors that could blight what might be a successful relationship with the markets.

As a trader and mentor, I have stayed very close to the trading community over the years. For the last few years, I've been a moderator for a stock chat room that allows me to learn each day about other traders' profiles and personalities and what makes them tick. I've also been a speaker at various seminars and workshops, and, because of that exposure, I've had the good fortune to speak to and learn from those who are hungry and willing to travel long distances to become educated about trading. I also make it a point to keep a close watch on the pulse of what traders think.

I previously worked as an assistant to one of the largest stock traders in the nation and currently am a full-time professional trader who has been personally mentored by New Market Wizard Linda Bradford Raschke. In fact, I am now her partner. Thus, it might appear that I had it easier than the next person. However, I am no different than Mary in many respects. I have stood in her shoes. I have gone through the same type of growing pains that many traders do. I have questioned my talents and abilities many times, and I chased my tail for years until I found the right game for me.

Pablo Picasso created more than twenty thousand works. That does not mean, however, that anybody could use Picasso's brushes and be as great an artist. Just because someone sits at Liberace's piano does not mean he or she will be able to play like Liberace. They had their game, their style, and what works for them, but not for others.

Define Your Game and What Works for You

We hear some of the better traders say that they have a business plan or a game plan. What exactly does this mean? If they want to have a chance, traders have to ask themselves a score of questions before they risk capital in the markets. To start, do they have a sound methodology that has a high percentage of winners to losers?

Do they have the right tools to assess the market environment on a particular day, such as:

- Has the market been consolidating so much that it is in a breakout mode? For example, is it looking for a trending market that opens on one extreme of its range and closes on the other extreme?
- Or has the market been trending so much recently that we are looking for a consolidation environment, where volume dries up leading to a dull sideways trading range, before the cycle begins again in a breakout mode?
- Or are we trading in a holiday environment, an expiration environment, or during a week where the Federal Open Market Committee (FOMC) is a factor?

Speaking to Mary, my questions led to questions that led to even more questions until we were able to define her game. I asked her, what stocks do you like to trade the best? Do you like the Dow stocks or have a favorite index?—the banks, biotechs, oils, drillers, Nasdaq100? How about the utility stocks or broker-dealer stocks? This was the first of several steps in building a plan. Once we got the process going, it became less of the overwhelming task I originally had anticipated.

She finally explained to me that many of her losses came while attempting to get filled properly while trying to enter and exit NYSE stocks. She hadn't been very successful. On the flip side, she loved to trade the more volatile Nasdaq stocks—KLAC, QLGC, BRCM, MSFT, EBAY, QCOM, etc. (in all, fifteen to twenty stocks based on their volatility and prices). Other favorites included the QQQ (Nasdaq tracking stock), SPY (S&P tracking stock), and the DIA (Dow tracking stock). Finally, she indicated fondness for the S&P and NASDAQ futures indexes and the E-minis, due to their leverage and hedging benefits. So, there's step one—we defined her stocks and also her indexes.

How many of us trade every single stock out there and find that, for us, getting filled on some of the NYSE stocks is not the easiest? Or maybe we feel that the Nasdaq is too volatile for our likes and we like the NYSE ever-so-much better. So, gut it out and ask yourself the question—what is my stock list or my futures list or whatever? What specific products fit my comfort level? Oils? Drug stocks? NYSE or NASDAQ? E-Minis? The Dow? Do I even have a favorite list or do I just trade anything that moves?

What's the Time Frame?

After we locked in the type of stocks that Mary liked to trade, the goal was to find what particular time frames she liked best. Working a one-minute chart, for example, is a very short-term time frame, but short term is a relative term dictated again by a trader's own comfort level. Some traders dislike short time frames and would rather hold for a few hours or a few days. There are other traders who simply cannot be in the markets that long or they will pull their hair out, and Mary was one of those. From experience, she felt that, mentally, she could not hold on to stocks for a few hours or a few days. Yet, she wanted to stay away from an extraordinarily short-term time frame as well.

Her weakness and subsequent losses came from swing trading on daily charts or using large time frames like 60-minute or 120-minute charts. She could not stand the heat when a trade went against her. For Mary, those longer time frames were tortuous, but scalping on a 1-minute chart was too fast and noisy. As a result, she ended up scalping in and out of the market fifty times a day, and that resulted in paying predictably larger brokerage commissions for her small wins.

We concluded that her favorite time frames to trade were 5-minute and 15-minute charts, with the 5-minute time frame the clear favorite. Does this mean she only watches a 5-minute chart? No. In fact, Mary watches a number of time frames across four monitors for support and resistance levels on higher time frames. However, she executes and trades patterns on only the 5-minute chart. That's her comfort level. So, the question is, have you defined your time frame? What is your best time frame? Are you a day trader scalping fifty to one hundred times a day on a tick chart or a 1-minute chart, or do you like to put your positions on and wait it out for a few hours to a few days?

With a defined stock list and the chart time frame best suiting her personality well in hand, we moved on to other factors.

FIGURE 1: Five-minute chart of the S&P 500 E-mini futures contract

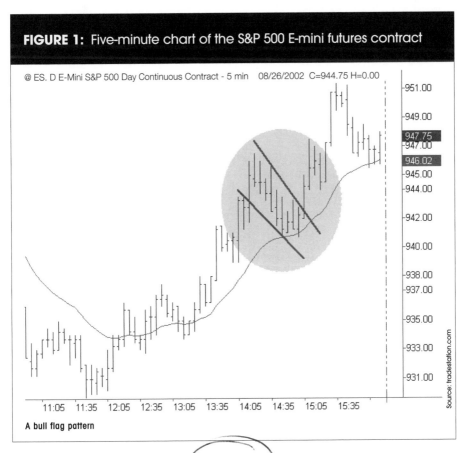

@ ES. D E-Mini S&P 500 Day Continuous Contract - 5 min   08/26/2002 C=944.75 H=0.00

A bull flag pattern

Recognizing Friendly Price Patterns

Next step? Identifying price patterns that Mary was able to recognize without forcing herself too much. I asked her if she preferred channels, triangles, or wedges, bull or bear flags, head-and-shoulders patterns, Fibonacci retracements, or breakout plays from a consolidation mode. If the markets wind down to a point of breakout, perhaps she'd like the idea of buying new highs or shorting new lows after the first thirty or forty-five minutes of the day. Or maybe not.

Mary felt her eye was best at seeing higher-probability patterns, like bull and bear flags (a flag pattern is a continuation pattern in the direction of the trend). Flags have been around since the early days of technical analysis and are considered to be one of the higher-probability trade setups. Simply, a bull flag is a buy pattern in an up-trend, and a bear flag is a sell pattern in a down-trend. Mary felt that since this was a very easy pattern to recognize and that working with the trend is bet-

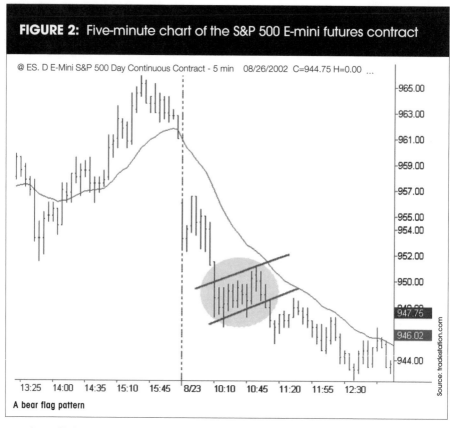

FIGURE 2: Five-minute chart of the S&P 500 E-mini futures contract

@ ES. D E-Mini S&P 500 Day Continuous Contract - 5 min   08/26/2002 C=944.75 H=0.00 ...

A bear flag pattern

Source: tradestation.com

ter than fighting it, this would be the best price pattern for her to trade. (See *Figure 1* for bull flag example and *Figure 2* for bear flag example.)

At this point, it was time to begin defining risk and profit objectives based on the stocks and futures Mary liked to trade and the time frame and chart pattern she felt most comfortable using—connecting the dots, so to speak. I explained to Mary that I personally like to use a twenty-period exponential moving average on all my charts and felt it would help her as a short-term moving average support in an up-trend... and resistance in a down-trend. Thus, we included that in her game plan. *Figures 1* and *2* show this moving average plotted on the chart examples.

What's your pattern? Have you found one good pattern that repeats itself over and over in a consistent manner that allows you to enter and exit the markets each day? Or do you have many different set-ups and throw darts until one hits the target? Find your favorite pattern and master it.

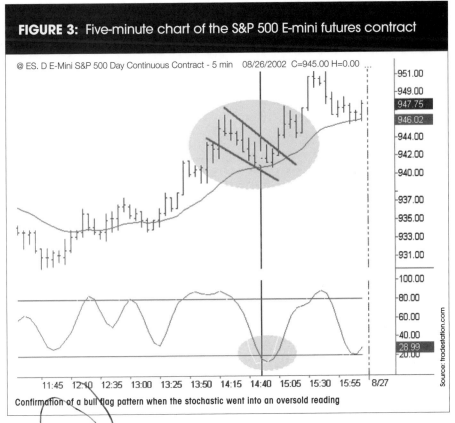

FIGURE 3: Five-minute chart of the S&P 500 E-mini futures contract

@ ES. D E-Mini S&P 500 Day Continuous Contract - 5 min   08/26/2002 C=945.00 H=0.00

Confirmation of a bull flag pattern when the stochastic went into an oversold reading

Which Indicator Rocks Your Clock?

The next step was to learn if she had a preference for any indicators—an RSI, stochastic, or an MACD, for example. With the variety of studies available, we concluded that she felt best using a short-term slow stochastic with a 5,3,3,1 setting for her 5-minute chart time frame. I also needed to explain to Mary that indicators only confirm what the price pattern is telling a trader. For example, the retracement in an up-trend would be a buy, and the slow stochastic would confirm the price pattern when it became oversold (*Figure 3* shows confirmation of the price pattern when the stochastic went into an oversold condition). She had used several indicators at one time, and I explained to her that if she used more than one indicator, she might find herself facing a buy and sell signal at the same time and not be able to trust either of them. It's similar to wearing two watches, one on each hand; if each tells a different time, one will never know what the true time is. So, a trader should look toward the one particular indicator that he or she feels good about using.

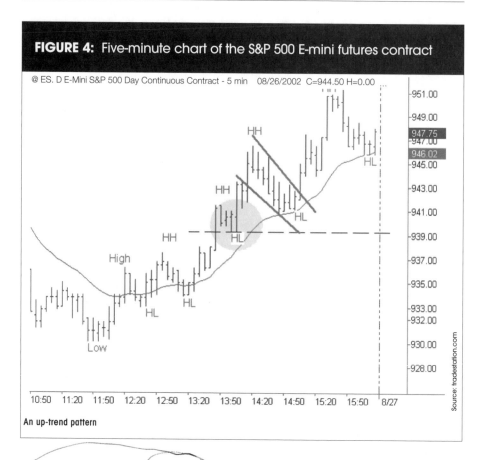

FIGURE 4: Five-minute chart of the S&P 500 E-mini futures contract

@ ES. D E-Mini S&P 500 Day Continuous Contract - 5 min   08/26/2002 C=944.50 H=0.00

951.00
949.00
947.75
947.00
946.02
945.00
943.00
941.00
939.00
937.00
935.00
933.00
932.00
930.00
928.00

HH
HL
HH
HL
HH
HL
High
HL
HL
Low

10:50   11:20   11:50   12:20   12:50   13:20   13:50   14:20   14:50   15:20   15:50   8/27

An up-trend pattern

Source: tradestation.com

What Can You Afford to Risk?

The next consideration is defining risk and target levels, based not just on a dollar value but also on the chart, pattern, and trend of the market. An up-trend is defined by higher highs and higher lows. In *Figure 4*, we see an up-trend. For this trend to stay valid on this time frame, we want to see if the price retracement has a higher low to its last higher low. In this example, the last higher low was 939.00, and the market retraced to 940.75. Therefore, the risk on this trade was around two points. I explained to Mary that sometimes the risk of a trade is too high—maybe four to five points—and sometimes the risk is not as great—maybe one to two points. That risk, I explained, also will determine the size of the position she will enter. One S&P E-mini futures contract equals $50 per point, and for the larger S&P contract, it would be five times that size, or a point value of $250. And, of course, her risk level would be a factor in her position size. A full position would be five E-minis, and risk would normally be two points or $500 ($250 x 2 points). If, on the other hand, the trade required a four to five-point risk, her contract size would have to decrease to accommodate the dollar value she was willing to risk.

We determined that her account was funded such that she could afford to trade one large S&P contract (or five E-minis), and that the average risk per trade would be around two S&P points, and further, that the greater the point risk in the S&Ps, the fewer contracts she would trade. The same applies to the stock side of the equation if a trader is trading five hundred shares with one point as the average risk. Intuitively, the greater the risk in price, the fewer shares the trader can assume for that set-up. Have you determined your share or contract size and risk level based on the time frame of your trading?

Another cog in the wheel is in knowing when to get in and out of the market so as to reasonably maximize profit and avoid undue losses. Those decisions, though, need to be made before Mary puts on a trade, so an exit price is predetermined both for a loss and also for a win. The pattern she felt most appropriate for her trading is based on a trending market environment in an intraday time frame; typically that occurs when an intraday trend exists and, based on other factors, a trader expects the market to open on one extreme and close on the other extreme. Mary's profile pointed to the fact that she did not want to stay in too long, but still didn't want to get out too fast. It was important to lock in a profit, and the plan unfolded: to bring the risk exposure to a minimum when the price rallies from its bull flag pattern, she would raise her stop loss to just under the last low. When the markets retested its prior highs, she then would take a profit on the position. Before you enter, do you know your risk level and when to take your profits?

Putting all of these factors together, Mary learned how to play the right game for her personality. Some traders will never look at a bull flag pattern, never consider a 5-minute chart, nor use a stochastic or anything less than a 50-period average. Some traders prefer the 5-minute chart as a time frame and love to use a 14-period RSI. There are as many variations as there are traders.

I've taken you through a journey—a journey that puts together a custom game plan for someone who lacked one. Mary no longer has to trade fifty times a day and does not need be in the market every waking moment. With help, she was able define a clear, concise trading plan with:

1. the financial products she enjoys trading the most;
2. the time frames that fit her comfort level;
3. a solid chart pattern that has endured the test of time, with an indicator to confirm what the price is telling her;
4. a clear concept of risk, and the realization of how much she can reasonably risk; and
5. a profit objective.

Mary now can go in and out of the markets three to five times per day in both stocks and stock index futures. The patterns described above also have taken into consideration the higher time frames for support and resistance levels. Mission accomplished!

Christopher Terry is a full-time professional trader in both the index futures and equities markets. He speaks regularly at derivative conferences and has written articles for *Active Trader*, *SFO*, and *Stocks and Commodities*, among others. Terry has traveled extensively and spoken on the psychological approach to achieving success. In the last few years, he has focused on speaking and training traders on technical analysis and the methodologies that have helped him in his trading. In addition to trading, Mr. Terry and his partner, New Market Wizard Linda Bradford Raschke, provide free educational information for both stock and futures traders at www.lbrgroup.com. This article originally appeared in *SFO* in October 2002.

TRADING COACHES NEEDED!

BY JOHN FORMAN

Trading coaches are a worthwhile investment. But one must fully understand what separates a coach and a mentor to find the right fit.

I define a coach as someone who is at core a teacher and who is well educated on the subject in question. For example, as a volleyball coach I teach players the ins and outs of the sport and I help them develop their skills. I do this with a variety of approaches, including specific training regimens and video reviews. Beyond the skill development, though, there is also motivation and strategy development

A mentor is more like advisor. He or she helps guide you through the learning process from a broader viewpoint. A mentor is often someone who has achieved success and who can provide advice and suggestions, offering a sounding board for thoughts and ideas. Good coaches can certainly be mentors, and they often are. Mentors, on the other hand, are not as likely to be coaches.

In many arenas it is easy to define a coach. They are the folks who go through training programs and work under other coaches as they enter a field. I started coaching by helping out my own high school coach. Later, I assisted under other experienced coaches and then coached my own teams under the supervision of others. I read tons of books on the topic, joined the American Volleyball Coaches Association, and went through USA's volleyball coaching accreditation program. I've gone to seminars and clinics, talked with coaches from all over the country, worked at camps, and coached teams of all levels. In other words, I've developed my coaching through education and experience.

Mentors, on the other hand, are more likely to be experienced in a given field. They can share their war stories and provide advice based on having had an experience similar to the mentee's. Older players on a team can be mentors to the younger ones. In my role as a college coach I not only worked with players in developing their volleyball acumen, but I could also share with them my own playing experience. Even more, I could advise them on academic, career, and other life issues at times as well.

The Making of a Coach

The whole topic of trader coaching is something I have thought about at length. In trading there is no real development structure for coaching. There are no coaching certification processes and not much in the way of opportunity for a prospective trading coach to apprentice under an experienced one. As a result, it is hard to clearly identify coaches and know what they can offer. Much of trader coaching has been closer to my definition of mentoring. A budding young trader develops a relationship with a successful trader who has a good deal of experience in the markets. That's great, but only to a point. Why? Because mentors do not always make great coaches.

Here is the classic example. In sports one hardly ever sees top athletes as successful coaches. The best coaches and managers often come from the ranks of relatively average players. There are any number of reasons for this. It may be that being less gifted, the average athlete worked harder learning the game, trying to find ways to compensate for his shortcomings in talent. It may be a basic communication issue. We have all had teachers or professors who were absolutely brilliant in their field but awful in the classroom. They simply could not present the material in a useful, coherent fashion

The same sort of thing happens in trading. So many novice traders attempt to learn at the feet of superstar traders because they think the fact that someone made five hundred percent in the markets over the last three years means he can teach someone else how to do it. Frankly, things just don't work that way. Being able to teach someone else how to match your trading results requires you to understand exactly how you achieved them in the first place. Many traders simply cannot do that because they don't really know. They might think they know because they have a system of some kind, but there are often other elements involved in the process, some of them unseen—for example the psychology of the superstar trader. And even if that superstar trader can tell you exactly how he or she does it, there is still the question of being able to teach it effectively. Not everyone has what it takes to teach. It requires an understanding of how to communicate with students in ways that allow them to grasp the material. It also requires a great deal of patience, which not everyone has—especially hyperactive traders! Make sure you don't mistake teaching for coaching. They are not the same.

There are loads of trading courses, seminars and classes out there. Some of them use coaching in their titles or descriptions even though there really isn't any coaching involved. It's instruction. They are teaching you something—generally about a particular market, a style of trading, a trading system, etc. That's not the same as coaching.

Coaching, at least in my mind, is very personal and is more comprehensive. The coach works with the individual to help develop his or her specific skills and then utilize them during the game. Even in a team situation, a good coach spends time with each individual player, observing her and working on her specific strengths and weaknesses

A good trading coach does the same thing. It isn't just about presenting the right information. The coach learns about the player, understands his strengths and weaknesses, and customizes the training program to his needs. Coaches also help in the implementation of trading terms—similar to actual game coaching which is vastly different from practice coaching.

Finding a Good Coach Starts with You

So where do you find good coaches? That's the ultimate question. Unfortunately, it's not an easy thing to answer. Since there is no "Association of Trading Coaches" you're going to have to do the leg work yourself. Clearly you need to go looking where there are traders and do some research.

The first part of finding a coach actually involves deciding what you are looking for—what you feel like you need to learn or do better. That can include things like:

- learning the details of a new market;
- improving your risk management;
- developing a deeper understanding of how to use volatility in your trading;
- understand how to evaluate trading systems;
- learn a specific type of trading (scalping or day trading, for example).

These are just a few examples. There are many others that could come in to play. The important part of the process at this stage is having a clear notion of what exactly you want to get out of a new coaching arrangement.

Here's another example in volleyball. In this sport there are several specialized positions. Each player must know the overall rules of play, understand the system the head coach is employing, and train in the basics (conditioning, quickness, ball-handling skills, etc.). These things are usually accomplished in group practice sessions.

Often, however, the player will also spend time working on skills specific to his or her particular position. The focus here is narrower and may be geared toward either the individual or a smaller group. This training is generally done by a coach with a better understanding of the specific position and how to develop the skills involved. Sometimes, to get even more focused and individual attention, a player will get involved with an outside coach who specializes in the position in question.

In trading, you can do the same thing. There is one level of general coaching that can cover a broader scope—trading forex, for example. Then there is the much deeper level which goes into more specialized territory—such as how to trade using market profile charts. You just need to find a trading coach who knows exactly what your needs are.

Coaching Takes Knowledge and Communication
The next step in finding a good coach is to look for someone who has demonstrated great knowledge of trading and the markets—especially in those you are looking to learn. That's obvious. But there are experts everywhere. How do you find one that can work with you?

You need to narrow it down to people who can effectively teach the subject. As mentioned before, knowledge doesn't necessarily equate to teaching ability. It requires communication. Look for someone who is good at expressing things and can articulate ideas and concepts clearly. This might not be easy to figure out. Some potential coaches can be observed presenting classes or seminars. Others have written articles or books. If that's the case, it will be fairly easy for you to evaluate their ability to communicate.

However, if you don't have access to the writings and/or oral presentations of a coaching candidate, you are going to have to take a more direct approach. That means you need to speak to them yourself in order to make that judgment.

After you have a candidate in mind, the process becomes much more personal and individual. You need to be able to communicate well with your coach and she with you. That means, ideally, spending at least some time getting to know her—certainly enough to establish whether there is a reasonable level of compatibility.

It's important for the prospective coach to be focused on you. If possible, before you give him any real information about yourself and what you are looking to accomplish, ask the question "What would you do for me?" This is a bit of a trick question. If he starts rambling on about all the stuff he knows and doesn't talk about your particular needs at all, look elsewhere. In actuality, the ideal answer would be no answer at all. A good coach would first try to get an idea of what you need, and that means asking questions. If your prospective coach asks you questions about your experience and objectives, take that as a good sign.

Make sure, in your discussions with a prospective coach, that you also discuss the way the coaching will be handled. Will it be in person? Will it be over the phone, through e-mail, or some other online connection? What sorts of support resources will the coach provide? Will you be required to purchase any other books, products, or services? Before committing to any arrangement, you have to know the full details.

What it Costs

If you can find that person and get her to coach you, then you've got something special. Keep in mind, though, that coaching is rarely free. After all, a good coach will commit a decent amount of time to the process. Additionally good coaches will only work with people they know they can help, and only they will be able to assess that. They won't just take on anyone.

I have seen per hour coaching rates that range from $100 up to $300, and there are those who charge even more. A good coach is worth the money, but obviously you don't want to put yourself in bankruptcy for the sake of it.

Often coaches will offer discounted rates for making a longer-term commitment. This is great, but you don't want to lock yourself into something you cannot get out of if you find things are not working out the way you had intended. Give yourself enough time to get into the coaching relationship and see where it's going, but don't lock yourself into something longer than that until you know it's what you want.

Having a trading coach is most definitely a worthwhile objective. A good one can help you go far beyond where you were likely to be able to go by yourself. Make sure you don't just go for someone who has achieved spectacular results (especially if they were accomplished over only a short period of time). Knowledge and practical experience are important, but teaching ability is equally so. Ask lots of questions and make sure any prospective coach wants to get to know you. If you do that, you are more than likely to find yourself in a positive and rewarding coaching relationship. Best of luck finding the right one for you.

John Forman is a near twenty-year veteran of the markets and author of *The Essentials of Trading: From the Basics to Building a Winning Strategy* (Wiley, 2006). He can be reached through his website, www.TheEssentialsOfTrading.com. This article originally appeared in *SFO* in April 2007.

SECTION TWO
Managing Mind Games, Emotions, and Risk

No question about it. The mind has an enormous bearing on a person's ability to achieve. Nearly every trader confronts issues like controlling emotions and fear, managing risk, and sticking to the plan at some point in his career. Learning some basic strategies to tackle these before they become unmanageable can be key factors in averting major problems.

In this section we'll talk about how to self-diagnose some of the most common psychological trading problems and address them with basic behavior modification. Understanding your habits, thought and behavior patterns, and personality traits and how they relate to your trading practice is the first step to conquering your own personal mind games. And sometimes what seems like an emotional problem is really a case of poor trading habits or inadequate training that is easily resolved.

Trading is a high-risk, demanding career that takes enormous discipline. Sometimes the hardest part is simply following your plan—whether it be an inability to pull the trigger or an inability to pull out of a losing a trade. Developing the right methodology, timing, and rules for your trading practice is important, but it's even more critical to follow your plan when you start to second-guess yourself. Our writers share practical strategies like self-analysis, blogging, mental rehearsal, and stress inoculation that can bring back your edge.

Thanks to recent research, we now understand the importance of resilience in many walks of life, including trading. Long-term success requires persistence, creativity, and strong coping strategies. The good news is that everyone can build their resilience, and we've included some key strategies for conquering stress and strengthening coping skills.

Intuition? Education? Patience? We'll explore the qualities of successful women traders compared to their male counterparts and the lessons we can learn from each other.

DIAGNOSING THE TRADER:
Enhancing Performance
Through Self Assessment

BY BRETT N. STEENBARGER, PhD

For nineteen years before I came to the world of proprietary trading in Chicago, I taught in a medical school department of psychiatry. My job was to help medical students and residents become better helpers. The medical world is steeped in the ethic of "above all else, do no harm." That means that physicians need to take the time to understand problems before they undertake cures. Diagnosis precedes treatment.

Alas, this is not always the case with traders, whose motto often seems to be, "above all else, keep trading." When traders detect problems with their profitability, rarely do they undertake the equivalent of blood workups and imaging studies. Without examining their trading in detail, it is difficult to accurately diagnose performance problems—and figure out what to do about them.

I suggest a simple diagnostic scheme for trader performance problems that might guide traders in the process of self-assessment. Because the cure to trading ills generally must follow the diagnosis—solutions must be tailored to problems—such a diagnostic effort can pay off handsomely. Ready to become your own psychologist? Let's go!

Eliminating Garbage Categories: Trading and Lack of Discipline

When people don't understand the nature of their problems, they generally turn to simplistic explanations. Couples that come in for marriage counseling invariably attribute their difficulties to "communication problems." Traders cite "lack of discipline." These are garbage categories—catchalls that reflect the results of problems, not their causes. Before we embark on a more promising diagnostic scheme, it will be helpful to understand why that ubiquitous term in trading psychology—"discipline"—is of limited value.

When people seek help for problems, it is because they have a pattern of thought, emotion, and/or behavior that is disrupting their life, creating unwanted consequences. Think about what that means:

1. Our behavior is patterned;
2. Some of our patterns are unwanted;
3. We cannot always change our patterns on our own.

Every psychological problem has, at its root, a pattern that is not fully in our control. It might be an emotional pattern such as depression; a behavioral pattern such as substance use; or a cognitive pattern such as perfectionism. Indeed, we might say that every psychological problem is a problem because it takes away a piece of our free will. When we are under the influence of a psychological pattern, we do not fully control what we do or what happens to us. That is why some of our patterns are unwanted.

Every psychological problem, in that sense, results in a lack of discipline. If free will enables us to act in a deliberate manner and seek goals of our own choosing, our negative patterns are the reverse: they disrupt our plans and interfere with the achievement of our goals. When I got married, my marriage vows were part of my life plan. To the degree I cannot control my anger, my gambling, or my closed-mindedness, I am diverted from that plan. Such lack of discipline is not the cause of my problem, but the effect. All psychological problems have the effect of making us less purposeful, less able to act upon our priorities.

FIGURE 1: A diagnostic grid for traders

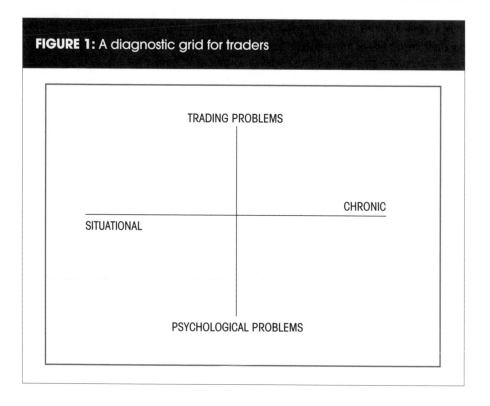

Traders are all too familiar with the forces that interfere with their plans. When we set stop-loss points or establish maximum position sizes and then violate these, the results are painfully apparent in our profit/loss (P/L) statements. We might over-trade and take trades that don't meet the criteria of our setups; we might under-trade and fail to act upon valid setups. Either way, we have a problem with our ability to act upon our plans. Something is diminishing our free will in the marketplace. The loss of discipline is the result of this something. The goal of diagnosis is to figure out just what that something is.

The Diagnostic Grid

Figure 1 is a fourfold scheme that I carry in my head whenever I begin work with a trader. It is my way of making sense of a trader's difficulty in following his or her plans. The grid consists of two intersecting dimensions: the primary source of the problems and the chronicity of the problems.

The source of the problem reflects whether the disruption of trading plans is caused primarily by a trading problem—a deficiency in how the trader is approaching the markets—or whether it can be traced to specific, psychological difficulties. In other words, what we're trying to differentiate are emotional problems caused by bad trading and trading problems caused by emotional upheaval. This, as we'll see, can be challenging to sort out, as trading problems and emotional ones can affect each other in a circular fashion. Determining which is primary, however, is absolutely crucial to improving trader performance.

The chronicity of the problem reflects the degree to which the difficulties are longstanding and consistent versus recent and situational. Sometimes problems only appear in very limited circumstances, often because of a difficulty that has arisen in a particular situation. Stress over a job change would be a common example; grief over the loss of a loved one would be another. Other times problems are chronic: they have been present for a while and do not markedly change with circumstances.

The intersection of these two dimensions creates four quadrants, which are my diagnostic categories:

1. **Chronic trading problems.** These are generally the result of poor trading habits developed over the course of a trading career;
2. **Situational trading problems.** These often result when traders change markets or when markets change on traders, reducing their edge;
3. **Chronic psychological problems.** These reflect ongoing psychological difficulties among traders;
4. **Situational psychological problems.** These occur when recent events in traders' personal lives interfere with their trading.

That's it. I like to keep the categories simple and straightforward. When I first meet with a trader, I have a little checklist in my head:

• Does this person know how to trade? Has he ever been truly successful?
• Has something changed in the trader's market? Has volatility or trending shifted significantly during the period of trading problems?
• Does this person have a history of psychological difficulties outside of trading?

- Has something recently changed in the trader's personal life during the period of trading problems?

If I cannot answer these questions accurately, the odds are good that I won't be of much help to the trader. I have to know the person as a trader and as a person. Similarly, when you are diagnosing yourself, you need to sort out what is ongoing and what is situational; what is a function of trading and what is a function of your personality.

Trading Problems: Chronic vs. Situational

Let's face it—some people don't know how to trade. It's not their fault. Most traders have never been trained in trading. Surgeons and musicians go to school to learn their craft; athletes train in team sports throughout childhood and young adulthood. There are few comparable training programs for traders, however. A seminar, book, or video course wouldn't teach us how to master golf or chess; how could it possibly train us for trading?

Chronic trading problems generally are the result of a lack of training. That is how people develop bad trading habits. A good example is poor risk management. A trader starts with a small trading stake and puts a large portion of it at risk each time he or she makes a trade. The result is that P/L swings wildly as a function of portfolio size. These P/L swings cause emotional swings, which in turn further interfere with trading. But the primary root of the problem is poor trading.

Suppose, for instance, that a trader with a $25,000 portfolio has sixty percent odds of winning on each trade. The trader trades once a day, trades ten lots on the S&P e-minis, and limits each trade to a stop loss of five points. Such a trader has a near mathematical certainty of encountering five consecutive losses in the course of a year. If each loss draws the portfolio down by ten percent (five points on a ten-lot), the trader almost certainly will lose a substantial portion of his or her trading stake. This is likely to generate frustration, anger, depression, and faulty efforts to change the trading system.

Such a trader may think he or she has an emotional problem, but the root of the problem is a lack of understanding of risk and trading fundamentals. Poor training has created a chronic trading problem.

As a rule, if you have never sustained success as a trader and you are experiencing frustrations with trading, the odds are good that you need training, not psychotherapy. Your trading methods may lack a valid edge; your frequency or size of trading may be eroding your profits and exposing you to excessive risk. These are not problems that will be solved by emotional self-help tools.

Other times, the trading problem is situational. The trader may have fine trading behaviors and will have a history of trading success. Recently, however, the P/L has gone south. Profits are no longer flowing and trading is becoming frustrating. Very often, this is the result of changes in the marketplace. Markets periodically shift their trends and volatility. What worked and provided a solid edge in one market no longer works in another. I recently conducted a series of studies that showed the S&P 500 index to be at historically low levels of both trending and volatility. The result is that traders who used to make their money by riding the back of momentum can no longer count on this strategy. The market offers less movement, and it tends to reverse movement when it does occur. Once again, the answer is not to consult a shrink. Either you need to find a new market that will follow momentum, or you need to develop a new, countertrend method of trading your current market.

The best way for me to identify a chronic trading problem is to watch a trader trade. If we're watching the screen together and I make a comment such as, "The large locals are leaning to the short side," the trader might respond, "How do you know that?" At that point, I have a pretty good idea that the trader is having trouble discerning supply and demand in the market auction. That tells me that training, not counseling, will be helpful, and we'll end up discussing how to track volume occurring at different price levels, the proportion of volume occurring at bid versus ask prices, etc.

If I see that the trader can read supply and demand, however, but is staying in trades too long or entering with too much size, I have a sense that the problem is situational. Often this occurs when a trending market consolidates and becomes slower and more range bound. The trader does not adapt to the shift in market conditions and overtrades the slower market. Such traders might simply need a tool to help them identify market shifts as they occur, such as a monitor of current market volume as a proportion of the usual volume at that time of day.

As a psychologist, my training taught me to look for psychological causes of problems. Having worked with traders every day in a professional firm, however, I have learned to respect the fact that many emotional disruptions of trading are caused by trading problems. A lack of training and difficulties adapting to changing market conditions can hurt P/L, and that can disrupt emotional well-being.

Emotional Problems: Chronic vs. Situational

There are other times when emotional difficulties truly are at the root of trading performance concerns. A chronic psychological problem is one that predates trading and that shows up in facets of life that have nothing to do with trading. An example would be a tendency toward depression or anxiety, a personality trait that psychologists call neuroticism. Such traits show up early in life and tend to persist. Their expression can be modified, but they don't radically change. If a person was active and highly distractible as a child, for example, the odds are good that he or she will carry some of these features into adulthood. These can interfere with trading and create subsequent frustrations.

Not all chronic psychological problems are the result of diagnosable disorders. Sometimes personality traits of traders do not match their trading styles, creating chronic problems. For instance, there are personality traits that are associated with the ability to tolerate risk. People who are risk averse but who try to trade aggressively will experience considerable stress on a regular basis. They are unable to cope with the swings generated by their portfolios. The upset generated by this mismatch can disrupt trading over an extended period.

When such chronic emotional difficulties occur, psychological assistance can be invaluable. Such problems as major depressive disorder, bipolar disorder, and attention deficits are highly treatable with the right medications. Many such problems can benefit from talk therapy as well. Cognitive therapy, for example, has a proven track record in treating depression. Behavioral techniques have a similar record of reducing stress and anxiety.

In cases where chronic distress is generated by a mismatch of personality and trading style, tweaking one's trading will be more helpful than trying to change one's personality. My experience is that two variables—trading frequency and trading size—are two of the most important variables to tweak. Both are related to risk and the volatility of returns; both also affect the cognitive process of trading. For instance, traders who make decisions analytically may need longer time periods between trades than traders who process information more intuitively. One's trading frequency and holding time for positions should reflect one's cognitive style.

On other occasions, situational personal problems can interfere with trading and reduce profitability. For instance, emotional disruption from relationship problems or trading slumps can cause traders to lose their focus. One of the most common situational disturbances involves trader finances. When traders incur unexpected expenses in their personal lives, they often alter their trading to try to make more money. The result is that they lose their edge in the marketplace and actually perform worse. Many times, such added expenses are the result of positive life events, such as marriage, a new home, or a new child. Anything—even a positive—that leads to an overemphasis on P/L has the potential to divide attention and interfere with performance.

When trading difficulties are situational, short-term counseling can be extremely helpful. Performance anxiety due to slumps or heightened expenses can be conquered through such stress management methods as systematic desensitization and exposure therapy. Similarly, cognitive methods to change self-talk patterns are useful. Tweaking indicators or order execution methods when life is intruding on trading is less likely to help.

What This Means for You

What we have here is a chicken and egg problem. Trading problems can cause emotional disruptions, and emotional disruptions can play havoc with trading results. The steps you need to take to cure trading woes depend crucially on the nature of those problems. Some trading challenges benefit from teaching and training; others from self-help methods; still others from professional assistance. There is no one size fits all.

If you are underperforming as a trader, ask the right questions before you pursue answers. If you seek mentorship, make sure your mentor knows enough to ask those questions. Proper treatment always follows from accurate diagnosis. It's amazing how quickly traders can turn their problems around if they just figure out what those problems are!

Brett N. Steenbarger, PhD, is associate clinical professor of psychiatry and behavioral sciences at SUNY Upstate Medical University in Syracuse, NY. As director of trader development for Kingstree Trading, LLC, in Chicago, he mentors professional traders and coordinates a trader training program. An active trader of the stock indexes, Steenbarger uses statistically based pattern recognition for intra-day trading. The author of *Enhancing Trader Performance: Proven Strategies from the Cutting Edge of Trading Psychology* (Wiley Trading, 2006) and *The Psychology of Trading: Tools and Techniques for Minding the Markets* (Wiley, 2002), Steenbarger maintains a trading archive and blog at www.brettsteenbarger.com and a blog of market analytics at www.traderfeed.blogspot.com. This article originally appeared in *SFO* in July 2006.

TRADE DEMONS SHRINK YOUR POTENTIAL: Four Experts Discuss the Mind Games of Trading

BY GAIL OSTEN

A friend of mine just came back from a weekend in Las Vegas, and I chuckled as I listened to his stories of bravado at the tables. High stakes, high hopes, high drama. It interested me to hear his mental rationale for taking chances and tales of woe when the odds didn't work out. His own personal mind games were present in spades. While I would not equate investing with gambling—the only real capital formation stays at the tables in Vegas or Atlantic City—the games investors and traders play in their heads may be quite similar.

Enormous discipline is needed in trading; it's not for the weak of spirit nor for the lazy. It's not a sure-fire, get-rich-quick scheme. Successful trading is very much dependent on proper mental gymnastics, preparation, practice, and psychological self-help. To that end, I asked four professionals to comment on the psychology of trading, the people that do it well and not so well, and a variety of other questions, the answers to which you will find enlightening…and helpful as you travel this road.

Here's our line-up:

Ari Kiev, MD, is a psychiatrist and attorney; author of more than fifteen books, including best-sellers, The Psychology of Risk: Mastering Market Uncertainty (Wiley, 2002) and Trading in the Zone: Maximizing Performance with Focus and Discipline (Wiley, 2001). His most recent work is *Hedge Fund Masters: How Top Hedge Fund Traders Set Goals, Overcome Barriers, and Achieve Peak Performance (Wiley Trading, 2005). Kiev has lectured widely in the highest of investment circles and coaches traders with financial institutions and several large hedge funds.*

Ruth Barrons Roosevelt is a traders' coach, attorney, and author. She works with traders around the world to help them achieve their optimal effectiveness. A futures trader, she is a former vice president of Pruden-tial Securities and of Thomson McKinnon, and once head of the Interna-tional Moneyline Trading Desk at Rudolf Wolf and a stock and futures broker at Drexel Burnham Lambert. She is the author of Exceptional Trading, The Mind Game (Traders Press, 1999) and 12 Habitudes of Highly Successful Traders (Traders Press, 2001).

Brett N. Steenbarger, PhD, is associate clinical professor of psychia-try and behavioral sciences at SUNY Upstate Medical University in Syracuse, NY. As director of trader development for Kingstree Trad-ing, LLC, in Chicago, he has mentored numerous professional traders and coordinated a training program for traders. An active trader of the stock indexes, Steenbarger uses statistically based pattern recog-nition for intra-day trading. The author of Enhancing Trader Per-formance: Proven Strategies from the Cutting Edge of Trading Psy-chology (Wiley Trading, 2006) and The Psychology of Trading: Tools and Techniques for Minding the Markets (Wiley, 2002), Steenbarger does not offer commercial services to traders but maintains a trading archive and blog at www.brettsteenbarger.com and a blog of market analytics at www.tradersfeed.blogspot.com.

Adrienne Laris Toghraie, MNLP, MCH, is a trader's coach and interna-tionally recognized authority in the field of human development for the financial community. She is founder and president of Trading on Target (www.TradingOnTarget.com). Toghraie's eight books on the psychol-ogy of trading including, Winning Edge 4 (Traders Press, 2002), have been highly praised by financial magazines. Her public seminars and private counseling, as well as her television appearances and keynote addresses at major industry conferences, have achieved a wide level of recognition and popularity.

GO (Gail Osten, former SFO editor): First, thanks to each of you for participating in this roundtable. Each in your own way has something to offer the trader from a psychological point of view. I'm interested to see how your responses may shed light from different angles. To start off, what would you say sets trading apart from any other profession?

ALT (Adrienne Laris Toghraie): When most traders first come into trading, they truly do not handle trading as a profession. In other professions, people endure long, arduous years of education to make decisions that become embedded for an automatic response for their neurology to handle. Without this training, trading sessions in the beginning are not only an intellectual choice, but an emotional choice. When dealing with losses, a trader goes into the psychological place where he stores all losses. Since human beings avoid losses, a trader who does not operate out of an automatic response will make an emotional choice. Emotional trading builds negative anchors that keep a trader from following good money-making strategies.

GO: It's been my experience that a lot of traders do indeed seem to jump in without any experience or education at all—particularly after a bull market where they have profited quite well from investments. It makes them feel like they're already experts. Any other ideas?

AK (Ari Kiev): One thing that differentiates trading from other activities is that you're constantly being measured. A long-term investor buys stock, holds for a year or two, and rides out the fluctuations. A trader who's taking advantage of short-term moves is very much influenced by the intra-day volatility and, so, he is measuring performance daily. A trader's performance is constantly judged, recorded, and measured. There aren't too many other activities out there where your performance is measured so closely. In a regular business you can say, "We'll get our figures quarterly, and we'll make projections and plans based on how things have been going." So in regular business, you're protected from the scorecard 'til the end of the game or 'til the end of the quarter.

RBR (Ruth Barrons Roosevelt): It's also different from a regular business because politics don't help. You can't charm your way through the markets. Maybe you can persuade people to do things, but your personal magnetism alone will not draw winning trades to you. Second, the everyday things are different. With trading, the future is completely unknown. It's not like walking into an office every day with a routine. In a day of trading, many more surprises will pop up than in a day in a cubicle. That's not to say that there aren't similarities, though. I would say that there are at least two similarities between trading and other types of professions. One is that risk taking is rewarded, but it needs to be managed risk. Second is that optimism is rewarded.

BS (Brett Steenbarger): You're right. There are definitely similarities. In fact, my focus has been on looking at the similarities rather than the differences, trying to identify fields that are similar to trading in several different respects, where they have a high case of activity, a high degree of risk and reward, and a high-performance demand. And, so, my search for similar fields has led me to professional sports and elite military services like the special forces. I have been trying to see how they are similar to trading and how people are trained in those fields as a way of getting some insight into how people might be trained to become effective traders.

GO: Interesting. As long as we're on the topic of similarities, what professions does everyone else think are similar to trading?

ALT: A surgeon, a trial lawyer, an athlete, concert performer, or any kind of person that performs and has to do it live.

GO: Because of the necessity for spontaneity?

ALT: Right, because you have to be continuously on alert. You have to be conscious, while at the same time perform somewhat intuitively. So, you have to be able to go with the flow of your education. You have to be able to go with the flow of what's coming next, even if you're not sure of what's coming next.

GO: Well you certainly don't know what's coming next in trading. What do you think, Ari?

AK: I agree with Adrienne. Sports, surgery...really, any job where you've got a limited amount of time to do something which is very complicated. If you're a surgeon, for instance, you may be in control of some of the variables, but when you have an elderly patient that has had some systems break down, and you have a limited amount of time to get the procedure done, you can't always predict how the patient is going to respond.

GO: And it's very life or death, probably more stressful than trading.

RBR: Actually, speaking of life and death...the insurance policies of floor traders, in terms of their health insurance etc., pay premiums just as high as skydivers, deep-sea divers, and all the most dangerous professions. In terms of stress, it's probably as high as any other. In other professions, while you could lose your job, you're not going to lose all your money in a given moment. So stress is higher in that sense.

GO: Are there any positive things regarding the kind of profession that trading is?

RBR: Oh, it's exciting. It's different every day. It can be infinitely rewarding. And it's so interesting, and every day is a whole new array of events. Because there's no limit to how much you can make with it, it's very, very rewarding. Every day is like Christmas! You've got these packages under the tree, and you don't know what's in there, but you know it could be something wonderful.

GO: That's a unique comparison. I've never thought of trading as being like Christmas. On that positive note, let's move on. So, we've established that trading is a high-stress, high-performance field, but people in other professions experience stress too. Do traders need specialized psychological advice? Couldn't they go to a regular therapist?

ALT: Usually, they can go to a regular therapist, but most therapists are trained to deal with issues over an extended period of time. Traders don't have that time. They need instant transformation. If the issues are handled over a long period of time, they might not have the money to continue the profession when they finally have the transformation necessary to follow the rules. In addition, most traders would be diagnosed as gamblers and treated as such by therapists. The truth is that to be exceptional at anything you must be obsessive-compulsive. The difference between someone who is a gambler in trading and a professional trader is that a trader is obsessive-compulsive about following rules.

RBR: You're exactly right, and a regular therapist may or may not understand what is involved with trading and could offer the worst ideas. Adding to that, though, I would say a lot of it also depends on the values of the therapist. For example, I was telling a colleague of mine that I had a client who was making $5,000 a day on the floor of the New York Stock Exchange and that he wanted to make $10,000. She replied, "Well, that's just disgusting." And I looked at her and said, "Well, that's why I work with these people, and you don't." He made up his mind to make $10,000. I believe that it's not wrong that if I make money, somebody else will lose. It's our obligation to be successful. So you could run into a difference in values of the person.

GO: Brett, you're a psychologist, do traders need specialized psychological advice?

BS: Some do. The key here is making a distinction between traders who have pre-existing emotional problems that are seeping into their trading versus traders who are really trading poorly, and that's creating their emotional problems.

GO: These are clearly two different scenarios.

BS: It's two different scenarios, and you really have to separate them. There certainly are people who have emotional problems. They may have relationship problems, and the fallout from those interferes with their processing of market information and making decisions in the market. And, yes, a general, competent therapist would be helpful in such a case because the primary problem is an emotional or a relationship problem. But if you have someone who's under-capitalized and not managing risk properly, then talking to the best therapist in the world will not change their outcome. Instead, they really need very specialized advice from someone who is a competent trader as well as someone who's capable of providing therapy.

AK: I don't think that being a good trader's coach entails being a good trader yourself necessarily. All that's really needed, I think, is somebody who understands the market, the impact of the market and the suggestibility of people in certain situations. For example, I talked to a client this morning who was running about a billion dollars, and he said, "These things have been tough lately because there are so many hedge funds, and trades are getting crowded." So all these hedge funds are out there shorting stocks and covering their shorts while he's trading them. He's trading against them, hanging in there and not getting taken out, but at the same time he was getting uncomfortable and wanted my guidance. To an extent I understand him, and to the extent that he truly believes his methodology, I could guide him to stay in his shorts by using a contrarian signal—to just stay with it and that in the long run, he'd be rewarded. I'd have to have been here a few times to feel confident about making that recommendation.

GO: I suppose it's really a matter of the trader's preference whether or not his coach or therapist is a trader himself. Many articles and books focus on the discipline trading requires, but don't you need discipline and training in other professions as much as you do trading? Is there a difference?

RBR: You need discipline in all areas of your life. Discipline is doing what needs to be done to get you to where you want to go. Whether you want to or not, whether you feel like it or not. You need discipline to exercise. You need discipline to get up in the morning. You need discipline to go to bed at night. You need discipline to go to work every day. It takes discipline in life to succeed.

GO: Is there more discipline that's necessary as a trader?

RBR: Well, if you don't have enough discipline, you'll slip much faster. It'll take longer in an ordinary job for a lack of discipline to show up. It could happen in a day if you're a trader.

AK: I would add to that, that trading successfully, trading to win, trading in the zone, mastering the markets—all those kinds of things require the ability to act counter-intuitively, which means when you're losing, the natural inclination is to hold on, to go into denial, to hope that things turn around...you stay attached to your original analysis because you believe it. Now, sometimes you want to stay in a losing position if you've done the work and it's an opportunity to really multiply the potential for profit, but the natural inclination for most people is to hold on to losers.

GO: So, in other words, it does require a lot of discipline.

AK: You have to practice, practice, practice, until you get comfortable doing the uncomfortable, like letting go of losing trades.

GO: Not being able to let go of losers seems to be a very common weakness among traders. How can traders assess their own work? How can they identify their strengths and weaknesses, such as not being able to let go of losers?

BS: Well, one of the things that is extremely helpful in that regard is that at the end of the year, I do an audit of each and every one of my trades.

GO: On each and every trade?

BS: On each and every trade, and I do hundreds in a year. I literally write out each trade by hand, including when I placed it, how many shares, contracts, whatever, and whether I was long or short, what my profit or loss was, trades that made the most and least money. I see what I was doing right and wrong and formulate one or two big goals. For instance, this past year, a relative handful of my trades were accounting for the majority of my profits. Fortunately, I was profitable on the year. So, I looked particularly at where those trades were coming from, and they were occasions where I was able to catch the sweet spot of a move where the short-term trend and the more intermediate-term trend were aligned.

And I realized I could be trading less frequently and really limiting myself to those good-trending opportunities, and I still could be making just as much money. So, part of my goal this year is to trade more selectively, to be more rule-governed in my trading, based on trend readings.

AK: It's interesting that you say that. Sometimes I'm able to get people to keep a diary, to keep real track of where they got in, where they got out, what they were feeling at the time they were getting out and then how much further the stock ran, how much did they leave on the table and how much did they give up because they were too anxious. Then they begin to identify those feelings. I have some people, who've become good at it, to even time how long their discomfort with certain trades would last. Once they knew how long it lasted, they had a better handle of the situation. Each time, the discomfort doesn't happen as much, and then the next time it happens even less. And then pretty soon, a trader can get comfortable with separating feelings from what the trade is.

GO: And that's exactly what traders need to be able to do. I think generally having a solid trading plan in place also enables a trader to separate feelings from the trade or avoid giving into emotion, wouldn't you say?

ALT: Well, I can't speak for everyone else, but, yes, traders need a business plan and part of it is like a regular business plan that you would put together if you were a shop owner, let's say. You'd have to have all of the information, the financial information and all of the information that you need for a business. Now, beyond that, a trader needs a methodology spelled out in a set of rules, even if those rules are intuitive. Going beyond that, they need contingency planning—everything that can go wrong and everything that can go right and seeing themselves with the best possible outcome, so that they can prepare themselves for any kind of situation. If you do not prepare for contingencies, you're like most traders in that once the flow of the markets change, you panic, and you create a lot of losses and negative anchors. This is one of the reasons a trader has to do a periodic review. The periodic review, by the way, is not every time you get huge draw-down trades. A periodic review should be done every three to four months when you can go back and look at your trading.

BS: I would say, it's not the plan, it's being planful that helps a lot. The term I've used—and it fits for me better as a trader and as a psychologist—is being rule-governed, that you have certain rules that you follow. Every little wiggle in the futures is not going to throw you for a loop or have you asking questions because you have a rule. The rule tells you when you get in it. The rule tells you when to get out. The rule tells you how much capital you're going to allocate to the trade. You have all of these rules that make it more automatic.

RBR: But sometimes they have those things planned out, and they violate the plan. They second-guess the plan in the excitement. Traders have to have confidence in their strategy, confidence that it will most likely work. They have to have confidence in the probability, because probabilities are all that they have, but probabilities ARE enough.

Another problem is that a lot of people will have so many indicators to tell them what to do that they get lost, and they've got so much stuff on their screen they can't even see the prices. So they can't make decisions. Sometimes the strategies that are the simplest are the wisest.

GO: So what should be in every trader's plan? What would you tell people who came to see you?

RBR: You need to have a strategy for entering the market and a strategy for exiting with profit and with a loss. And you need to have something that tells you what the trend is, whether it's up or down or flat.

GO: In addition to a plan, having a coach at your side may help take some of the trader's bias out as well. Having said that, how does a trader or investor determine if she could seek personal coaching, or maybe just when he or she really needs to be her own therapist?

RBR: Well, first of all, you can't be your own therapist because you're too subjective. You're in the middle of it, and sometimes you need somebody outside yourself to perceive what you're doing and to help you hold you to your commitments. It's just like nobody would go into the Olympics without a coach. They just wouldn't dream of it. You might have a physical coach and a psychological coach. Why shouldn't we, when we're in the biggest game of all time, have a coach?

BS: Well, I think any kind of good coaching or counseling is directed toward helping people become their own therapist. That's my goal in working with everyone, and I tell clients that. I tell them I want you to put me out of business. And so you're teaching people skills that they can utilize on their own. And typically that takes a certain form, so that you'll first describe the skill to the person. You'll then model it for them, show them how it's used. You'll then have them try the skill out in front of you, so that you can see that they know how to do it, and then you'll assign it as homework and then you'll have them do it on their own. And that way, they learn, they see, they can ask questions and they develop that skill on their own, and they don't need to use you.

RBR: I would agree with that. As a coach or therapist, you're not building a trader's dependence on yourself. You're building that person to be strong, to operate without you, but a trader can't necessarily start out being his own therapist.

AK: And traders definitely benefit from coaching. I would liken it to...why does an actor need a director? You know the actor knows how to act, but the director helps the actor to transcend his limiting notions about his own identity, about his own ability and so on. A coach can do the same for a trader.

GO: At what point in their trading/investing journey do you typically see traders or investors, personally? What types of situations typically bring them to you?

RBR: There are several. One would be that they've spent years de-

Blogs: A Tool for Cultivating a Winning Mindset

By: Brett N. Steenbarger, PhD

As a psychologist and an active trader, I am my own trading coach and client. Much of my self-work has little to do with resolving conflicts from the past, learning coping skills, or other such therapeutic staples. Rather, I find myself working on consistently implementing the cognitive, emotional, and behavioral patterns that distinguish exemplary performers across a variety of disciplines. There is rich research literature on the psychological factors that distinguish creative, successful individuals in the arts, sciences, sports, and politics. Dean Keith Simonton, psychologist at the University of California, Davis, and K. Anders Ericsson, psychologist at Florida State University, are two of the more prolific contributors to this body of knowledge. Both emphasize that high levels of achievement in any field are the result of continuous, intensive, deliberative practice, in which skills become internalized to the point of becoming automatic.

An insightful article about legendary baseball pitcher Sandy Koufax appeared in the May 16, 2003, issue of *Investor's Business Daily*. Koufax observed, "As much as you can do to get the variables out of the delivery, the easier it is to repeat. That's the key to a repeated golf swing or pitching motion or batting swing...The pitcher wants to do exactly the same thing every time." Jane Leavy, author of Koufax's biography, noted, "The hardest thing in sports is no single act, it is the replication of that act."

Working on my own trading, I have been able to achieve a higher degree of replication by developing a set of rules to guide my entries, exits, and position sizing. Most of these rules are based on research that I have performed regarding the trending qualities of the SP and ND futures. In general, I want to be entering directional markets when the market's trendiness is expanding, exiting when the trendiness is waning, and adding to positions when the short- and intermediate-term trends and trendiness are aligned.

To keep myself grounded in these rules, I maintain a daily weblog, which is an online diary that allows me to follow each trend-related measure, assess its status and formulate my ideas for the coming day's trading. The blog forces me to focus on basics and get the variables out of my trading. I have found that it reduces my internal mental chatter during trading by taking much of the discretion and potential impulsivity out of decision making. It takes me out of the mode of trying to pick tops and bottoms and concentrates my efforts on riding the sweet spot of market movements. It also makes all of my market mistakes quite public—a useful tool in cultivating humility!

signing a system to trade and now they can't pull the trigger on the system. That's one. Another would be that they're losing money over trading or not getting out of losses, and they come to a forced awareness that they need help. They'll come to me then.

GO: Those are the most typical problems that you see?

RBR: Yes. Or maybe they work for a bank and they'll ask the bank to send them to me and they will.

GO: OK. So, you do both individuals and individuals trading for institutions. Interesting. You work with institutional traders as well, Ari.

AK: Right. I work with a number of hedge funds, and I work with individuals within these hedge funds.

GO: Because you're there to help them anyway, in the context of the hedge fund, what are the most typical problems that you try to help them through?

AK: I think the biggest problem is getting people to size their positions, and I try to do that typically by getting them to set some goals. One is to really develop a methodology where there is a consistent kind of track record of performance. Somebody can have more winning days, but they don't make as much money on their winning days as they do on their losing days, which means they're holding on to their losers and not getting out.

GO: That's very typical, isn't it?

AK: Yes, so I would use these kinds of parameters. How much can you make this year? Given what you know, given that you have some control of sizing, given that you have so much capital, maybe you can make X dollars this year. OK. Say you have Y dollars of capital, so the next thing would be to get them to say, "To make X dollars a year means to make Z dollars a day. And to make Z dollars a day, how many positions do I need? How big should they be? How long should I hold them? How much work do I have to do to give myself the confidence to be able to buy those kinds of things." So, managing loss and developing that discipline, building a kind of methodology, finding a group of financial instruments that you really can do the work on. It's not just automatic.

GO: But to be able to ingrain a skill, to make it automatic, doesn't that take a certain type of personality? Are there certain types of personalities that make better traders than others? Or are there certain personalities that should probably avoid trading altogether?

ALT: One is the opposite of the other. Entrepreneurial people–and that means self-starters, motivators, risk-takers—make some of the best traders. People who are not only analytical, but who are creative as well. Most people think that to have the analytical skills is to be a great trader, but I found that to be a really great trader you also have to be creative and synergistically combine the right brain with the left brain. Emotionally self-confident, optimistic, self-disciplined—that's how I would describe a good trader.

GO: What about smart?

ALT: There are different kinds of smart. There is emotional smart. There is street-wise smart. There is wisdom. There is intellectually smart. I find that intellectually smart very often gets in the way of being a great trader. People that are street-smart, wise, and intuitive are more likely to be better traders.

BS: I was doing questionnaire research awhile back with Linda Raschke, looking at traits and coping styles. The successful traders were high in a trait called conscientiousness, meaning they were very dependable, very reliable. The successful traders had coping styles that were more problem-based. When something went wrong in trading, they would say, "OK, what can I do about this trade?" The traders who were having problems were high in a trait called neuroticism, which is a tendency toward negative emotional experiences, like anxiety and depression. And when the unsuccessful traders were having a problem with trading, they would get emotional and they'd say, "What's wrong with me?" and "Nothing ever works."

GO: So there are certain personalities that probably should avoid trading altogether?

BS: I think so. No one ever wants to hear that, of course.

RBR: I don't think so. If they want to trade, we've got to find a way for them. They come to me to find a way, and so I'll find a way, with their personality, to do it. But basically, good traders are optimistic. They are optimists who can apply discipline on top of their optimism. Good traders are risk takers. They're people that are comfortable with uncertainty. They're adventurous. They're able to think quickly and make decisions. They're able to act. They're willing to admit when they're wrong, and they don't have a fear of being wrong.

GO: Do you ever turn anyone away?

RBR: No, I don't, because they've come to me and said, "Help me." I've had some really difficult clients, and I've been able to get them trading.

GO: Well, for those people who really want to trade, but need help, how do they find a good coach or therapist? How would you define a trader's coach or therapist?

ALT: First of all, recommendation is the best. Credibility, evidence of work and accomplishments, speeches, articles, books. Ask for testimonials or ask for people to call. A good coach takes an investment in your life, someone who makes a long-term commitment to you–not just there for you right in the beginning, but at each new level of success. And the good coach makes a trader as independent as possible as soon as possible. That's really important. In a typical psychology class, you're really taught to keep a client coming. A coach gets the best results when a client trusts and follows the advice the coach gives, so it can't only be a one-way street. There has to be a bond between the coach and the trader to get the best results.

BS: A good coach or therapist is part expert, part teacher. I think if you don't have experience and expertise in the skill domain, you're going to be limited in what you impart. I don't think a person could be a good basketball coach if they had never played basketball. That being said, just knowing a lot about something or having done it oneself doesn't necessarily mean you'll be effective in imparting it to others.

AK: I think a good traders' coach is somebody that understands the trading process, the challenge, the dilemma that traders face as regards the realm of uncertainty in a disciplined way...the balance between the willingness to take risk against the need to preserve capital. That creates a certain amount of inner tension and frustration, and you have to be able to deal with that. You need somebody that's interested in working with people who are in a game that lends itself to high performance. Not everybody likes to do that because you're talking to people who are—if they're successful—able to do things that are beyond what most ordinary mortals could do. So, these guys are, as a result of their willingness to play in the game, like sports stars. You have to be able to work with them and help them and not put a value judgment on their lifestyle or the fact that they're making such an inordinate amount of money. And yet, do it without feeling envy or jealousy, which isn't necessarily the easiest thing.

GO: I'd like to switch gears here. There are probably more investors than traders, so I want to address the investors out there with this question. What do you do differently for traders and investors? Is there a difference?

BS: I think it's a completely different thing. They're not even related in my book psychologically because in investing you are making longer-term decisions and it's a very conscious, deliberate, analytical process. In trading, very, very often, you're making short-term decisions in very active markets, and you're relying on skills that you have honed over time and that you're executing relatively automatically. The shorter the time frame you're holding a position, the more automatic your skills have to be. You don't have time to engage in elaborate analyses.

RBR: Yes, but it shouldn't be too much different, it's just a different time frame. That's where people in the stock market get robbed. If they have more of a trading mentality, they would get out or go short. But they don't. So we really don't want to think of investment as just staying put. With any good investment, you have to see if it's still a good investment. You need to reassess it. Investing is just slower-term trading, and I think if you look at it that way, and reassess all the time, you would be much better.

ALT: Psychologically, a trader and investor go through the same process, but those who make quicker decisions are more likely to have more emotional issues to deal with. For both, I start out with an assessment.

GO: In other words, we have some very different ideas out there about what it means to be an investor and a trader. It's definitely something to consider for anyone who is seeking a trading or investing coach. This is always something I love to ask because I think it is exceedingly helpful for traders–if there were three pieces of advice you could offer the new trader, what would they be?

ALT: First, to have a good education in trading. And while there's a lot of stuff out there, there's a lot of people teaching and everything, you really need to self-educate. Just read, read, read, read and read. And then have a plan, a business plan which includes rules for entering and exiting a trade. And follow those rules, and if you can't follow those rules, then hire a coach.

GO: Brett?

BS: First of all, if your goal is to become proficient, that takes, like in any field, a number of years of concentrated practice. In trading, start with a very small account and very small positions, so that you can survive your learning curve. And, then, as you gain success, as you gain experience, you can always add to your size.

The second thing is that, if a newcomer's going to be a full-time, very active trader, he must be adequately capitalized. If he's under-capitalized, he's subjecting himself to very high potential drawdowns. So when

Stretching into a New Comfort Zone

By: Adrienne Laris Toghraie

Robert has been a consistent trader for many years. Each morning, he awakens knowing that his mortgage is going to be paid, his children will remain in private school, and his wife can impress friends with elegant entertaining from his trading profits. When Robert stopped at my booth at his first trading conference and looked at my sign, "Problems with Discipline, Stop Here," he said, "This is the most important part of trading," and asked if I could bring him to a new level of success in trading. I suggested that he take an evaluation and see if there was anything that was actually preventing him from reaching his next level of success. Though Robert's evaluation indicated that he was in great psychological shape, he wanted to kick up his trading and his life a notch. He decided to work with me in private consultation.

Robert had a remarkably good life without the trials and setbacks that most traders experience. But I was to find out that being safe in his level of comfort was why he never made it to exceptional levels of trading success. His practical and loving parents who never wanted to risk or stretch beyond their comfort zone passed those ideals on to their son. When I asked him why he wanted to go beyond his level of security, he said it was because his son's achievements as a golfer inspired Robert to do more. The athletic coach had inspired his son's success, which then inspired Robert to become the best that he could be. Robert joked, "I cannot be outdone by my son."

In order to motivate the best performance in Robert, we had to change his values about money and risk, which meant that we had to increase his neurological system's comfort zone. We accomplished this transformation by replacing his current mental images of his life and the feelings of comfort those pictures inspired, with new pictures of how he would like his life to be and feelings of comfort with a more enriched life. In addition, we developed an overview of his entire life, accentuating and expanding on the things that gave him more pleasure in a progressively more ambitious lifestyle.

I am pleased to report that Robert is actually working fewer hours, making more money by cherry picking, and risking more with his better trades than ever before. This process has given him twice the amount of time he is able to spend with his son on the golf course, and he and his wife are spending more quality time together. Their life together has been revitalized. He is taking better care of his health and has a new interest in learning more about himself. Now, Robert lives his life finding enjoyment and excitement in the process of reaching towards the best he can be in all areas of his life.

a trader is under-capitalized, he goes through more emotional swings because the drawdowns are affecting a greater percentage of his total equity. So, being well capitalized is also a psychological strategy.

GO: I don't think most people would have considered being well-capitalized as a good psychological approach to trading. And your third piece of advice?

BS: My number three piece of advice: Find a mentor. Find someone who you can emulate and learn from that person. That was certainly true when I learned how to do therapy. I could pick up things from their style and synthesize those into my own style. And I think it's the same with traders.

GO: Ari?

AK: First, keep your losses down. Be willing to face the facts, tell the truth, admit to being wrong, and get out to preserve your capital. Don't get attached to your ideas to the point that you are losing money.
    Second, as you build up a cushion, begin to size your positions commensurate with your level of conviction in your ideas and consistent with your profit targets. This is tougher than it appears, and most people tend to be too conservative and cautious and miss opportunities. Be willing to be guided by your objectives and do the work necessary to justify your conviction.
    Third, review what you have done, be flexible, keep course correcting and improving your performance and adjusting to the new and changing demands of the marketplace. Successful trading requires attention and intention and commitment.

GO: Brett, there is one other thing that you said to me that I'd like to add as refers to how trading, or working on it, can be of benefit generally. One more time, because I think it's a good way to end this piece.

BS: When done properly, I think that working on trading is a way of working on yourself. As you work on the trading, it forces you to deal with pressure in certain ways, and it improves you as a person. And as you improve yourself as a person, and work on your ability to handle risk and work on those analytical abilities, it helps the trading as well. So, in the best of all worlds, you get a certain synergy going, your trading is improving and you're improving. That makes it a noble pursuit.

GO: Excellent comments from you all today. Thanks again for your insights.

Gail Osten has been involved in senior marketing, advertising, and corporate communications positions in the derivatives business and commercial real estate business for more than thirty years, including positions with Chicago Mercantile Exchange, the Chicago Board of Trade, and MidAmerica Commodity Exchange. She is a former executive editor of *SFO* magazine and produced forty issues of the magazine. This article originally appeared in *SFO* in July 2003.

ARE YOUR MENTAL FILTERS POLLUTED?

BY TONI TURNER

As an industrious and conscientious society, we are all about clean. We expect our retail, entertainment, and business environments to sparkle. We scrub our homes, our garages, and ourselves. There's another area, however, that we tend to neglect and leave in a state of untidiness: our personal mental filtering systems.

What if we could settle into our desk chairs each morning and face our trading screens with our mental and emotional operating system completely clear of concerns, prejudices, negative memories, and cloudy personal belief systems? What if the mental and emotional filters through which we sift and categorize incoming information were free from judgmental clutter and acquired "soot?" Clearly, we would observe the market with crystal-clear perceptions and trade our plans with clarity and confidence. In other words, we'd make more money!

Every time we study a chart or other research material, then click on buy or sell, our decisions have had to wiggle through the gamut of our own established belief systems and thought associations—in short, mental filters. These filters are lined with the gauze of a lifetime of feelings and experiences. While they are designed to keep us safe, some filters actually choke our progression as traders. Negative mental clutter—most of which we're not aware of harboring—can act as virtual clogging agents that limit free-flowing decisions and the nimble mindset so necessary to success.

In this chapter, we'll talk about three pollutants that get stuck in our mental filters and gum up our trading decisions. They are: personal value and deservability programs, loss remorse, and performance anxiety.

Do they look innocent? You bet they do. That's why they're so hard to spot. But just like greasy, grimy street dirt, they gather silently under the hood where you can't see them or hear them, until your engine (trading career) lurches badly or grinds to a stop.

Check Your Personal Value Programs

As traders, if we are asked, "Do you deserve to make money fast and without physical effort?" most of us will raise our chins and answer, "Of course!" Deep down inside, though, some of us don't really believe it.

The United States long has been a leader in the world economy, mainly because of our work ethic. We stress a steely-jawed, "by the sweat of our brow," "no pain, no gain" mentality. We sleep less, endure longer workweeks, and take shorter vacations than any other culture. "After all," we insist, "money doesn't grow on trees!" (Translation: earning money demands hard, backbreaking work.)

It's no wonder that when we, as traders, seize hundreds or thousands of dollars—in minutes to hours, with very little physical labor—a tiny voice deep inside may whisper that we simply don't deserve it. (Yes, we study and research for long hours, but it's possible to grab profits without that work. We all know newcomers to the markets who have made lucky trades that netted them a profit.)

If we subscribe to the work-ethic mentality, it's important to realize that making money quickly is a characteristic of our occupation. And those of us who have survived this game for years can attest to the fact that while the labor isn't back-breaking, it stretches and strains every fiber in our brains!

Another deservability program comes to us courtesy of, "The love of money is the root of all evil." As traders, we focus on price and money all day, every day. If we unconsciously subscribe to this "loving" money-is-evil association, and if we fail to recognize it and replace it with a prosperity-is-good concept, it can sabotage our profit-making abilities.

Finally, some of us unwittingly drag around old reprimands from our youth. "You're so lazy, you don't deserve to make money," or "You'll never amount to anything," can haunt us into adulthood, run deep under our personal self-image and seep into our trading decisions.

Does this pattern sound familiar to you? Think back to your childhood. Did anyone tell you that you were undeserving of good fortune? Or did someone just give you that feeling? The feeling alone will anchor a thought pattern into your subconscious that can usurp your trading (and many other) goals.

Insidious because of their invisible nature, deservability issues cause many successful traders to sabotage their own careers. Afflicted traders produce a string of winning trades, but they inevitably lose all their profits.

I knew such a trader. This man was an excellent trading guru with enormous knowledge. He also was a talented trader. He traded his own account—a large account by anyone's standards. There was only one chink in his armor: he'd make hefty gains, and then give them all back. He continued this cycle for years, with bigger and bigger drawdowns.

One day, he did it. He totally blew up his account. He told me privately that he was relieved! Deep down inside, he'd always thought himself to be a pretender, and he really didn't think he deserved success. When he finally lost his entire account, he unconsciously played out and confirmed what his deeply rooted belief system assured him was true.

To remedy deservability programs that may lurk under the surface of your conscious mind and slow your trading career, ask yourself at the beginning of each day if you are ready and deserving to earn money easily and quickly. Do you hear an enthusiastic yes? If you don't, hold off trading until you re-examine your thought processes and replace all negative beliefs with positive, proactive versions.

Next, reserve a special slot in your trading journal to jot down thoughts and feelings you experienced during the trading day. Before you fluff off this exercise, know that it takes guts and determination to write down these associations. Some feelings and thought patterns can be painful to examine, but keep in mind that the benefits of doing so can result in a much more successful trading career.

Think of it this way: a negative deservability program that undermines your progress could be compared to a splinter in your heel; it's tiny and nearly invisible to the naked eye, but hurts like heck when you walk on it. When the pain irritates you enough, you sit down, put your glasses on, turn the sole of your foot up and rub your finger over your heel until you locate it. (Yes, the process is tedious, and it hurts, but you have to do it or you can't walk.) After you pluck the splinter out, the pain disappears instantly and the spring returns to your step.

Banish Loss Remorse

The next association that corrodes our mental filter is loss remorse. Basically, as traders we generate two kinds of losses: defined and undefined. Good traders define their risk parameters—and, thus, their losses—before they enter each trade. (Depending on account size and experience level, many traders take this step further by defining their maximum account drawdowns for the day, week, and month.)

On the flip side, impulse traders jump into trades hootin' and hollerin' about the big bucks they're going to rake in. Tap them on the shoulder and ask them to define their risk, and they'll answer "Huh? Risk? Whassat?"

If they find themselves caught in a violent market storm, they have no clue where the emergency exit (read: protective stop point) is located. Their only choice is to chase the price down (or up, if they're short) and throw a market order at it. Remorse City.

Now, if we're honest, most of us will admit that at one time or another, we've ignored our risk parameters. We've held stubbornly onto a losing trade and then clung to it while it sunk to gloomier and gloomier price depths. Trouble is that when this occurs, we don't merely lose money. The experience almost always results in feelings of guilt and remorse that stay glued in our subconscious long after the position is closed.

And if these feelings aren't dealt with and remedied, they cloud our perspective. Moneymaking opportunities can step into our path, but we may not recognize them because of the film of regret and shame that stains our perspective.

Unlike deservability issues, loss remorse is easy to spot. Happily, though, it can be cured with a strong dose of discipline ("...and from this day forward, I'll always follow my plan"), a written-out list of trading criteria (example: "I trade in the direction of the longer-term trend"), and a well-thought-out plan for each trade (entry price, initial protective stop price, and initial profit target determined before trade execution).

Here's another technique you can use when making changes that require steely self-control: "corner" yourself. Tell a friend that you've established new techniques for money management, and that you're committed to them. Just knowing that your friend will bring up the subject and ask how your new plan is going will remind you of your promise and help keep you from deserting it. Plus, you won't want to admit to your friend that you didn't follow through with your commitment.

Finally, your dedication to discipline and money management applications soon should produce profits. Once you begin to see green on your screen, any residual loss remorse will be replaced by new levels of self-confidence and self-worth.

Eliminate Performance Anxiety and Perfectionism

Critical self-examination is a symptom of type-A personalities and common with high achievers—which most traders are. Still, nit-picking and judgmental self-talk during the trading day fogs our perspective and causes us to second-guess the way we perceive incoming information. These negative tapes keep us from being mentally nimble and recognizing market reversals.

Most types of performance anxiety are rooted in the personality trait known as perfectionism. Those of us afflicted with this trait (I am a card-carrying member of the Perfectionists' Society) habitually establish stratospheric goals for ourselves, and then berate ourselves for not being able to achieve them. In trading, this could mean setting unrealistic monetary goals for the day or week. When the goals aren't attained, we scold ourselves for the perceived failure.

With novice traders especially, this scenario sets off the chain of emotions that segues into overtrading. The trader hopes to reach the monetary goal set—so he overtrades, even in a low-odds market—and loses money.

To trade his account out of the loss pit, anxiety-driven internal pressures urge him to trade even more. Now, frantic actions bring more losses...and more negative self-talk...which goad the trader to trade more...which causes more losses. On and on the cycle goes.

Another form of performance anxiety comes with increasing share size. For example, a trader used to executing trades of 300-share-lot sizes usually feels apprehensive if she increases her position to 1,000-share positions. That stands to reason. A quarter-point loss for 1,000 shares is $250; for 300 shares, it totals $75, or one-third the drawdown. Just knowing the possibility exists to lose three times the usual amount tolerated can promote increased performance anxiety and fear-driven tactics.

How do the perfectionists among us purge our mental filters of the limiting traits that result in profit-blocking actions?

First, shift your focus from performance-driven goals to process-driven or method-driven goals. For example, instead of saying, "I'm going to make $1,000 every day this week," substitute, "I will strive to plan each trade carefully and then trade my plan at least eighty percent of the time." When you achieve eighty percent, raise the bar to eighty-five percent and higher, until trading with your plan becomes second nature. Over time, you'll make more money this way because decisions will be clear of the pressure of unrealistic demands.

If you've ever over-traded, you know that action leads directly into the frantic zone. That's another reason we learn to carefully monitor feelings that simmer just underneath the surface of our thoughts when trading. The only emotion you want to feel is a sense of calm confidence born of discipline, knowledge, and experience.

Any form of fear that creeps into your trades, from nervousness to outright panic, should trigger you to stop. Stand up and move away from your desk. Reassess the markets and your actions. Are you in sync with the markets, or out of sync? You may want to take some profits off the table, tighten stops, and take the day off. Knowing when not to trade truly is the mark of a professional. Next, if you decide to increase share size and it makes sense with your account size and money management goals, go for it. But do so a hundred shares at a time, over a week or two time period. That way, you'll get used to handling larger increments slowly—and with the least amount of pressure.

Clean Mental Filters Promote Free-Flowing Decisions

Successful trading is ninety percent mindset and attitude. So, take time to give your mental and emotional filters a regular inspection and clean-up. Identify and eliminate accumulated perceptions that clog your decision-making abilities.

Then when you settle into your chair each morning, you will approach the market with your mental and emotional operating system clean, healthy, and running at maximum capacity!

Toni Turner is the best-selling author of *A Beginner's Guide to Day Trading Online* (Adams Media Corporation, 2000), *A Beginner's Guide to Short-Term Trading* (Adams Media Corporation 2002), and *Short-Term Trading in the New Stock Market* (St. Martin's Press, 2005). She is also a popular speaker and educator at financial conferences and forums nationwide. For more information, please visit www.toniturner.com. This article originally appeared in *SFO* in June 2005.

9

HOW TO BE A RESILIENT TRADER

BY BRETT N. STEENBARGER, PhD AND MARK D. COOK

The destruction of the World Trade Center buildings was a watershed event for America. It also was a landmark event for those individual Americans who either directly experienced or witnessed the attack. Counselors worked overtime following 9/11, assisting individuals who were displaying symptoms of traumatic stress. A large number of people, however—including some who escaped from the buildings— were not traumatized by the horrific events of that day. Shortly after the attacks, they reached out to help others and somehow went about the business of life. These hardy souls displayed a quality that psychologists refer to as resilience. Even when exposed to overwhelming stress, they managed to function effectively, without delayed, dysfunctional consequences.

Thanks to recent research, we now know more about resilience than ever before—and that understanding is of tremendous relevance to traders.

Stress and Coping

To get a better handle on resilience, let's start with the basics. We use the term stressors to refer to events that create emotional wear and tear for people, and these can vary in their impact. Stressors typically

TABLE 1: Common Coping Strategies

Confrontation Facing the source of stress head on; deciding on fight instead of flight

Distancing Retracting one's emotions by convincing oneself that the stressful event is not important; that there are more important problems to worry about in life, etc.

Self-Controlling Making active efforts to restrain one's impulses by holding back anger, tears, displays of nervousness, etc.

Seeking Social Support Relying on the advice and support of others to handle a stressful event

Accepting Responsibility Taking the blame for adverse outcomes; refusing to make excuses for failure

Escape or Avoidance Active efforts to run away from threatening events through the use of fantasy, drugs or alcohol, alternate activities, etc.

Planful Problem Solving Active attempts to identify what went wrong in an adverse outcome and develop strategies for dealing with the problem

Positive Reappraisal Efforts to find the silver lining in adverse outcomes by identifying what could be learned or gained from the experience

Research on resilience suggests that there is no single coping strategy that characterizes the resilient individual. Rather, resilience appears to be the result of having many strategies that work for a trader and being able to retain access to these strategies under difficult conditions. Rehearsing these difficult conditions as realistically as possible expands the trader's ability to retain access to coping during the heat of unanticipated market events—good and bad.

Source: Adapted from The Ways of Coping Test by Susan Folkman and Richard Lazarus

affect people in direct proportion to their threat value. A traffic jam is a particular threat if we are in a rush; the loss of a loved one is threatening if we counted on that person for love and companionship.

Our emotional, behavioral, and physical responses to stressors are known as coping. People employ a variety of coping strategies in day-to-day life, many of which are closely correlated with their personality traits. An extroverted person may rely on social coping strategies, sharing problems with others, and seeking support. Others may employ problem-focused coping strategies, actively attempting to solve the challenge at hand (see *Table 1* for a description of common coping strategies).

Most people manage daily stressors successfully with their usual coping strategies, but when stresses become overwhelming and normal coping methods no longer suffice, trauma results. And trauma leads to erratic and unpredictable emotional and behavioral responses.

Here's a simple trading example. You are a swing trader of the E-mini S&Ps, have a $100,000 trading account, and have just purchased three contracts. Within moments, the market hits a down-draft and you are down three full points on the position. Cursing your poor timing, you notice that the up-trend is still intact, and you hold the position, eventually exiting for a nice gain.

Imagine the same scenario, except you have just purchased thirty contracts. The full point loss means that your account has taken a paper hit of $4,500, not $450. Realizing that your account is now down 4.5 percent in a matter of moments, you suddenly think, "What if this continues? What if there's economic news that I don't know about?" In a panic, you get out of the position, only to see later that it continued its up-trend and would have made a nice winner.

This scenario, with which most short-term traders (including ourselves!) can empathize all too well, is an illustration of how coping strategies can be overwhelmed in the face of threat and stress. On paper, the three-lot trade was no different from the thirty-lot one. Psychologically, however, they were quite different.

Most traders don't realize that their well-planned trading strategies fly out the window once stress overwhelms their ability to cope. Once the body enters the flight-or-fight stress mode, blood flow patterns shift away from the brain's executive center—the frontal cortex—and toward motor regions and the body's periphery. When stressed traders feel as though they are losing their minds, they are quite literally correct!

Resilience: The Triumph of Coping

A resilient person is one whose coping remains intact even during threatening events that would traumatize others. A resilient, trend-following thirty-lot trader would have sat through the $4,500 down-draft as if it were a $450 drawdown. That doesn't mean that the resilient trader wouldn't feel some heat, only that the stress would not overwhelm attempts to cope.

Such resilience goes hand-in-hand with another personality characteristic: persistence. Resilient individuals are not apt to break down or give up when threatened. They persevere under difficult conditions. Interestingly, this is a characteristic found among highly talented people who leave their marks on their fields, from the arts and sciences to athletics and politics.

One of the earliest studies of geniuses, an investigation of 301 gifted individuals by Catherine Cox in 1926, found that the persistent drive for achievement was one of the most important predictors of eventual eminence in a particular field. Recently, Dean Keith Simonton, a psychologist and researcher at the University of California, Davis, has found that greatness is Darwinian: creativity provides mutation/variation, and the responses of scientific/artistic/political communities comprise the forces of selection. According to Simonton, persons most likely to influence their fields are those that persist in the face of selection, offering so many creative variations that, eventually, a few contributions break through to make a difference. Such persistence, however, is only possible when there is a high degree of emotional resilience.

We don't typically think of traders as creative geniuses, but the analogy does prove instructive. The common trading strategy—the canned indicator with parameters preset by software—is not the one that consistently makes money. Rather, it is the strategy that views the market in a unique way that can obtain a sustainable edge.

For example, in testing short-term trading strategies for his website (www.brettsteenbarger.com), Brett noticed that when the semiconductor stocks (the SOX index) rallied stronger than the S&P 500 (SPX) stocks during an up move, the rise was more likely to continue than if the semiconductor stocks lagged the S&P. Similarly, when the SOX fell harder than the SPX during a bear move, the decline was more likely to persist than if the SOX displayed relative strength. Out of this relationship, he developed a "SOX and STOCKS" indicator that tracked the relative movements of SOX and SPX. This later proved useful in determining holding periods for positions during intra-day moves.

If the successful trader generates variations of a strategy that offer an edge, the market provides the forces of selection. Victor Niederhoffer and Laurel Kenner, authors of *Practical Speculation* (Wiley, 2003), are well known for their ideas regarding ever-changing cycles. The strategies that work in one market (think buying opening gaps to the upside during the tech stock bull market of the late 1990s) tend to fail in other markets (the bear market of 2000 to 2002).

To succeed over the long haul, the trader must persist in generating creative variations: ever-changing strategies for ever-changing markets. Traumatized traders—even talented ones—do not succeed over time simply because they are unable to finish the race. That is why resilience is so important to trading.

Understanding Resilience

An important review of research pertaining to resilience appeared in the January 2004 issue of American Psychologist. Written by Columbia University psychologist George Bonanno, the review makes several important points:

- **Resilience is different from recovery** People who recover from a traumatic stress typically undergo a period of dysfunction soon after the threatening event and then return to their baseline functioning. Resilient individuals, however, never experience this initial reaction. They maintain their baseline functioning even under the most challenging conditions.
- **Resilience is common** As in the aftermath of 9/11, the majority of people exposed to those events did move on with their lives. Although we were all touched by the tragedy, full-blown posttraumatic stress was the exception rather than the rule. Similarly, among people who lose a loved one, only ten to fifteen percent display chronic depression and distress. More than half report relatively low levels of distress and sustain their functioning throughout their period of grief.
- **There are multiple pathways to resilience** Resilient individuals do not use a single set of coping strategies to maintain their functioning during stressful times. Rather, they employ a variety of strategies that best fit their personality and retain access to these even during periods of high threat.

Bonanno describes the common belief that, if one does not actively talk about or deal with losses, there will be some delayed grief or stress reaction at a later juncture. He points out, however, that this has not proven to be the case among resilient individuals. They do not simply sweep stress under a psychological rug. Rather, they cope with that stress throughout the period of exposure, proactively minimizing its impact.

One of the characteristics we have consistently noted among successful traders is persistence in the face of success as well as failure.

High levels of success require that a mind be prodded to levels beyond the norm. An Olympic athlete readies him or herself for levels not thought possible before the training. Similarly, a trader pursues profits that the normal working individual cannot fathom. A person who stops at his goals will atrophy to mediocrity. The resilient trader responds to success by raising the bar and jumping higher, realizing that the elevation he reaches can very well be beyond his line of vision. Most people stop assimilating what they do not see. The true entrepreneur—and every successful trader is an entrepreneur—looks and sees what isn't evident to most.

The evolution of their viewpoint is what all successful traders endure: I have seen myself and it is ugly! I have seen myself and it is fixable! I have seen myself and it is pleasurable! Resilience takes the form of self-flagellation to persevere. The first step in any change process—the willingness to take a hard, accurate look at oneself and acknowledge the ugliness—is itself a manifestation of resilience. In his seminars, Mark teaches that time is an ally for acquiring wisdom. He uses the formula knowledge x experience=wisdom to illustrate how persistence, driven by resilience, helps one accumulate an understanding of oneself and the markets. Wisdom, he stresses, must be continually fertilized with facts and time.

Can We Improve Resilience?

So now we get to the heart of the matter: what can traders do to build resilience?

Research on the short-term treatment of anxiety and trauma suggests that we can indeed build resilience. The cognitive-behavioral psychologist, Donald Meichenbaum, for example, developed a technique in the 1970s that he referred to as "stress inoculation." His idea was simple: just as a low dose of an inactive virus can stimulate the body's defenses during a vaccination, perhaps a low dose of a stress can marshal our psychological defenses: our coping.

Meichenbaum's technique required clients to identify stressful events that were likely to occur in the near future, such as a public speaking engagement, a first date, or a final exam. They were then encouraged to vividly imagine these events while picturing themselves engaging in successful coping maneuvers. The imagined stressors were not as threatening as the actual events, but like a low dose of an inactive virus, they were real enough to trick the mind and body into activating ways of coping. The key to the stress inoculation was that the clients were not simply talking to their therapists about stress. Instead, they were actively experiencing stressors via imagination, recruiting their best coping in the process. Not surprisingly, Meichenbaum found that individuals who prepared for stresses with such inoculation coped far better than those who dealt with situations without emotional preparation.

The variation of stress inoculation that Brett has found most helpful for traders is known as "flooding." In some ways, this represents the flip side of Meichenbaum's method. Instead of using a mild version of the anticipated stressor to activate coping, the psychologist encourages the trader to vividly rehearse absolute worst-case scenarios. For example, a trader who is afraid of having his sell stop hit is encouraged to imagine the market gapping sharply lower, well below the stop point. Or, instead of imagining feeling like a loser after a period of drawdown, the trader is asked to create an image of being publicly ridiculed for his shortcomings. The goal is not simply to evoke coping, but to allow traders to experience their fear, shame, and anxiety as fully as possible in as extreme a form as possible.

At first they are reluctant to allow themselves to feel such negative feelings. Once they allow themselves to live through a worst-case scenario, however, the reaction is almost always, "That wasn't as bad as I thought it would be." That recognition is extremely liberating.

Such therapy works by building an individual's resilience. The repeated exposure to a stressful event helps to normalize it, making it less scary. This principle underlies the "crawl, walk, run" training procedures of Special Forces in preparation for dangerous missions. By repeatedly rehearsing the missions—first slowly, then in growing degrees of simulation—soldiers are able to anticipate events that might go awry, activating their planning and coping. This makes it more likely that the missions will succeed when the frictions of war inevitably interfere with the best-laid plans.

The implications for trading are profound: resilience is not built by education, and it does not develop as the result of self-analysis, self-help techniques, or psychotherapy. Resilience is a function of training. Nietzsche's dictum—what does not kill me makes me stronger—is the training formula for building resilience. This is why post-traumatic stress responses respond significantly better to therapies that provide prolonged exposure to actual stressors than to traditional psychotherapy. It is also why exposures that are prolonged work better than briefer exposures. To no small degree, the exposure therapies such as flooding are training regimens, not mere counseling approaches.

So, how can traders take advantage of this research? Investigations of the treatment of traumatic stress make clear that it is the exposure to threatening events—and not learning of skills or development of insights—that facilitates emotional reprocessing. Moreover, it is clear that prolonged exposure is a critical ingredient in accelerating emotional change by stimulating the development of resilience. At this juncture, we don't really know how far the relationship between prolongation of exposure and reprocessing of stress extends. If a ninety-minute exposure is much more effective than a standard forty-five-minute session, might a three-hour exposure be more powerful still? We don't know the answer to this question, because insurance companies will not pay for three-hour sessions, and therapists are too leery of liability suits to put their clients through psychological Hell Week.

Brett's experience with traders in this area suggests that the relationship between the duration of exposure and the development of resilience is an exponential one. Very small amounts of exposure are insufficient to challenge the individual and build his or her coping. More intensive exposure, along the lines of Army Ranger School or Navy SEAL training, greatly accelerates the pace at which coping skills become routine and unfamiliar threats lose their power. It is likely that five consecutive hours of realistic rehearsal would yield far more dramatic results than five hourly sessions conducted weekly.

If that which does not kill us does indeed make us stronger, it behooves us to move well outside our comfort zones. Vivid flooding—highly prolonged exposure to worst-case trading scenarios under emotional conditions—is a rapid means for divesting stressors of their threat and building a trader's resilience. When you have repeatedly experienced the worst that could happen to you and made it through to the other side, you have gone a long way toward stress-proofing your trading.

Brett N. Steenbarger, PhD, is associate clinical professor of psychiatry and behavioral sciences at SUNY Upstate Medical University in Syracuse, NY. As director of trader development for Kingstree Trading, LLC, in Chicago, he mentors professional traders and coordinates a trader training program. An active trader of the stock indexes, Steenbarger uses statistically based pattern recognition for intra-day trading. The author of *Enhancing Trader Performance: Proven Strategies from the Cutting Edge of Trading Psychology* (Wiley Trading, 2006) and *The Psychology of Trading: Tools and Techniques for Minding the Markets* (Wiley, 2002), Steenbarger maintains a trading archive and blog at www.brettsteenbarger.com and a blog of market analytics at www.traderfeed.blogspot.com.

Mark D. Cook won the 1992 U.S. Investing Championship with more than a five hundred-percent return and was one of the traders profiled in Jack Schwager's modern classic, *Stock Market Wizards*. As part of his continuing commitment to instruct and encourage traders of all experience levels, he hosts regular seminars at his trading office in East Sparta, Ohio. Cook also issues a twice-daily advisory service for professional traders. He can be reached at cookfax2@aol.com, or via his website at www.markdcook.com. This article originally appeared in *SFO* in July 2004.

WHY CAN'T YOU PULL THE TRIGGER?

BY NED GANDEVANI, PhD

A common problem among novice and experienced traders alike is at some point they fail to implement their trading plans. They may spend countless hours developing a trading plan, but for some reason, when the time comes to execute their plan, they lose sight of the goal and let the trading opportunities presented pass them by without reaping any of the benefits.

For example, you may see the market approaching your price level to buy, but you fail to pull the trigger at the critical time. As the market moves up, you feel compelled to act, yet you do not. You feel angry and begin to beat yourself up psychologically. You keep asking yourself why you didn't take the necessary action. To get a better understanding of this phenomena, let's look at factors that make up our behaviors.

Behavior of a dynamic system results from two factors: internal dynamics and external factors. A dynamic system is any type of system that exhibits a behavioral change over time. A dynamic system, be it a stock market or a human being, moves and interacts based on the outcome of two primary forces, internal dynamics and external forces. For example, when you arrived at your office this morning, you used a means of transportation (an external factor) to meet your immediate objective (your want and desire, internal dynamics) to get to the office.

To identify the main cause behind the "not-pulling-the-trigger" syndrome, we will review these two factors in the following sections.

Internal Dynamics
In addition to external factors, your own internal dynamics can

dramatically affect your behavior. According to David McClelland, a psychologist with about forty years of research in human motivation under his belt, three variables interact in complex ways and cause an individual to elicit certain behaviors:

1. **Cognition** (your knowledge, beliefs, and understanding);
2. **Skills and Adaptive Traits** (your habits, abilities, and personality traits);
3. **Motives** (your driving force).

So, how does each of these factors affect a not-pulling-the-trigger syndrome?

- You did not have a trading system or have the proper knowledge for trading (cognition).
- You were not able to follow or implement your trading system due to your personality traits and habits (traits).
- You did not place your order due to lack of motivation and desire (motives).

In short, your understanding, psychological and emotional states, and your motivation collectively had a major impact, so you did not place your orders. Let's look at each of these three variables.

1. Trading systems and trading knowledge. Your cognitive understanding of the market, i.e., your knowledge and beliefs about your trading system, help you perceive outside information and filter it accordingly. To trade successfully, it is necessary to establish a trading plan that answers the following questions: What market(s) do you want to trade? Do you want to trade futures, stocks, or currencies? In which time frame are you interested? Long term (position trading), short term (swing trading), day trading? How do you want to trade? Do you want to use a mechanical system or a discretionary system?

The cognitive variable deals with your understanding and belief. Today, a majority of traders know that they should have some sort of trading system before they risk their hard-earned money in the market. Your trading system basically tells you when to enter the market by placing your buy (long) or sell (short) orders, and it also tells you when to exit and where to put your protective stop. You should look into your own trading system to see if its variables are compatible with who you are. Knowing how to trade and implement your system should enable you to bite the bullet and pull the trigger.

2. Applying your trading system and knowing your ABCs.
According to Dr. Ellis, the father of rational-emotive therapy, our beliefs about events, rather than the events themselves, determine our emotions and subsequent behaviors. His theory is based on the ABC model. When you see an activating event (A) in a particular way, because of your beliefs (B) about the consequences(C) of that behavior, you adapt your behavior to the perceived outcome of the action. The activating event (A) and what you believe (B) about it, creates the consequences (C) of your behavior. Your beliefs create and shape your behavior rather than the activating event, e.g., the market.

Let's look at an example of this theory. Suppose you are driving home from work, when a cyclist seemingly comes out of nowhere. You hit your brakes and the car screeches to a halt. Your heart is racing, adrenaline is coursing through your body, and you may even break into a cold sweat. Though you were surprised, the event was resolved quickly and no one was hurt, yet your physiological reactions were identical to those had you had an accident. This is due to the fact that your beliefs about the event, whether real or not, had a powerful effect on your experience both physically and emotionally.

Similarly, your beliefs establish a foundation for your reaction to market behavior. Though the market is the same for everyone, everyone's reaction to the market is not. For example, you may think that futures trading is high risk and akin to gambling. Since this is the basis of your belief, your action is based on this belief, and you exhibit gambling behavior. You might risk too much or try to make a killing in the market. The result is that you may not follow your trading system; you may pull the trigger too much or not enough. On the other hand, your friend views trading futures markets as simply another way to make extra when they traded consistently through a system. Because of your friend's belief about the futures market, he is likely to pull the trigger exactly when he planned.

Using the ABC model can enable you to understand and, more importantly, correct your behavior. So, it's important to analyze not only your beliefs about the market, but also the basis of your beliefs about the market.

Like our beliefs, our personality traits affect our actions and behaviors, even in trading. Think about your experiences trading. Do you become nervous as soon as you place a trade and end up not following your trading plan, or do you sit back and gauge the market's movement against your plan? On a trading personality profile (TPP) test, for example, a nervous trader will likely have a high score in neuroticism, a determining factor in your trading. Dr. Pierce J. Howard describes neuroticism or negative emotionality as one of the main dimensions of our personality traits. Behavior ranges from reactive to resilient. In that continuum, the middle ground is someone who is responsive, who may have a mixture of both traits. Have you noticed how some people are naturally cool under stress? You may even call them cold or aloof. They probably have a low score in neuroticism.

Perhaps you're not exactly nervous when you trade, but you always feel you can improve on your trading plan, and you're constantly tweaking it. Say that on a particular day you notice that a few signals were not profitable. Then you start playing with your system with the idea that you could improve on it. "Why not," you think to yourself. You could add a few more indicators that seem to have some validity and achieve a better performance. You check out a few indicators like moving averages or different periods for the stochastics. Subsequently, you get a signal from your new and improved system, and it is a loser. Now you realize that the old version of your system might have produced a winning trade. You get angry with yourself because you did not follow your system, and you kept modifying it.

You may have a high score in the openness dimension of a TPP test, meaning that you like to explore different options and keep tweaking your system while looking for the perfect system. You find that you keep repeating that same behavior and you wonder why. You repeat your behavior because it is part of who you are. Rather than beating yourself up over it, you may need to look for a system or an alternative method that is compatible with your particular personality traits rather than try to change the system or trade in conflict with it.

In order to quickly identify your strengths and weaknesses in trading, take a TPP test. If you are able to identify your particular traits, you then can create or select a trading system that is more compatible with your own personality, giving you a higher probability of success. As you can see from the previous example, we must have a better understanding of our own personality traits in order to become better traders.

3. Trading motivation and desire. Why do you trade? Do you like the action? Do you see trading as quick money? Your answers to these and similar questions will reveal your inner motivation for trading. Motivation is the underlying force that moves you toward or away from something. Many traders may come to trading—in particular day trading—because they enjoy the action. Some may trade solely for its potential monetary rewards. However, other people may trade because trading presents an intellectual challenge for them and keeps them sharp. They like the challenge of trying to figure out what the market will do next.

What is your motivation for trading? If, like many individuals, you started trading merely to make money, then ask yourself, "can I make the same amount of money without going through all the inherent financial risks and the emotional stress of trading?" What if you were offered a job that you could make the same amount of money, even more? Would you take the job?

Let's consider two traders who have just taken long positions in the S&P.

Trader A watches the market as it fluctuates around the entry point. Then, without warning, the market breaks three points straight down. The stop being used is a mental stop of two points. Trader A gets angry and exits his position with a three-point loss. Although upset, he realizes that this is just part of the cost of doing business and begins to look for the next setup.

Trader B also watches the market as it fluctuates around his entry price. Again, without warning, the market breaks and is now three points below the entry price. The stop is also a two-point mental stop, yet the trader does not exit his position. He gets very angry and begins cursing and banging on his monitor. He is yelling at the floor traders, brokers, whoever might be responsible for this move against his position. Now the market retraces about two points toward his entry. He is now feeling much better about things and is validated for not exiting his position and following his plan. Then, just as suddenly as the last break, the market drops another four points. Now he is fuming. His position is now underwater five points. And, yet, he still does not exit his position. His anger is fueled by the fact that he could have exited with only a one-point loss, but now has a five-point potential loss.

Considering the pain vs. pleasure principle, why has he not exited his losing trade? Often traders feel pain from losing trades but don't follow their plan or make the necessary change in strategies. Did Trader B enjoy his feeling of loss and regret? What was his motivation for not exiting? Did he not like being wrong? Or was it something deeper? Was it denial? Or was it about control. These questions require serious consideration before one can answer them, and it is essential to identify the motivating factor behind your behavior before you can change it.

The blanket view of the psychology of trading focuses on fear and greed. Fear as a primary motivation may show itself in different variations. Fear and greed may be utilized as general concepts to understand market psychology. To break it down, fear is primary, but it does not provide the answer for the causes underlying all problems. The trader in a losing trade fears losing more. It is human nature to manage risks, so he manages his losses and stays with the losing trade longer than he should. Another way in which a trader exhibits fear is when he cuts his winning trades short. He takes the profit quickly out of fear of losing whatever money he has gained. Further research of the psychology of human behavior reveals that we are risk averse in our gains; we try to protect profits by exiting trades quickly. Nevertheless, understanding that motivation is a critical component of internal dynamics should shed more light on trading behavior.

Many times motivating factors are clear, and many times they are not. Motivation and emotions interact with each other in a complex format. Sometimes the motivation might be easily distinguishable from emotions. Other times, the line between them is blurred, making it difficult to find the underlying cause for behavior. One way to identify your inner or subconscious motives is to look at your value system. What do you value most? How do you define good and bad? How do you define success and failure? The answers to these questions can help you figure out your motives for being in the market and help you define or redefine your value system for faster goal attainment.

If money is your primary motivation, then you will experience emotional swings associated with your performance. In some cases, when the market moves against you, you may get frightened and exit your trade prematurely. Then, after you exited your trade, the market goes in your favor, as was indicated by your trading system. Or when your position starts to show a bit of profit, you are compelled to exit quickly. Then, much to your dismay, you see the market continue going in your favor for a much larger profit. This type of motivator creates behavior that, in turn, results in an emotional roller coaster. You start beating yourself up psychologically and your self-confidence is shaken.

For the same reason, you may not pull the trigger since you had a losing trade and are concerned that your next one may be a losing one too. So, you tell yourself that this time you will look for more confirmation before you enter your trade. This time the market moves away from your potential entry point too quickly. Now you feel that you acted too slowly and missed a great deal of profit on the trade. So the next time you decide to be more aggressive and not wait for confirmation to enter your trade. As luck would have it, the market moves against you and you end up with a losing trade. "@!#%$$," you repeat to yourself and curse the market and whoever is close by. You again start the negative internal dialogue and feel there is no end in sight.

Trading is a business and, like any other business, you need some basic requirements before you start. A love and passion for trading. A motivation for trading far beyond money. A sound trading system or methodology, a sound trading plan, and the ability to implement that plan. If you trade only for the money, you would do best to find another career and avoid risking both your emotional and financial capital. Your motivation for trading is an important component underlying your behavior or lack of it. If you are not able to pull the trigger, I encourage you to find the real reason you are trading.

External Factors

External factors and your environment, such as your trading location, may also play a large role in why you can't pull the trigger. Are you in an office or at home? If you are in an office, are you alone or in a group setting? Are there any windows? Is the room light and airy or dark and subdued? What color are the walls? All of these may or may not affect your trading. In addition, there are other external factors. Your Internet connection, your PC, your account size, your broker, etc., all can affect your trading. Though external factors may influence your behavior, they affect you only to the degree that your personality shows sensitivity to them.

External factors are like catalysts; they affect your behavior and your ability to implement your trading strategies. However, the decisive factors are internal dynamics: your motivation, knowledge, and personality traits. Among your personality traits, you have one dimension that is called the extroversion dimension. This dimension of your personality deals with your preference for being actively involved or engaged with other people and environments.

Depending on your score for the extroversion dimension, you could be categorized as either being an extrovert or an introvert. If you like to take charge, assert your opinions, and work with people, you are most likely an extrovert. If you tend to be more independent, steady, reserved, and comfortable being alone or working alone, you are most likely an introvert.

An environment suited to your personality facilitates better trading results. Therefore, you need to pay close attention to your trading environment and arrange or modify it so that it best suits your personality.

Understanding the internal dynamics and external environment will help you implement your trades and help you avoid the not-pulling-the-trigger syndrome. You need to acknowledge and identify your habitual behavior patterns or personality traits in order to be a successful trader. Paying attention to your personality will aid you in making the right decisions and increase your willingness to pull the trigger. A proper trading environment and support group, along with a clear understanding of your trading system, habitual patterns, personality traits, and true motivation, all hand in hand eliminate the not-pulling-the-trigger syndrome and help you achieve trading success.

Ned Gandevani, PhD, is the author of *How to Become a Successful Trader: The Trading Personality Profile* (Writers Club Press, 2002). He is a professional trader and the developer of the winning edge system, which is based on chaos theory (www.winningedgesystem.com). Gandevani developed the trading personality profile, a quantitative method for matching traders and fund managers with their best trading and asset management styles. He has conducted trading psychology seminars throughout the U.S. and Europe. Gandevani currently teaches MBA courses at Keller Graduate School of Management in New York City. He holds a Masters in business administration and a PhD in finance. This article originally appeared in *SFO* in July 2003.

STICK TO YOUR TRADING PLAN

BY PETER KAPLAN

From our first day as traders, most of us hear a lot about the need for discipline in our profession. The question is, what exactly does discipline mean, as it applies to trading? Trading discipline is all about doing what we know to do and not doing what we know not to do.

Or, if one wants to make this really simple: discipline means following our trading plan. That's it. That's all it means. Every one of the separate issues that people tend to associate with trading discipline: religiously utilizing stop losses, holding until we hit targets, automatically taking a break after too many losses, focusing on only a few set-ups, choosing the best of the best trades and refusing those which are sub-standard, etc. Every one of these issues falls under the umbrella of a well-constructed trading plan.

Here's the astonishing thing about discipline and trading plans: having a great plan is actually less important than following it! Now, granted, this presupposes that our plan is founded on some of the basic tenets of trading and is backed up by a legitimate education. But assuming we know a thing or two about what we are doing, applying discipline ends up being more important than the specifics of our plan. Let me tell an interesting little story to illustrate this point.

My Story
A few years back when I was first learning to day trade, I was going through the usual travails that lie at the start of the learning curve: disheartening losses, an endless string of stupid mistakes, missed

opportunities, a multitude of emotionally driven decisions leading to dreadful timing, etc. And yet, despite the fact that I was losing almost every single day I traded, I had a strong sense that my trading education up until that point was sufficient to produce profits. There was just a strange, terrible disconnect between what I knew to do and what I was actually doing.

One day, after a particularly agonizing session of losses, I finally drew a proverbial line in the sand. I said to myself, "OK, Smarty Pants, if you really think you know enough to make money, let's see what happens if you actually force yourself to do it!" That night I scrupulously wrote down everything I was permitted to do in the course of a trading day and, even more important, everything I was forbidden to do. I made it all crystal clear to myself. Understand, up until that point I did have the vague shell of a trading plan. The problem was, I viewed it more as some nice trading "suggestions," rather than a code. In other words, it was a useless little description of what might happen in a trading day.

This time, to counteract that, I made sure to add the special pixie dust that makes the labor of composing a trading plan worthwhile—integrity. I swore to myself that I would follow what I had written, no matter what results it produced. I viewed the whole thing as a fascinating piece of scientific research, and my only job as the scientist was to conduct the experiment correctly. The results were no longer my business. The next morning, I fervently reread my plan fifteen minutes before the market opened and then placed it right beside my monitors as the seconds ticked down to the opening bell. Then...ding ding ding!!!

Take the Anxiety Out

When the session began I noticed within seconds that something was different. I was used to feeling a rush of adrenaline akin to a hot flash when all those little numbers and charts started skittering around my screens. While this sensation tried to pose as excitement, the far better word was terror or, at the very least, anxiety. On the morning that I employed my new trading plan I felt none of these things. My heart wasn't pounding, my palms weren't sweating. No hot flashes to speak of. I just carefully scanned through the charts, looking for set-ups that conformed to what was written in the plan. Even more important, I rejected dozens of things that I was forbidden to touch. Already this was an astonishing change.

My main Achilles' heel up until that point was my tendency to get involved with several sub-standard trades before I entered the ones that had the potential to actually make me money. This time, I simply sat calmly, waiting for the trades that I knew were the right ones, and I passed over a whole host of trades that I knew were the wrong ones. How strange this was! Why hadn't I simply made these choices before? After all, I hadn't acquired a whole encyclopedia of new trading knowledge overnight. I was "Smarty Pants," remember? The guy who actually knew what to do each day, but somehow never seemed to do it.

That first day of the test was a clear winner. By 11:00 a.m. I had made more money than I ever had as a day trader—which wasn't very much. Still, I was thrilled with it and decided not to trade any more that day. The next day the same exact thing happened: complete calm and poise at the open, uncanny restraint as I passed up a whole host of dogs, the ability to nail a few choice winners that fit perfectly into my plan...then done for the day by 11:00 a.m. with several hundred more dollars in my account. Day three was no different. In fact, over the next eighteen trading days I had only one losing day. For a guy who couldn't put together two winning days in a row and who usually lost four days out of five in a trading week, this was a miracle! Now, these days weren't exactly blockbusters, mind you—$200 to $600 after commissions on average—but I was so ecstatic with my newfound success I felt like I was walking on air. After all, soon I would drastically increase my position size and make the money I deserved. (If you are hearing the rumbling of storm clouds on the horizon, you're not hallucinating. Indeed, the story is about to take a not-so-pleasant twist.)

Why Does This Work?

But before we go there, let's look at some of the implications of what I've described so far. One of the most telling aspects of my eighteen-day streak was the fact that the plays I had listed in my trading plan weren't exactly God's gift to day traders. In other words, they were legitimate trading candidates but hardly the best patterns out there. And yet this only serves to hammer home the point: the precise quality of our plan is less important than the fact that we actually have one and that we follow it. Why is that? Because the human tendency to override what we actually know to do, in favor of what we feel like doing is simply too powerful and too dangerous for most of us to handle.

Anyway, back to Smarty Pants and his trading plan. Right about now, Smarty was flying high from his miraculous seventeen-out-of-eighteen day winning streak. As he saw it, the world was now his oyster, and he was already making plans to start his own hedge fund. "After all," thought Smarty, "all I need to do is add a few zeros to the share numbers in my order entry screen, and presto, I'm practically George Soros!"

Sorry, no more hiding behind this Smarty character; it was me, and my delusions of grandeur by the end of that period were downright mythic in proportion. I even remember briefly shopping for a penthouse apartment. Now, here's how I messed the whole thing up. As you might have already gathered, a sudden, irresponsible upping of my standard position size was part of the problem. But that wasn't all. I was uppity in other ways as well: tripling the number of patterns permissible under my plan, raising the number of trades I could take in a day, expanding the hours that I could sit there in front of my screens and play around... pretty much increasing everything in the trading plan. The logic was very simple. If I'm doing this well with this little, imagine how much better I will do with more! Time out. Some special attention must now be given to this insidious four-letter word: more.

It's All Around Us

Let's face it, we live in a society that constantly promotes the concept of more. More money, more beauty, more things to buy, more things to eat...more everything. In virtually every facet of life, more equals better, and for this reason, a huge psychological brick wall waits in the path of most aspiring traders—particularly those who have been successful in other endeavors and have been well-rewarded by the "more principle."

In trading, more does not equal better! Better equals better. Better discipline, better quality to our picks, better restraint, better record keeping, etc. But more? That usually means more losing. If you don't believe me, just ask Smarty Pants. He learned this lesson the hard way. There I was, touring penthouses with real estate agents and

STICK TO YOUR TRADING PLAN

planning the logo for my hedge fund. I can viscerally remember the Monday it all changed. I had spent a decent part of that weekend adding all sorts of goodies to the trading plan. The way I saw it, the trading plan was my golden-egg-laying goose, and if I just stuffed the thing until it was fat as a hog, it would plop out bigger eggs, and more of them. What was once a concise, one-page document had now become a small opus, and it contained more patterns than John Murphy's *Technical Analysis of the Financial Markets,* rev. ed. (New York Institute of Finance, 1999). This way I was sure not to miss a single opportunity that the market might offer me, and I would make that much more money.

Can you guess what happened next? Do you think Smarty Pants got his penthouse? No, he pretty much lost his shirt! Over the next two-and-a-half weeks, following the deployment of my newly ex-panded, deluxe trading plan, I had two winning days in total, and they were dinky. The rest were all losers—at the increased size, mind you—and by the end of that demoralizing stretch I had wiped out all of the gains from my miraculous eighteen days and then some. And my poor real estate agent. That was the last time she ever went out showing apartments to a day trader!

The truth is, this unpleasant episode turned out to be a criti-cal part of my learning curve. I had gone from pretty much ignoring the concept of a trading plan to thinking it was some sort of mystical document. Emboldened by my great winning streak, I actually came to believe that anything I wrote down on that magical parchment would instantly transform into a winning strategy. And herein, at last, we find the true moral of the story.

The Take Away

The "more principle," this driving force, though helpful in other areas of life, is an accident waiting to happen in the trading universe. Suf-fice it to say that my once-miraculous trading plan had become badly afflicted with a case of more-itus. When I started dumping things into it like a gift basket, the restraining, focusing power of the docu-ment was lost. Suddenly I had just another useless description of all the things that might happen in a trading day, rather than a reliable map through the dangerous no-man's land of the market. All of this became very apparent to me after much back-testing and soul searching. And once I had this insight, the remedy was quite simple: I put my golden-egg-laying goose on a strict diet and removed all the extraneous, lower-odds plays from the list. I went back to the tight little plan that I started with, and within a few days my impressive results returned.

These days my trading plan is a very focused, very reliable blueprint for my actions. There is really never a doubt in my mind about which actions conform to the plan and which do not. While my overall approach to the market has slowly shifted away from the intense intra-day universe and into the world of longer-term positions, I have never forgotten the lessons of my Smarty Pants episode. Do I sometimes step outside the tight parameters of my trading plan? I rarely take a full step out, but sometimes I sneak a pinky toe over the line, and I'm almost always sorry when I do. The learning process goes on for me as well, and after every single trade, and particularly every single quarter, I do a very thorough investigation of my actions to see if I have added something overly complicated to the equation. I'm always on the lookout for any element of my trading that smacks of the "more principle." Heaven knows, Smarty Pants performs best when he isn't being too smart for his own good!

Peter Kaplan began trading securities in the early 1990s, following an extensive education in technical analysis at New York University. He specializes in intermediate and longer-term trading, which he has melded into a comprehensive approach to the equities market. He is the co-founder of Nexus Capital Management, LLC, and can be reached at peter@nexuscapitalmanagement.com. This article originally appeared in *SFO* in July 2006.

WHAT CAN MALE TRADERS LEARN FROM SUCCESSFUL WOMEN TRADERS?...AND VICE VERSA

BY GAIL OSTEN

Let me just get this off of my chest. I have heard over and over again for a number of years that women are better traders than men. Though I, too, am a woman and always love hearing positive things about other women, I figured that this was a gross generalization that ranked right up there with blondes being airheads. I originally started out conceptualizing this story as men versus women, but quickly realized that this simply would do no one any good. Yet, after twelve separate, lengthy interviews, some overwhelming consistencies about the differences between women and men in their trading universes made me sit up and take notice.

Generalizations? Yes, to some degree they are, because it's not possible that all men are one way, and all women are another way. And everyone I interviewed hedged their comments appropriately. Even macho men explore their feminine sides occasionally, and women, too, can be hunters rather than merely gatherers given the proper circumstances. The yin and the yang often can co-exist nicely.

But here's the deal. I am going to lay out what these very generous and knowledgeable interviewees had to say as they outlined their vast experiences. Then you'll have an easier time figuring out what successful women traders can teach men and, likewise, what successful male traders can teach women. Generally, the plus comes down on the side of the ladies, so if you are a man and your ego can't take it, stop reading now. On the other hand, for both sexes, the ability to open your mind may lead you to greener pastures for your trading success in the future.

Perhaps most importantly, the world has changed, and the anonymity of traders and investors has leveled the playing field. Gone are the days when women traders could be in on the action only if they were in an institutional trading room or on a trading floor. Now screen trading has made gender a non-issue. Today, as New Market Wizard Linda Bradford Raschke, says, there is room for both. You can just as easily be "a boy named Sue" as John Wayne.

The Knowledge Conundrum

David Bennett, founder of WomensWallStreet.com (WWS), a micro-portal destination for women to research, compare, and manage their personal finances, offered a telling statistic from a WWS survey of five thousand men and women: seventy-six percent of women feel that the primary factor holding them back from financial security is knowledge, versus sixteen percent for men who feel that way. And yet, women control seventy percent of the financial assets in the United States.

Though this does not directly relate to trading per se, one can easily transfer these results to the lower number of women now involved in active trading and investing as compared to men. Putting their ducks in a row before they jump into such a financially and time-intensive pursuit is one result of this mindset.

Unlike their male counterparts, women believe they need more education of one sort or another to become involved in trading; yet, each possesses the same human brain. "Their responses are broader than just investing or trading, but there's no question," says Bennett, "that women like to be comfortable with things before they move forward. And, versus men, eighty-three percent of women feel that financial institutions don't cater to their unique needs of communicating financial information in an understandable way." So, it seems evident that women feel underserved, whereas men do not, or simply don't express it.

On top of that, women, particularly when starting out, often are more timid in trading and more conservative in the use of their money. While this has advantages, it also can hold them back from feeling comfortable and confident in the beginning. They seem to suffer from more feelings of guilt in the loss of funds during the "tuition" stage of learning to trade.

"Men, on the other hand, seem not to have the same reservation or feeling of guilt regarding their initial funding or the price of tuition," offers Barb Magio, a trader, educator and moderator in woodiesc-ciclub.com. "They take these losses merely as part of the learning process and seem to feel less guilt or necessity to explain why instant profitability is lacking."

On the plus side,"women aren't afraid to search out mentors and ask questions," says Rhonda Reskin, a former stock broker and one who mentors traders via Firetraders.com, a live audio trading room. Men are a little foxier on exposing their soft underbellies while looking for advice.

Bennett agrees. "Women tend to investigate and/or talk about their investment decision and/or strategy more openly than men do. That is one of the underlying, common characteristics that make a well-informed female investor have a leg up over their male counter-parts. They communicate."

Does that communication help the ladies master the market? Definitely not, according to Mark Likos, senior analyst at the firetraders. com. "Women generally don't look at the market as something that is conquerable. They look at it as if it's a project or an endeavor that you never really master; rather it's just something that you need to continually change with and improve on. It isn't something that they complete and that they'll study and master in a year or a day or a month or whatever, and they seem to grasp that early on. Men sometimes take the attitude that the market is something to be beat or something that they have to master and control."

Tempus Fugit

The market is constantly on the move, and men in general want to get going, rather than devote a great deal of time engaging in some of the preliminary learning steps that women feel are so necessary.

"The idea of paper trading doesn't seem to be very enticing to men," notes Christina DuBois, a trader and instructor for Optionetics. "The men students I have just want to get in, where women take the concept of paper trading a little more seriously, and they tend to have a broader view of things by making decisions based on more information. Additionally, they tend to consider more strategies, whereas men want to pick one or two things and learn them fully, but start with a narrower range of tools."

Many of those interviewed indicated that the great majority of women are great students of the market and are highly inquisitive.

Rita Whitfield is a partner in programtrading.com, an investment advisor that differentiates itself by offering information on computer-assisted trading programs, buy-and-sell program execution levels, and the effect on trading and investments. She's watched the way women and men approach the markets on a continuing basis.

"You know, I've seen it over and over," observes Whitfield. "Women by nature are more curious about details, and they seem to have more patience for the tediousness involved in studying that detail." The men she has observed are looking for quicker answers in black and white and want a mechanical system to tell them when to push the buttons. Says Whifield, "Men are much more prone and susceptible to the BS flying around the floor or a hot tip, whereas a woman has that right brain that allows her to process twenty-five details coming in and ignore the ones that are unimportant to her trading decisions."

There are two sides to being analytical, however. Those interviewed indicated that a highly analytical mind, over-attention to the numbers, too many technical indicators, etc., can weigh down one's ability to take action. All agree that both men and women can possess overly analytical minds and can be too precise.

Are women slower than men in their deliberations? There is disagreement on this point. Magio says women are not necessarily slower, but instead more cautious and deliberate. "Women are not generally the overtraders of the world. That's where the deliberation comes in. They also tend to evaluate somewhat faster than men, because they can see the world more easily through visual patterns. This ability to see the markets quite visually is not unique to women, but more dominant than in men."

Others see it differently, viewing women as generally more reluctant to pull the trigger than men without the planets being in alignment. Annie Young, a trader of seven years and former elementary school teacher in Indiana, believes that women are more prone to perfectionism. "When they want it done, they want it done just right. I'm looking at the ES [E-mini S&P futures] right now, and there are three levels of support coming up. In my opinion, men will be more likely to go ahead and go long the market before we get down close to there. Women will be more likely to wait until it hits it exactly. I do think that women have a little more problem with the perfectionism issue."

Young adds that overly analytical traders—and that would include perfectionists, whether male or female—might consider eschewing day trading and start trading on a longer-term basis to be more successful.

Is There Something About Mary?

There's another aspect to the analysis paralysis where our experts believe men need to take the introspective look: too many indicators, too many programs, too many everything, which makes analysis confusing at best.

Hank Camp, founder of programtrading.com, says of the probably ninety percent of guys that are trading (S&Ps), "They've got a computer, they've got a data feed, they've got CQG, they've got relative strength, MACD—and I'd say to them, 'You know, you guys have been trading for a year and you haven't made anything.' And their response is, 'Yeah, well, we've got a new program we're working on, and it back tests great.' Believe me, I'm painting the picture that I've gotten after thirty years of watching people."

"Yet," says Camp, "we have spent thirty years programming computers to make buy-and- sell decisions. We have found that women have something you simply cannot computerize, and in all of those years, I've never figured out precisely what it is, but I'll call it a feel for the markets—intuition. Guys go out and look for a new formula, since they don't have the feel. A woman will walk in the trading room and look at the chart and say, 'Well, I feel it's going to do this,' where guys don't feel. There's no such thing as male intuition; men think it's more computer power that makes a difference, but it isn't."

Linda Bradford Raschke, one of the lone voices in the crowd who believes that gender means very little to successful trading (though she does concede there are some differences), believes that both men and women use intuition. Others believe that a sort of intuition can be acquired if only men were to try to visualize more often than simply pouring over numbers and stop amassing multiple indicators.

"Women do have a tendency not to look so hard at the numbers, but more to what resonates with them," according to Linda Ram, full-time trader since 1998. "A man's intuition is based more on, 'We went up 140 points on the Dow today, so OK, we're going up,' whereas a woman will sit there and look it from all of these other angles. We all should remember that you can overwhelm yourself with too many

Men and Women: Differences as I See Them

By Sam Seiden

The most profound realization during my years as a private trading coach is how different female and male traders can approach, analyze and trade the markets.

Without offering outrageous generalizations, it has been my experience that women possess a particularly logical mindset that can give them a substantial advantage in trading. Simply, my trading method quantifies the supply-demand and human behavior relationship that ultimately determines price in any market. It is based on a very objective and mechanical set of criteria. In other words, the goal is to learn the method and then simply follow the rules. The female mind has a much easier time doing this than the male mind.

Here is an example of how this works. The chart in this sidebar is a trading idea I recommended to my clients: buy AMD at a certain price based on anticipatory analysis. One of my female clients took the trade and did well with it, while a male client saw the trade but did not enter it. I had discussions with the two of them, and the conversations were truly fascinating—how could two human set of eyes look at the exact same chart, be told exactly what to do, and yet, treat the trading opportunity so very differently?

For privacy purposes, we'll call them Lucy Logic and Eddy Emotion.

So, here's the scenario: AMD had been declining to an area of support (demand) from where it had recently rallied. Eddy quickly asked me what I thought of the opportunity, and Lucy did not. Eddy then asked if I thought the support (demand) level would hold and produce a reversal, or would prices decline through it? Lucy would never consider asking that question with any trading opportunity because she knows it's a waste of time trying to predict the future. Eddy doesn't feel the same way. But let's face it—no one on earth knows for sure if the support will hold. All we can do is properly assess the odds and risk. If the odds are stacked in our favor and the risk is acceptable, we take the trade.

When the trade neared our entry level, Eddy abandoned objective thought and gave into emotions that still control his decision-making process today. Lucy remained logical and objective. Instead of worrying about what may or may not happen at support (over which no one has control), she explained to me why a high-odds/low-risk trading opportunity was at hand. She said that sellers were now selling after a multi-day decline and into an area of support (demand), exactly where the consistently profitable trader would be buying, not selling. When her entry price was reached, she took the trade with a low-risk stop in place and an objective target identified. She ended up profiting nicely on the trade. Eddy never entered.

How can we all benefit from this information? It is clear to me that females in general don't worry all that much about things that are not in their control, and this allows them to naturally focus on the objective information, which is key in

continued on next page

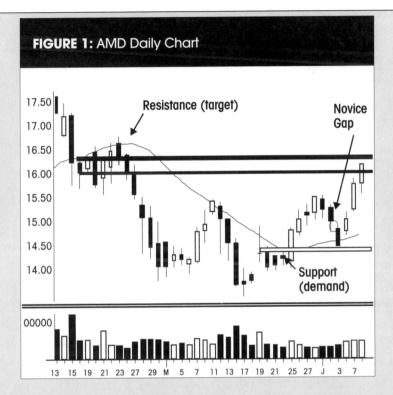

FIGURE 1: AMD Daily Chart

successful trading. In trading, it is the objective and logical mindset that gets paid from the subjective emotional mindset.

I have found that the difference between mindsets is most evident at a specific time. When a trading opportunity arises and it is time to take action, the female mindset tends naturally to execute the trade that has been planned out. At the same precise time, the male mindset tends to drift to subjective and emotional thought, which can lead to trouble. It appears that, again generally, the female mind has the naturally logical mindset needed to understand the material quickly, whereas the male mindset has difficulty keeping things simple, naturally trying to complicate the process. An example would be to constantly add subjective indicators and oscillators that can lead to trouble for any trader.

What validated my thoughts on this topic are what my female clients and other successful male traders out there have in common. Each of them share two common traits. First, they realize the power of human emotion and that a trading plan absolutely must be followed. Second, the successful male clients I have worked with have the ability to not let subjective information enter into their brains. It is almost as if they have a special filtering process going on when they read trading books, take seminars and take coaching programs such as mine. In other words, successful male traders succeed with tools a female brain naturally possesses.

continued on next page

From my experience, men tend to be focused on trying to predict the future, whereas a woman uses simple logic to consistently make the correct choice. They have the natural ability to keep things objective, simple and logical. The man tends to have trouble in these areas, which can make trading for him more difficult than it has to be. This is no different than how men and women make choices in other parts of life outside of trading.

Though trading is still a career dominated by men, I would expect this to change in the near future for a few reasons. First, the barrier to entry is not what it was years ago. Second, from my experience, the female mindset is likely to last longer in a trading career than a male mindset, as a woman's mindset is much more suited for the challenging task of consistently profitable trading.

indicators and too much information. You have to choose which information really is important to you."

Whitfield of programtrading.com adds that many men by nature will put the bulk of their faith in a mechanical system. However, "successful women will learn the same mechanical system, but will recognize the nuances and exceptions when the mechanical system doesn't work and want to know why the hell it doesn't work." Adds Whitfield, "If I could figure out why it didn't work today, I could make money the next time that exception happened."

Sticking with a Trading Plan

When I called Denise Acosta in New York at around noon for the interview, she was on a break, and I heard baby noises in the background. Acosta, who trades the Euro futures early in the morning, the E-Mini Russell index futures early in the afternoon, and was just beginning to trade the Hang-Sang Index in the evenings, is the mother of triplets. With that much on her plate, I had to ask about how important it was to stick with a trading plan.

Working on a daily basis remotely in an online trading room with both women and men, Acosta says the men she knows say they have plans, but generally don't stick to them. "I literally have a book, and I have my trading plan outlined. I have a daily journal, and I write down my trades. Men are more likely to break their own rules."

"I don't want to sound old-fashioned, but maybe it's that women are a little more in touch with their emotional side. I think that often men kind of dismiss that because they believe that if they have a mechanical system, it should work," says Acosta. "Men that have trading plans say, 'OK, this is the outline of my plan,' and then a half an hour later they're doing something totally contrary to something they say their plan entails."

So what about emotions? Mark Likos says that the strong women traders he knows are very well-disciplined, and have good emotional stability. "When they are in the heat of battle when their P/L is going against them and all the technical aspects of trading are holding strong, they seem to be able to ride out the panic that some of us get into from time to time better than the men. I've seen that over and over and over again."

Toni Turner, best-selling author of three books on trading, observes that quite without Western men's conscious knowledge, "they have to be right." Right or wrong, that's they way they are brought up—when you're right, you're strong; when you're wrong, you're weak. "If they go into a trade and buy five hundred shares of Microsoft and tell everybody at a cocktail party that that's what they did, and the next day Microsoft starts tanking, it's very hard for a man to admit to his buddies that the trade went against him. It makes him wrong, and while that's not the actuality, it's certainly the appearance."

Taking it full circle back to the trading plan, says Turner, "The need to be right and the fear of being wrong jumps into the male consciousness and they say, 'Oh it'll come back, it's alright, I'll ignore my stock. I'm not going to follow my plan. Two days ago I sold a stock, and the thing turned around and went straight up, so that'll happen again.'" Many times it just doesn't work out right. The plan has disappeared.

Barb Magio of woodiescciclub.com, concurs with Turner. "I've had both men and women traders sitting right next to me at my desk while I've been trying to teach them. I can have a plan written right there in front of them, and men will say you know 'yes, I understand this, I believe this, and this is going to be my trading plan.' And they're fine for an hour, and then it somehow goes by the wayside. I find women, in general, to be much more disciplined and have more self-control in evaluating what it is that they're doing before they do it. I think that that is one of the first issues that differentiates men and women in trading."

Mini S&P trader Annie Young agrees. "Unfortunately, men more than women have a tendency to overtrade. Sometimes they will get a good entry into a trade but don't let it develop. They may get a couple of ticks down, and then take it off. That's what I call a nervous trader. In 'revenge trading,' you start overtrading in order to make back what's been lost...and then have commissions to worry about. And anytime you do a lot of the in-and-out trading, you are generating a lot of commissions."

"I think that men have a harder time dealing with that than women because, unfortunately, society expects men to be the breadwinners and to be the success of the family," says Young. "Our society has come a long way with that, but there's still an awful lot of that out there."

Anyone who feels they have to make a living for his family by trading is going to be under pressure, after all. Dealing with a mortgage payment adds even more stress to the pressure of the markets. Becoming a full-time trader means you really have to be financially set up before you ever get into it.

Get a Life

Finally, balance in trading versus other life pursuits generally falls into the plus column of more women traders than men.

"I find that women have a life at the end of the day," contends Rhonda Raskin, "and those men that don't, should. You know, we might sit at our desk for a long time, not eating or going to the bathroom until a certain phone call or price target or tick occurs. On the other hand, we can also learn to trade for two hours, stop, and then go to the beach for the rest of the day."

Others, particularly those who are checking in and out of online trading rooms, often find the same men online at 6 a.m. and also at 10 p.m...and they've been engaged all day long. Not a healthy situation. "We're either with the kids or tend to be out among people more. Men still are sitting at the computer trying to tweak their systems," adds Raskin.

Interestingly, and perhaps to be expected, stay-at-home trader dads may have cornered the market on balance, says Anne Young. "I have a good friend online that is a stay-at-home dad, and he does a marvelous job trading and balancing everything. His wife works outside the home, so it can be done. He has learned balance. He truly has a life outside the trading, but I know some men that don't." Go, Daddy, go.

So, what have we learned? Well, for one thing, the scale seems to tip to the side of the women—it seems that the good ones generally are more balanced, more able to multi-task and follow a plan without veering from it, are less emotional, and are alright with being wrong.

Maybe they are even more intuitive and have more fun. And men are the opposite?—No, of course not, but if the shoe fits, wear it.

Women, on the other hand, might need to realize that caution is not always a good trait to have. The markets are not perfect, and perfection is a goal you can't achieve either.

There are great male traders and great women traders, but Linda Ram makes an excellent point, which is food for thought: "If you were to take a man at an eighty-percent success rate and a woman at an eighty-percent success rate, I would bet you that what they are good at would have very little overlap. The solution is that men should get a woman trading partner, and women should get a man trading partner. Multi-sex partnerships are better than single-sex partnerships." In fact, that's what Hank Camp did when he hired Rita Whitfield, and he's never looked back. "Every man should trade with a woman," he contends. "They will never be sorry."

Gail Osten has been involved in senior marketing, advertising, and corporate communications positions in the derivatives business and commercial real estate business for more than thirty years, including positions with Chicago Mercantile Exchange, the Chicago Board of Trade, and MidAmerica Commodity Exchange. She is a former executive editor of *SFO* magazine and produced forty issues of the magazine. This article originally appeared in *SFO* August 2004.

SECTION THREE
The Science of the Trade

No one needs to tell most investors that when immersed in the high-stakes world of trading, our minds aren't always logical, and our decision-making skills can be compromised. While traditional economics focuses on theory and the rational conclusions reached in a perfect world, behavioral finance looks at the irrational decisions we make in the real world.

This relatively new discipline uses data collection, scientific research, and economic modeling to analyze why we make economic decisions. Behavioral finance is economics through the lens of a psychologist. It helps to be aware of the broader patterns revealed through behavioral finance to decipher tricks the mind can play and avert our potentially self-destructive tendencies.

The average investor's portfolio dramatically under-performs the market in which he's investing. Why is this? Many investors who lose money do so because they do not have an understanding of themselves and how their personal psychological makeup affects their market decisions. This section will explore broad psychological patterns prevalent among traders, such as controlling emotions, managing risk, and the impact of personal biases.

We also know that groups function differently from individuals—this includes investment groups, trading buddies, or even followers of certain trading methodologies. Group-think can affect your bottom line. We'll share some tips on assessing if this is a factor in your trading.

Pervasive feelings of regret are sometimes the most obvious symptoms of psychological difficulties. We have practical strategies to identify, understand, and manage regret in order to become an emotionally intelligent investor.

Bernie Schaeffer, one of the top options experts in the field, offers an interesting twist on crowd psychology. Learning to react in the right way to investor sentiment may give you the edge you seek.

THE PSYCHOLOGY OF TRADING AND BEHAVIORAL FINANCE

BY MIKE ELVIN, PhD

The psychology of trading and investment is both a theoretical and practical discipline that can be used as a tool to preserve your capital and to improve your overall performance. The psychology of trading applies research, methods, and models developed in the field of psychology to the challenges facing traders on a daily basis. It includes perceptual and emotional biases, stress control, and offers models of learning that can be used as a map or guide. The comprehensive model of trading competence (see *Figure 1*) highlights the composite areas of tactical and strategic actions required by traders to achieve competence. If a trader can understand and define the composite skills required, learning will be fluid. Traders also should strive to incorporate attainable goals, which can act as milestones in their personal development.

As a trader, I need to know how to improve my performance in an understandable and relevant format. As a simple working definition, behavioral finance examines how groups of individuals perform in an economic context, while the psychology of trading examines how the individual performs under conditions of uncertainty. Moreover, the psychology of trading provides methods and techniques that apply to specific challenges an individual trader may encounter. Much of economic and financial theory is based on the notion that individuals act rationally and consider all available information in the decision-making process. However, empirical research in cognitive psychology demonstrates that this is not the case. When faced with uncertainty,

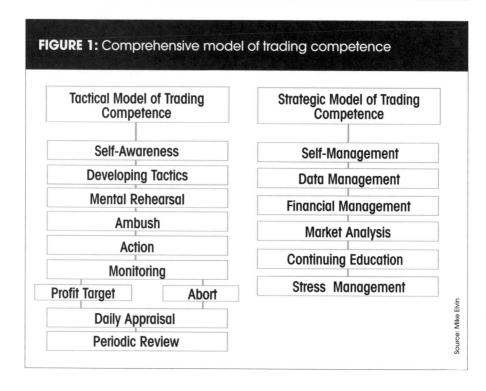

FIGURE 1: Comprehensive model of trading competence

Source: Mike Elvin

the evidence reveals repeated patterns of irrationality, inconsistency, and incompetence in the ways we arrive at decisions and choices.

The recent academic discipline called "behavioral finance" examines theories of cognitive psychology and attempts to understand and explain how emotions and cognitive errors influence investors and the decision-making process. Many economists believe that the study of psychology and other social sciences can shed considerable light on the efficiency of financial markets as well as explain many stock market anomalies, market bubbles, and crashes. Some researchers believe that these human flaws are consistent, predictable, and can be exploited for profit.

The Art of Speculation

Speculation comes from the Latin root "speculatus," meaning to watch for or observe. This derivation implies that investors must be guided by an accurate picture of the facts and awareness of the cognitive and emotional pitfalls that relate to making investment decisions. The biases of decision making are often referred to as cognitive illusions,

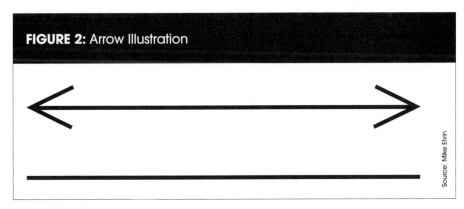

FIGURE 2: Arrow Illustration

Source: Mike Elvin

and as with visual illusions, the mistakes of intuitive reasoning are not easily overcome.

Consider the visual illusion in *Figure 2*. The second horizontal line appears longer than the first. You may wish to use a ruler to clarify for yourself that both horizontal lines are the same length, but even following accurate measurement, you will perceive the second line as longer than the other. This example provides a salutary lesson: that simply learning about illusions does not eliminate them.

The purpose of learning about cognitive illusion is to develop the skill of recognizing circumstances in which bias is likely to occur and where critical and analytic thinking must support intuition. As investors, we are vulnerable to numerous cognitive biases that lead us astray. We each have a personal inclination to succumb to certain biases of thinking and perception, which may or may not be shared to any great degree with our investor colleagues and friends. Let us examine a common perceptual bias and how it influences our beliefs regarding investment software and training courses.

The Halo Effect

If a person has one salient good quality, his other characteristics are likely to be judged by others as better than they really are. Handsome men and women tend to be rated highly on intelligence, athletic prowess, sense of humor, and so on. In fact, physical appearance has little to do with such characteristics. There is a small correlation between being handsome and being intelligent, but it is not enough to account for the mistakes people make in their judgments. The opposite effect is known as the devil effect. The presence of one salient bad trait like selfishness in an individual can lower people's opinion of all his other characteristics; he tends to be seen as more dishonest and less intelligent than he really is.

Although psychologists have known about the halo effect for more than seventy-five years, it is remarkable how little notice is taken of it. Traders are prone to be influenced by the halo effect, and it is one of the strongest influences on a trader's decisions in purchasing trading software or courses and developing a trading style. People marketing trading courses appear to have a good level of expertise, good physical looks, and extensive interpersonal and verbal skills. Furthermore, they are people with whom we are familiar, to whom we feel close, and to whom we are attracted. Such people are able to exert more influence on us than others. The appearance of credibility to promote a trading course or software is important and used extensively by marketing folks.

Some famous investment gurus have used the halo effect to support their theories and views, whether the theories are accurate or not. For example, some traders who have no formal training in psychology have invented anecdotes to demonstrate the psychological dynamics of fear and greed at work in the individual and how this influences their trading. Some have even become experts in neurophysiology by making unsubstantiated claims about the functioning of the brain and its relevance to trading. In addition, I have seen traders run seminars using psychometric tests with little understanding of how to interpret the scores. But they can easily convince the audience that they know what they are doing and label their actions as methods of behavioral finance. The halo effect in these circumstances is potent and has been used equally effectively by stage hypnotists. Many of you have completed psychological tests in trading books. Have you ever stopped to think, "On what data is this test based to ensure a reliable and valid score?" Traders would certainly ask this question of any trading system or methodology where they would invest time and money.

Be wary of traders who pretend to be gurus or Nobel Prize winning psychologists. (In fact there is only one Nobel winner in psychology of finance: Daniel Kahneman in 2002.) Be aware of how the halo effect biases your own perception. Many investment gurus have recognized that their credibility has been questioned as a result of not holding psychology qualifications and have aligned themselves to the relatively recent discipline of behavioral finance. There are many valid reasons why the new discipline of behavioral finance is becoming popular. However, it is generally more credible for a trader to be an expert in behavioral finance than in psychology, especially if he or she has no formal qualifications whatsoever.

Don't Be A Sheep!

Let us now explore the psychology of groups and how our decisions and beliefs may be influenced. Traders are generally aware that a person's behavior tends to conform to that of any group of which he is a member. Belonging to a group, however, has other implications, and the interaction between members has significant effects on attitudes and their behavior toward other groups. As individuals, it would be reasonable for us to assume that our attitudes would drift toward the mid-position (regression to the mean) held by the rest of the group. However, research demonstrates that if there is a prevailing attitude in the group, it becomes accentuated in its members. For example, a group of traders who has an affiliation with, say, Elliott wave theory will see their techniques and methods as far superior to those employing other methodologies.

Experiments have been designed to analyze the decision processes of investment clubs, and the results have been replicated and confirmed many times. The research assessed the risk level acceptable to individual club members in purchasing stocks. After each member had independently given their acceptable odds, they discussed the risks as a group in order to reach joint agreement about the acceptable odds. The group as a whole opted for significantly different odds than the individuals. In other words, the group was prepared to take a greater risk than its members acting separately. This phenomenon has been termed the "risky shift."

The demonstration that group attitudes are more extreme than those of individuals has been replicated many times and in different circumstances. The phenomenon occurs for a number of reasons. First, group members want to be valued by the group. They may suppress arguments that are opposed to the attitude and beliefs of the group, and they may be prepared to be more extreme in the group because we know that membership of the group reduces individual responsibility.

Research also indicates that investment groups manifest an illusion of invulnerability coupled with extreme optimism. For example, they ignore inconvenient facts; they hold stereotyped views of rival groups. Individual members attempt to silence dissent from others in the group, and each member suppresses his own doubts in order to conform. In addition, there is an illusion of holding a unanimous view, and they protect other members by concealing information not in line with the group's views. In fact, group leaders tend to pick those candidates whose ideas and attitudes most suit their own when a decision needs to be made regarding group membership. It is therefore likely that the group, through selecting these members, will become even more extreme in their views. I have been to numerous trading seminars where this phenomenon was evident, and I am sure that many readers have observed something similar.

Stereotypes: A Dangerous Trap

It is difficult, if not impossible, to think of one's own group and trading methodology as special without thinking that other groups or trading methodologies are inferior. Such prejudice against other groups is usually accompanied by the formation of stereotypes. Some reasons explaining the inflexibility and failure of some traders to adapt and learn new methodologies in response to changing market conditions are rooted in the same dynamic that forms stereotypes. One reason for stereotypes is that they are convenient; we do not have to assess the individual case. A second reason is we tend to notice anything that supports our own opinions but don't pay much attention to those that might not support our view. Third, we are attentive to the actions of another group, which appear more noticeable than those of the larger group. They are conspicuous because they are rare. Fourth, stereotypes can be self-fulfilling. Finally, when discussing the halo effect in relation to individuals, it is shown that the person who has one salient quality may be seen as having other related qualities that he does not in fact possess. For these reasons and others, prejudicial stereotypes are common and powerful and very hard to eradicate, and their basis in truth is unfounded.

It is comforting to belong to a cohesive group of traders showing a common philosophy, discipline, and method of trading. It is difficult to think of your colleagues and tutor as special without at the same time making others appear inferior. These prejudices against other traders holding different beliefs about market trading are not based on facts.

In other words, advocates of a particular method or members of an investment club are likely to pre-judge traders, their actions, and their methods based on a false belief system.

Understand Your Biases

The risky shift and halo effect biases are discussed in detail in my book *Financial Risk Taking* (Wiley, 2004). The challenge for behavioral finance is to identify the mechanisms of biases and provide a model of learning for investors. The challenge for the psychology of trading is to make those models relevant to the individual investor and also to provide tools to overcome the damaging effects of biases on our trading accounts. The rest is up to us because we are our responsible for our success and failure. Recently I managed to increase one of my trading accounts by 256 percent. I increased my leverage and added positions with discipline, but I became distracted and made an error. Weeks of concentration, effort, and profit were wiped out to near break-even, and even though my emotional control is competent, I can't help feeling discouraged. But I have a map, and I accept that I have no control over the markets; I only have control of myself.

Mike Elvin, PhD, resides in London and is author of *Financial Risk Taking: An Introduction to the Psychology of Trading and Behavioral Finance* (Wiley, 2004). He was a research psychologist and managed mental health services in the UK prior to his current employment at a futures exchange. He offers individual tuition and seminars. Further enquiries can be made to m.elvin@blueyonder.co.uk. This article originally appeared in *SFO* in July 2006.

BEHAVIORAL ECONOMICS: How Investors Really Make Decisions

BY PHILIPPA HUCKLE

"Buy when everyone else is selling, and hold until everyone else is buying. This is not merely a catchy slogan. It is the very essence of successful investment."

—John Paul Getty

Centuries ago, people facing difficult decisions would seek the counsel of a wizard, an oracle, or a soothsayer. Today, few soothsayers and even fewer wizards can be found in the telephone book, so sensible investors are forced to make decisions very differently. Thanks to the lifetimes of inspiration and analysis by literally thousands of the world's most sophisticated financial minds, particularly over the past one hundred years, a number of works have unravelled the dynamics behind investments to explain how markets work. Collectively, these brilliant minds have formalized the doctrines of modern finance and given us the formulas and rules for successful portfolio management, including asset allocation, diversification, and rebalancing.

But let's first take a look at what's really happening in the world of the individual investor. In a study by DALBAR, a U.S. financial services market research firm, the average investor's actual returns over twenty years were compared with the returns posted by various markets. The results are dismal. The average investor dramatically under-performs the market in which he's investing, failing even to beat inflation.

Available returns simply are not being reaped. This is not a criticism of intelligence because, frankly, even the smartest people are

TABLE 1: Quantitative analysis of investor behavior (QAIB) compound annual returns 1984-2003

	Average Investor	S&P 500	Difference
Equities	2.6%	12.2%	-78%
Fixed Income	4.2%	11.7%	-64%
Inflation	3.1%		

making serious investment mistakes. While the S&P 500 delivered 16.3 percent over the fifteen-year period from 1984 to 2000, the Mensa Investment Club (whose membership is restricted exclusively to the top percentile of the world's registered intelligentsia) clocked in an annualized return of just less than 2.5 percent.

Failing to capture market returns has a substantial and far-reaching effect on the quality of investors' lives, altering their life choices, the quality of education they can provide their children, and the legacy they leave. So, what has happened? Investors have the rules, guidelines, and formulas for successful investment—but what prevents these people from applying them? Because no one would consciously sabotage their own investment results, there must be other factors at work.

Why Investors Err

Neo-classical economics requires investors to be rational in order to profitably apply the rules of investment. About forty years ago, a group of psychologists spearheaded by Daniel Kahneman and Amos Tversky began exploring the way investors make decisions in real life, rather than in theory. Their work inspired the field of behavioral economics, a 2002 Nobel-prize-winning discipline which views economics through the eyes of a psychologist to scientifically explain the consistent, predictable, very human, irrational mistakes that decimate investors' results.

While neo-classical economic models explain what we should do, behavioral finance explains what investors really do—and why. Behavioral finance explains why the average investor commits the most fundamental investment mistakes: futilely chasing performance, ineffectively attempting to time markets, failing to capitalize on opportunities, and being overwhelmed by the crowd. It explains why the average investor ends up inadvertently buying high and selling low, even while meaning to do the opposite. DALBAR's Quantitative

Analysis of Investor Behavior (QAIB) confirms that poor investment results are the result of poor investor behavior rather than poor market returns.

In understanding these destructive tendencies, investors can consciously alter their behavior to dramatically improve investment results and transform the quality of their lives.

The basic requirement for profitable investment is to buy low and sell high as markets move through cycles. We've all heard this over and over again. But what may be a cinch for the objective, rational, neo-classicist so clinically described in economic textbooks is much harder for real people. After all, a statistician would say that if you stood with one hand plunged in a bucket of ice and the other on a hot stove, on average you'd be comfortable—but we humans feel things.

Price changes are unavoidably accompanied by a range of very human emotions. When an investment pounds home extraordinary returns in the above-average part of its cycle, it's perfectly human for exuberant investors to want to load up on and chase after the giddy, shiny assets inspiring this euphoria. The temptation to buy high is overwhelming!

Faced with plummeting prices in the lower part of an investment cycle, our deeply entrenched survival instinct kicks in. Webster's Dictionary defines risk as "the possibility of loss or injury; peril." As humans, we're wired to avoid loss, an instinct which worked very well for our ancestors but has a devastating effect on the average investor's results. In the face of loss, thousands of years of genetic programming flood investors with anxiety, dread, and panic, screaming at us to get out, to keep away, to sell, sell, sell. Investors who make decisions based on the emotions accompanying recent performance end up breaking the rules of investment and sabotaging their results.

These emotional instincts are reinforced by heuristics—or mental shortcuts—which our brains have developed over the centuries to swiftly handle information and speed decisions. While these tools are extremely useful in many areas of life, they can short-circuit when investing.

Representativeness is a mental shortcut we use to quickly categorize an event or item alongside other events or items with the same traits; indeed, this may be useful when shopping for cars, but dangerous when investing. In *Table 1*, the representativeness shortcut categorizes temporarily spectacular returns in the upper part of an investment cycle as typical of the type of investment which delivers good returns. It labels the investment as good and instructs us to buy (high). Investments temporarily in the below-average part of their cycle are categorized as representative of the kind of investment that delivers poor results. Labeling the investment bad, our brain instructs us to sell (low).

On top of that, our brains have devised a handy law of memory to speed decisions by rapidly gauging likely outcomes. Repetition welds strong mental bonds, and the stronger the bond, the easier the recall. In debating whether to encourage or dissuade an action, your brain tests how easily it can recall a previous outcome; a swiftly recalled outcome is assumed to have occurred frequently in the past, while more elusive memories (from uncommon occurrences) are considered unlikely to repeat. However, vivid, distressing events (a sudden market drop, bombings, a bad financial experience) instantly forge a very powerful memory which is as easily recalled as a frequent event.

Awful outcomes seem more likely than they really are, which explains thing like why vacationers avoided the seaside after Jaws was released in cinemas, why the threat of SARS reduced the Hong Kong economy to a standstill, and why most investors failed to build a sufficiently strong equity position into market lows after three tough years of a bear market.

Gambling on Positive Experiences

But, short-circuiting is equally prevalent with positive experiences. Our brains have evolved a highly tuned pattern-seeking ability which begins to extrapolate a pattern after just two iterations of a sequence. This is why gamblers tend to bet more when recent success burns bright in their memory—they feel lucky. This also explains why investors instinctively become more optimistic when markets are rising and are more tempted to buy. For example, a study showed that nearly ninety percent of Japanese investors expected further increases at the peak of the Japanese market (*Wall Street Journal*, June 13, 1997).

Outperforming investments clearly will catch people's attention. But investors often will wait awhile for proof of out-performance, then go ahead and buy (high). However, because investments move in cycles, the law of regression dictates that recent above-average performance will inevitably fade to normal, and prices will fall. Whenever you gamble that a very high or low return on any asset will continue, the odds are stacked against you.

Take the example of investors who chased meteoric returns by ploughing $200 billion into technology and Internet shares in 1999 before the Nasdaq caved in 2000. Euphoric investors poured billions into roaring emerging market funds before markets crumbled in the mid-1990s.

Investors stampeded into acceleratingly expensive small-cap growth before the 1997 collapse. Corporate and emerging market bonds have recently enjoyed a fabulous run, which is why investment advisors have been fielding a lot of calls from new investors looking to buy bonds on the back of extraordinary returns. This is a classic behavioral impulse, one which should cause investors to be cautious. After all, belated performance-chasing is more appropriate for travels in a time machine than for an investment strategy. With interest rates at historic lows (for a while at least) and bond yields matching record lows set in mid-2003, risks abound for bondholders.

Conversely, pattern-seekers tend to extrapolate temporarily poor returns out into the future and feel the pessimistic urge to escape the downward trend they've projected—by selling low or simply avoiding investing altogether. The thought process is muddled further because loss aversion reinforces this urge to flee from low prices. Worse, panicked investors often are dangerously compelled to replace low investments with ones inspiring excitement and euphoria—even though a basic requirement for profitable investment is to buy low and sell high as markets move through perfectly natural cycles.

By unintentionally using mental shortcuts, emotional investors become trapped in a vicious cycle of loss: frantically unloading underperforming assets (prematurely fleeing market cycles); belatedly chasing after last year's returns (buying too late into maturing cycles); and nervously guarding against remote risks (failing to capitalize on opportunities in down markets).

Professional forecasters are equally as susceptible to short-circuiting. In his excellent book, *The Fortune Sellers* (Wiley, 2001), William Sherdon analyzed the leading economic research from 1970 to 1995 and found that of forty-eight predictions for major turning points in the economy, forty-six were wrong.

Look at Investments in a Different Light

The rules for successful investing (asset allocation, diversification, rebalancing) are extremely effective. Permanent financial success requires a diversified mix of stocks, bonds, cash, and other asset classes running on different cycles. And, in order to make a profit, one needs to sell highly priced, popular assets that were bought when they were cheap and out of favor. There's really no shortcut to this formula.

Buying low requires going against the accompanying negative consensus to purchase an out-of-favor asset, and selling high means selling highly priced, popular assets currently enthusiastically endorsed by the world at large. To position yourself to consistently reap profits over meaningful periods (your lifetime, for instance), you need a systematic, long-term, rebalancing process which consistently sells in-favor investments and simultaneously buys those currently out of favor, methodically positioning for a profitable sale later. But this process requires investors to be rational.

DALBAR's QAIB confirms that the average investor succumbs to emotional and mental short-circuits and inadvertently ends up breaking these rules. Belated performance chasing is an irrational but very human curse that violates the doctrines of modern finance. Behavioral finance is the key to understanding why—and, most importantly, when—investors are likely to deviate from the rational outlook required to successfully implement investment strategies. By using the lessons from behavioral finance to understand investor psychology, we can recognize when we're likely to deviate from proven principles; with this awareness, we can begin to effectively adapt and control our behavior and then dramatically improve our results. In recognizing our destructive human tendencies, we can correct them.

Many anomalies we see in behavioral finance stem from the way information is framed—the way we view and interpret information before making a decision. Rational investors are required to be fungible, or to make financial decisions based on the net effect on overall wealth, but behavioral finance shows that investors routinely make buy-sell decisions by anchoring to and measuring profit or loss against the purchase price at which they happened to enter a particular investment cycle. This encourages representativeness and is a primary driver of selling low and buying high.

Knowing this, investment professionals need to help their clients evaluate their portfolio of investments in a new light. Focusing on investment weightings helps investors properly diversify across uncorrelated market cycles. Changes in relative investment weightings (rather than cyclical profit or loss) trigger rational rebalancing decisions which systematically take profit from maturing markets (sell high) and calmly reposition into cycles next due to bloom (buy low). Not only does this consistently capture market cycles while dramatically reducing volatility, but it frees investors from an emotional rollercoaster ride as investments move through cycles.

Reframing information, educating clients in the lessons of behavioral finance, and providing coaching through the inevitable periods of irrationality helps investors consciously avoid behavioral mistakes. In the end, that should translate into greater wealth, peace of mind, and a rational confidence in investment decisions.

Philippa Huckle is the founder and CEO of The Philippa Huckle Group, a leading investment advisory firm headquartered in Hong Kong. Huckle is regularly quoted and published in regional and international media including, the *Sunday Times UK*, CNBC, and *Asian Wall Street Journal*. She is the author of *Perspective*, an online publication read by more than five thousand people in forty countries. By successfully integrating classical economic methodologies with the discipline of behavioral finance, the group's highly personalized service guides each high-net-worth client to robust, sustained returns. This article originally appeared in *SFO* in July 2004.

DON'T BE A CAVEMAN: Curb Natural Instincts and Become a Rational Investor

BY KYLE HANDLEY

The complicated world of finance has developed rapidly over the past hundred years. But the wiring of the human mind occurred slowly over the past few million years and under very different forces of natural selection.

Ancestral human life consisted of hunting and gathering food while avoiding being eaten. For better or worse, humans still are emotionally driven by the neurobiological wiring of their ancient ancestors. While civilization has come a long way in the past twelve thousand years, how different is modern man from the stereotypical caveman? A caveman plucked from the Paleolithic age and placed into the modern world would have a tough time indeed.

Economic theories and models of behavior are built around assumptions of rational decision making with perfect information. In contrast to the caveman image, the models use a character armed with all the makings and trappings of modern finance. This rational man has the following traits: he is utilitarian, not confused by cognitive errors, has perfect self-control, is always risk-averse, and has no regrets. He can process all information available to him before making decisions devoid of emotion. The assumption makes the equations work beautifully, but it can fall apart with real investors.

Where Is This Rational Man?

Investor behavior doesn't always follow the models and may even contribute to market volatility. Investor sentiments can swing from the greed of the late '90s to the fear of the 2000-2002 bear market. Investors can be irrationally exuberant one day and irrationally pessimistic the next.

But does rational man really exist? The average mutual fund investor actually has a dismal record. DALBAR, a financial services research firm, studied the behavior of average mutual fund investors from 1984 through 2003. During this nineteen-year period the average fund investor achieved a paltry 2.57-percent annualized return. Inflation ran at 3.4 percent and the S&P 500 Index returned 12.22 percent over the same period, according to a 2003 DALBAR report.

It concluded, "Investment return is far more dependent on investor behavior than fund performance." Most investors hold equity mutual funds for just a little over two years. In reacting to news, emotions, and faulty logic, the average investor missed out on the greatest bull market of the twentieth century. Studies of human behavior and decision making amid uncertainty suggest the investor is his own worst enemy. Educated, knowledgeable individuals who understand the benefits of asset allocation, diversification and modern portfolio theory still make terrible decisions.

Why do some investors make such poor choices, despite all the tools and information available? For one, simple survival instincts compel humans to withdraw from danger or perceived threats. The brain's emotional control center is wired to manually override an otherwise rational course of action. The hiker hearing a noise that sounds vaguely like a bear engages the instinct to run away quickly. Survival instincts don't allow the brain time to evaluate the alternatives. "Is this a bear, a tree falling, a bird, or another hiker?" Because the hiker might be dead by the time he figures out the answer, it is advantageous to overestimate the probability that the noise is indeed a bear.

In the financial world, many investors run from bears (in the market sense) before they have the whole story. The human mind has quick-and-dirty shortcuts the brain uses to make quick, complex decisions; in the world of behavioral finance, they are known as "heuristic biases." Driven by emotions like fear, these shortcuts can be life-saving for the hiker above or deadly for investors.

The investor should understand and guard against the worst of his behavioral tendencies. No investor, except for the aforementioned rational man, is immune from making these mistakes.

Heuristics: Decision-Making Shortcuts

The most common bias is the "availability heuristic." Investors will judge the probability of a given event based on how easily it comes to mind. Said another way, traders are influenced by vivid imagery, recent events, or significance to the question at hand. It would stand to reason then that a news media that keeps good or bad news at the forefront is a major factor. The mind will mentally sample from readily available information.

Remember back—it was easy to imagine stocks continuing to go down in 2002 or always going up in the heady days of 1999. This bias can cause investors and humans in general to make very basic errors in probability. Consider the following scenarios and estimate their probability:

- There is a large bond market sell-off, where prices fall more than five percent in one day.
- The Federal Reserve Bank raises interest rates, triggering a bond market sell-off, in which prices fall more than five percent in one day.

Many investors incorrectly estimate that a Fed rate increase causing a bond market sell-off is more likely than a sell-off for any reason whatsoever. An overall sell-off is rather abstract, but the specific idea of Fed rate changes affecting the market is recent and constantly analyzed in the mass media. As a result, investors overweight the likelihood of a specific, retrievable event.

A related bias is the "representativeness heuristic." This tendency causes investors to estimate the probability of market events based on how representative the event is of a broader category or process. Investors will infer trends where none exist. After watching the market go down several days in a row, the investor infers the market is more likely to continue heading down. Because falling stock prices are representative of a market downturn, the investor attaches a high probability to that scenario.

But these limited daily observations are more likely to be meaningless in the big picture. Falling prices are symptoms experienced in a downturn, but are not necessarily indicative of overall malaise. Inferring general rules from small samples implies a "belief in the law of small numbers." This bias may have been very useful for survival ten thousand years ago in the small world of hunter-gatherer societies. It still has some use today in the right situations. But taken out of context, it can be very dangerous for investors to develop general rules with only small bits of information.

So what happens when the caveman is introduced to Mr. Market? Prehistoric instincts definitely contribute to behavior biases that cause market mistakes. This would actually be laughable if the biases did not hit the investor's pocketbook to the extent the DALBAR data indicates. The following is a rundown of very common behavioral errors and biases. Do you recognize any of them?

Chasing Winners and Timing the Market

Despite the preponderance of evidence that market timing is inferior to disciplined investing, especially after transaction fees and taxes, many investors continue to engage in this costly game. Every mutual fund prospectus contains the warning label, "past performance does not guarantee future results," but investors chase hot mutual funds and stocks anyway. Even the most astute investors will sell investments based on only one year of bad returns. They feel like everyone else is getting rich without them and jump into extremely risky investments with no regard for potential losses.

The investor may identify trends in the noise of investment returns. Convinced that he can make money with this information, large sums will be staked on the outcome. Consider a sequence of coin tosses for heads (H) or tails (T). Which series is more likely? Sequence (a) H-T-T-H-T-H, or sequence (b) H-H-H-T-T-T. Most test subjects would answer sequence (a), but they are both equally as likely to occur.

Most people just can't accept that a random process would generate a pattern-like sequence (b) and might subsequently base a major decision on otherwise random events. Like a gambler convinced he can predict the next spin of the roulette wheel, investors will see patterns in purely random processes.

The media and financial pundits encourage this error regularly. In 1992, *USA Today* cited the *Jerry Favors Analysis* newsletter as asserting that the "three-peaks-and-a-domed-house chart pattern has predicted every major market decline for two hundred years without a single mistake." Aside from being wrong, this is a typical example of reading too much into limited information. By covering these more sensational outlooks, the media bestow credibility on faulty logic. They give a lot of column inches and airtime to sensational theories and forecasts of experts. None of that information is going to make someone trade better on Monday morning. It reinforces bad behavior. I try not to do much forecasting in my market commentaries. I try to keep them interesting and entertaining, but the basic advice itself is rather boring. The process of successful investing is not exciting reading.

The Homer Bias
The availability bias also explains why an investor is predisposed to invest in domestic companies. Researchers have found that Europeans and Americans both over-weight holdings in their geographic areas. Think about it; both parties can't be right! Prudent investment principles would dictate reasonable portfolio diversification. Even so, many traders and investors perceive an advantage not only for American companies, but home state stocks and mutual fund companies as well.

This bias is compounded by the oft-repeated mantra of retired investing legend Peter Lynch to "buy what you know." Frankly though, just because an investor sees lots of consumers purchasing Tide doesn't mean Proctor & Gamble stock is ready to soar.

Overconfidence in One's Ability
Anyone who thinks he is too smart to make these mistakes should beware of overconfidence. Surveys show that most investment managers believe they are above average, a statistical impossibility. Data from fund tracker Morningstar confirms that most managers are indeed just average. A fund manager wouldn't be in the business if he didn't think he could add value above his peers. But what leads the investor to think he is better at stock picking than everyone else who has equal access to the same pool of information? And further, how can the investor confronted with his poor results continue to be confident in his ability?

Overconfidence is strengthened by media coverage of star performers. It's hard not to believe that prophets exist, when a manager with a great track record is on CNBC almost daily. But the emergence and subsequent "death" of successful fund managers conforms precisely to statistical expectation.

In his book, *Fooled by Randomness* (W.W. Norton & Company, 2001), Nicholas Taleb presents a version of the following example. Consider ten thousand investment managers, each of whom are given a fair coin to toss. Heads, the manager beats the market, and tails, he leaves the investment business in disgrace. Statistically, about five thousand managers will make it to the second round, 2,500 to the third, and so on.

So 312 managers—10,000 x $(\frac{1}{2})^5$ for those keeping track—will have five-year records that beat the market, and they will get interviews in all the major financial publications and media outlets. In ten years, only about ten managers will have managed to beat the market. They will be heralded as the next Warren Buffett or Peter Lynch, and investors will rush to copy their success. But wait, they were just lucky enough to flip heads ten times in a row. The sample started with ten thousand managers, about the same as the number of funds in the Morningstar mutual fund database. Maybe they aren't so skillful after all.

This lengthy but incredibly telling example demonstrates the survivorship bias. When investors, aided by media coverage, look at investment performance, they only see the survivors. It is more important to look at the cemetery. The investor who ignores the cemetery may die trying to match the results of survivors.

"I Knew It All Along" (The Hindsight Bias)

Compounding the overconfidence and survivorship bias is the old adage that hindsight is 20/20. The error of an investor's ways is so obvious in hindsight that he overestimates how much he should have known. In hindsight, it is obvious there was a bubble in technology stocks. But the investor caught up in the euphoria probably didn't see the writing on the wall until it was too late.

An investor who avoided the tech crash may overestimate his ability to predict the next bubble and sell out just before the crash. Even an investor who was decimated may think, "I knew it all along." With renewed confidence, he won't make the mistake again. The hindsight bias lends itself to convenient and simple after-the-fact explanations for bruised egos. Losses and bad earnings forecasts are attributed to random events that no one saw coming. Gains and correct prophecy are attributed to superior knowledge and skill.

Valuing Losses More Than Gains

The typical investor does not value equivalent gains and losses equally. The negative reaction to losing $1,000 is more severe than the positive reaction to winning $1,000. Quite simply, losses hurt more, and investors are more worried about potential losses than they are excited about potential gains. This heuristic is considered "risk as feeling." While finance views risk as volatility and standard deviation, the mind fixates on the abstract emotions associated with loss and uncertainty.

The popularity of lotteries with huge jackpots provides some insight. Individuals that never play the lotto will buy a ticket when the jackpot goes up. The feelings and imagery of winning huge sums of money outweigh the small cost of tickets and terrible odds.

Conversely, investors unable to see the big picture can't commit to an integrated financial savings plan. The vision of a secure retirement is distant, abstract, and remote. Investors don't want to think about being seventy years old, destitute and living from one Social Security check to another. Because the payoff is long term and abstract, saving $100 per month seems more like an immediate short-term loss.

"Risk as feeling" can lead to a propensity to overemphasize losses. The investor concentrates on poorly performing investments and ignores the portfolio as a whole. Dividing money into several different compartments is called mental accounting. This often results in piecemeal, inconsistent portfolio management where investors have separate accounts for "play money" versus more serious "retirement money." Or worse yet, they carry high-cost debt while maintaining a checking account elsewhere with enough money to pay it off. This compartmentalization allows heuristic biases to take over one investment after another.

Anchoring and the Refusal to Sell Dogs

For better or for worse, humans are still emotionally driven by the neurobiological wiring of their ancient ancestors. Investors must be on guard against anchoring to irrelevant and arbitrary details. While some anxious investors buy and sell too often, others hold winners and losers too long. Mistakes occur when the portfolio is anchored to variables the investor cannot control.

The investor may find himself fixating on a losing stock's fifty-two-week high of $47. He may not want to sell until it reaches $47, even though the price has no bearing on future performance. Once the investor has anchored to such a detail, all decisions are likely to be influenced by it. There are many examples, even investors who anchor major portfolio decisions to the political party controlling the White House.

Anchoring can be worsened by regret aversion. No one likes to admit they are wrong. Selling an underperforming investment feels like punishment. By holding on, the investor's mistake doesn't seem real. There often is no logic to the rule of thumb, "don't sell when you are down." It applies only if you already have a highly diversified portfolio. Regret aversion also leads to holding winners too long because investors regret selling and watching the investment continue to appreciate. The advice to ride your winners provides fuel for this bias but can fall apart in a logical portfolio context. Win or lose, investment decisions must be divorced from ego and emotions.

Toward Rational Man

Awareness of these mistakes and their causes should steady the hand of a disciplined investor. Controlling emotions is critical to achieving a successful investment experience. There are many processes at work in the markets each day. In the big picture, most of the daily movements and information will have no impact on long-term investment results.

Investors should avoid the anxiety of framing results into one-minute time horizons. The stock market is open for six-and-a-half hours per day. The investor checking prices every minute will see his mood and emotions change 390 times during the day and more than one hundred thousand times in a year. Hourly monitoring still entails about six anxious moments per day or about 1,700 per year. By monitoring and making major changes more than quarterly, the investor risks creating an environment where behavioral biases and irrational decisions can thrive. A rational and thoughtful annual review of a disciplined investment strategy can provide peace of mind year-round. Anything less would be uncivilized.

Kyle Handley has more than seven years of experience advising individuals about investments and retirement planning. He is currently a consultant and economic correspondent for McSherry Anderson, LLC, an investment advisory firm (www.maportfolios.com). McSherry Anderson provides portfolio management and financial planning services to individuals and company retirement plans. Kyle is a doctoral student in economics at the University of Maryland and holds a master's degree from the London School of Economics. This article originally appeared in *SFO* in October 2004.

WOULDA, COULDA, SHOULDA: Manage Regret and Increase Your Investing Profits

BY ELIOT BRENNER, PhD

"When one door closes, another door opens; but we so often look for so long and so regretfully upon the closed door, that we do not see the ones which open for us."

-Alexander Graham Bell

Successful investors and traders know the pain of regret. They have looked at the closed door, perhaps wishing they had bought Dell in 1993, or that they had sold short the Nasdaq in April 2000. Regret is the psychological pain that occurs when you realize that you have made a bad decision and could have done things differently. Emotionally intelligent investors know that it only pays to look at the closed door long enough to learn from one's mistakes.

Identifying, understanding, and managing regret are central to being an emotionally intelligent investor. Emotional intelligence involves four abilities:

1. Recognizing emotions in yourself and others.
2. Recalling emotions to guide current thinking and problem solving.
3. Understanding how emotions combine and change over time.
4. Managing emotions to achieve goals.

Profit from Your Pain

Investors can leverage these abilities to boost their profits and increase the enjoyment they experience from investing. To learn how successful investors can use these four abilities, consider the plight of Lisa, a struggling investor:

When Lisa bought $30,000 worth of stock, she anticipated making a sizable profit. Lisa was so hopeful and optimistic that she purchased the stock in one lump sum. Shortly after the purchase, the stock began to decline. Her position is now worth approximately one half of her purchase price. Lisa's hope and optimism have turned into regret and pain.

By being aware of her feelings of regret, Lisa has already demonstrated the first of four emotional intelligence abilities, the ability to recognize emotions in herself and others. She has also demonstrated the third emotional intelligence ability, the ability to see how emotions change over time. Lisa is aware of how her hope and optimism have evolved into pain and regret as she has watched the value of her investment diminish.

Emotionally intelligent investors use joy and pain to their advantage, recalling the feelings generated by past investing successes and mistakes to guide future investing decisions. When Lisa makes future decisions, she will have the opportunity to recall the regret she felt from her current investment. Emotionally intelligent investors intentionally recall their past joy and pain to remind them to use effective investing and emotion management strategies. There are a number of different strategies that Lisa can use to manage regret. These strategies are supported by scientific research in the field of behavioral finance, which considers how social and emotional factors influence economic decisions.

Strategies to Manage Regret

Cut Losses Research shows that the pain and regret that investors experience with a given amount of losses is considerably more intense than the joy they experience from the same amount of gains. Thus, it pays to protect yourself from losses.

The trading and investing maxim "cut your losses short and let your winners run" is integral to many models of investing and risk management. For example, William O'Neil, founder of *Investors Business Daily*, urges investors to exit losing positions when they fall more than eight to ten percent below the purchase price. Lisa's investment has to double from the current price just to break even. To avoid regret in the future, she could cut losses at ten percent, losing $3,000, rather than $15,000.

Pyramid Positions Behavioral finance researchers have found that investors who buy mutual funds in their retirement accounts using dollar cost averaging (purchasing over time) experience less regret than investors who make lump sum purchases. Similarly, investors who buy or sell short their positions all at once, rather than scaling into them, are more likely to blame themselves and experience regret if their timing is off. To minimize the likelihood of experiencing regret, it pays to increase the size of a position as the market moves in a profitable direction.

Like loss cutting, pyramiding positions also helps manage risk. Had Lisa scaled into her stock position and assumed a ten percent stop loss, she may have been stopped-out before allocating all of her capital, thus saving herself even more money than if she had made a lump-sum purchase.

Take Partial Profits Scaling out of positions—taking partial profits once the value of your position approaches the price target—is another way to minimize regret. Taking some money off the table improves the likelihood of locking in a profit on the overall position should it reverse direction. Using trailing stops for all or part of your position—adjusting your stop toward the current price as the investment moves in a profitable direction—is another way to manage regret and improve the likelihood of locking in a profit.

Beware of Hindsight Bias One reason that people are prone to experience regret is that they regard events in the past as more apparent than they actually were. Behavioral finance researchers refer to this phenomenon as "hindsight bias." Market bubbles are obvious in the rear view mirror. For example, in hindsight it is easy to see that in 2000 Internet and telecom stocks were overvalued.

One way to manage hindsight bias and regret is to learn to forgive yourself, acknowledging that no investor owns a crystal ball. Emotionally intelligent investors do the best they can to make complex financial decisions with limited information, forgiving themselves when they are wrong.

Don't Overpay for Emotional Insurance Investors sometimes avoid making decisions because they anticipate feeling regret if they are wrong. This is especially true when given a second chance to make an investment at a higher price, even when that investment is still a bargain. Consider the following scenario:

James had an opportunity to purchase the stock of a small biotechnology company but decided not to do so because he was unsure of the company's drug pipeline. A year later, after doing considerable research on the company, James determined that the drug pipeline was actually quite promising, but by that time the stock price had doubled. Although the company seemed more promising than ever, James could not bring himself to pay twice what he could have paid for the company a year earlier.

James's reluctance to buy the young biotechnology company because it had doubled in price demonstrates how some investors decide against good investments because they anticipate feeling regret if they overpay for them. In reality, investors underestimate their own ability to cope with distressing emotions, including regret. In doing so, they purchase unnecessary emotional insurance. If something is still a bargain, buy it. You can always use pyramiding and loss cutting to manage regret if the investment goes south.

Accept Responsibility One reason that people have experts manage their money is so they will feel less regret if things go wrong, since there will always be someone to blame. In fact, some behavioral finance researchers suggest that one of the reasons that foundations and universities hire outside money managers, rather than managing their money in-house is so these institutions have someone to blame if their endowments underperform. Given that most outside money managers under-perform their respective market benchmarks, endowments pay a steep price for using outside managers to control their regret.

Investors who wish to manage their own money have no one to blame but themselves when things go badly. This is especially daunting when you consider that the best investing returns usually result from being contrarian. Contrarians must have the fortitude to go against the herd, and to accept blame and regret when their ideas are wrong.

Be Yourself When you make investment decisions that deviate from those you typically make—and things later turn out badly—you can expect to experience regret. The more extreme the deviation, the stronger will be the feelings of regret.

Novice investors that have in the past delegated their portfolio to investment advisors are especially vulnerable to regret when they begin to make their own investing decisions, because they will be deviating from their past habit of having others manage their money. Novice investors should prepare to experience some failure and to forgive themselves when things do not go as planned. Gradually assuming responsibility for investments can also minimize the likelihood of experiencing regret. If a novice's first investment is a sizable one and it performs badly, he risks experiencing regret strong enough to undermine future investing confidence.

Aim for Imperfection Investors that aim for consistency and outsized returns are less likely to experience regret than those who aim for perfection. Emotionally intelligent investors know that not every investment will be a winner. Because markets reflect the collective actions of humans—who are by nature fallible—the markets themselves are imperfect. Thus, aiming for consistency rather than perfection is likely to minimize regret and to improve investors' satisfaction with their performance.

Opening the Door to Investing Success

Although regret is a painful emotion, each time it occurs it offers investors a learning opportunity. Successful investors learn to recall past regret and to cue themselves to use effective emotion management strategies. Emotionally intelligent investors do not wallow in their regret. Instead, they view the markets as ongoing opportunities for success. Like Alexander Graham Bell, emotionally intelligent investors recognize that when one door closes, another one opens.

Eliot Brenner, PhD, is a licensed clinical psychologist who has published articles on emotional intelligence in financial magazines and psychology journals. He has a private practice in Fairfield, Connecticut, where he coaches and consults with traders. Brenner can be reached at eliot.brenner@sbcglobal.net. This article originally appeared in SFO in February 2007.

THE PARAMOUNCY PRINCIPLE:
Emotional Intelligence and the Small Investor

BY MIKE ELVIN, PhD

Why is it that ninety percent of investors who trade the markets full time fail to earn an adequate return even when using systems claiming seventy percent accuracy? Perhaps it is because investors do not recognize the importance of the paramouncy principle.

The paramouncy principle suggests that you are the most important variable in the trading equation. Not you, the dispassionate arbiter of technical and fundamental analysis, but also you, the thinking, feeling, sentient being with all your human foibles, hopes, and aspirations. Most investors lose money because they do not have an understanding of the markets or of themselves. They trade without method, strategy or discipline. They fall prey to powerful emotion that leads to impulsivity and behaviors more akin to gambling than to genuine understanding. They give in to perceptual biases that lead to false conclusions and inappropriate actions.

Most Traders Focus on Method

A wide educational curriculum is crucial in addressing the paramouncy principle, yet most investors prefer courses on technical analysis that concentrate on method but neglect money management and mental processes. A quick perusal of the popular courses available confirms this view.

The predilection by investors for learning technical or fundamental market analyses at the expense of other important areas is not new. During the early 1900s, Jesse Livermore, the legendary character in

FIGURE 1: Emotional Intelligence Domains and Associated Competencies

Self-Awareness
- Emotional self-awareness: reading one's own emotions and recognizing their impact; using gut sense to guide decisions.
- Accurate self-assessment: knowing one's strengths and limits.
- Self-confidence: a sound sense of one's self-worth and capabilities.

Self-Management
- Emotional self-control: keeping disruptive emotions and impulses under control.
- Transparency: displaying honesty and integrity; trustworthiness.
- Adaptability: flexibility in adapting to changing situations or overcoming obstacles.
- Achievement: the drive to improve performance to meet inner standards of excellence.
- Initiative: readiness to act and seize opportunities.

Source: By permission of Dan Goleman

Reminiscences of a Stock Operator by Edwin Lefèvre (George H. Doran and Company, 1923), realized that his peers overrated the value of charting. Even great technicians like W.D. Gann and Richard D. Wyckoff are advocates for the development of method, the application of discipline, and the importance of money management. Yet even armed with this understanding, investors have the daunting task of identifying the psychological factors that lead to self-defeating behaviors.

More Psychobabble from Psychologists?
For some, the importance of emotional intelligence to the development of investment skills is considered irrelevant. Yet those are precisely the personal attributes outlined in Figure 1 that will sustain, inspire, and motivate the investor during times of duress. Emotional intelligence is as important to the investor as is traditional IQ. Those who think back to their school days will recollect that there were a number of students who always seemed to get A's and B's and probably just as many who got poor grades or failed.

However, we also all probably know that many of these so-called less intelligent students now have very successful businesses or have received public acknowledgement for their contributions to the community. They may have more affluence in its widest sense and in terms of personal happiness than those so-called more intelligent students.

Academics, teachers, and research psychologists have largely ignored the value of emotional intelligence until recent years. There are many domains and related competencies subsumed under the term emotional intelligence, and a number of personal qualities relevant to investors, including:

- the ability to control impulses;
- the ability to delay gratification;
- the ability to motivate oneself;
- the ability to persist in the face of frustration;
- the ability to regulate moods;
- the ability to keep worry and fear from thwarting the decision process during times of duress;
- the ability to empathize with others; and
- the ability to not lose hope and to communicate hope to others.

These are qualities that enable an investor to succeed where simply more cognitive intelligence will not be of singular value. We all experience emotions but sometimes find it difficult to understand their role and purpose. Ancient Greek philosophers laid the foundations for modern European and American psychology of emotions.

Plato wrote popular and influential philosophic writings consisting of a series of dialogues in which the discussions between Socrates and others are presented with erudition and charm. Plato thought emotions were like drugs; they pervert and distort reason. This assumption influenced the thinking of Victorian scientists and still permeates the beliefs and attitudes of investors today. For example, the works of evolutionary biologist Charles Darwin and American psychologist William James imply that emotions are merely biological events like a cough or a sneeze with no meaning and that they are the opposite of thinking.

Aristotle is the best known of Plato's students, and his contribution to the understanding of emotions is significantly different than that of Plato and more in line with the findings of modern scientific research into emotions. Aristotle's most fundamental insight was that emotions are connected with action and that they derive from what we believe.

Aristotle's book, *The Nicomachean Ethics*, is a philosophical inquiry into virtue, character, and the good life. Our passions, when they are exercised, have wisdom, and they guide our thinking, our values, and our survival. But they can easily go awry and often do so. Aristotle's view was that the problem is not with emotionality, but with the appropriateness of emotion and its expression. Aristotle's challenge is to manage our emotional life with intelligence.

Investors hold contradictory beliefs regarding the value of emotions. On the one hand, they act as the foundation for heroic and compassionate deeds, and on the other, they act as destructive forces that can cause self-sabotage during trading, faulty reasoning, war, and destruction. Not only do we have a contradictory belief regarding emotions; the well-worn phrase "emotion kills successful trading" is inculcated into the psyche of the novice trader.

Contemporary scientific evidence shows that emotions are central to establishing, maintaining, changing, or terminating the relation between a person and the environment in matters of significance to the person. Emotions now are viewed by the scientific community as both functional and indispensable to rational thought. The effect of moods and emotions on judgment is significant, and investors make judgments by combining how they feel with what they know.

The Need for a Model of Investment Competence

There are very few occupations that require the determination, strength, courage, and integrity of beliefs as does trading. Investors have only their knowledge and courage—in essence, we are on our own before the computer screen. There is no external examiner or line manager to help. There are tools, such as the computer, which help to analyze the market, charts that may plot strengths and weaknesses or resistance and support. Investors may have a fast order entry system giving depth of market, and market maker (Level 2) information. In the final analysis, for many, trading is a solitary pursuit without the immediate or the informal support of colleagues. In these circumstances, it is essential that investors have a comprehensive model of trading competence to guide them.

The paramouncy principle embraces the holistic notion that an investor can develop a range of skills over time to address all aspects of the person required to succeed in this difficult profession. In my

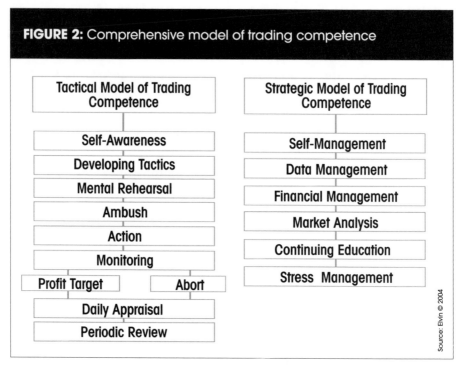

FIGURE 2: Comprehensive model of trading competence

book, *Financial Risk Taking* (Wiley, 2004), a comprehensive model of trading competence is presented to outline tactical (active trading) and strategic (planning and learning) skills requirements (see Figure 2). In addition to the comprehensive model of trading competence, eight standards and related criteria are presented in the style of a workbook to assist the investor to structure and facilitate learning. If investors can identify their weaknesses and strengths, they will be taking the first steps to trading competence.

Following a number of years assessing my own strengths and weaknesses as a full-time, home-based trader, I examined research in cognitive psychology and economics, applying theory to practice. The eight standards and criteria of trading competence were developed following interviews with thirty-eight home-based traders who identified critical areas of their own learning and development. (See page 160 for the eight standards).

The Planet of Market Wizards

Perhaps the strongest evidence in support of intelligent life existing in some distant corner of the universe is that they have not contacted us. Investors lose money by repeating mistakes time and again and view these blunders as business expenses on the road to market mastery. They look to self-professed experts for guidance, some of whom hold no qualifications apart from a certificate in audacity and the ability to convince people that they hold esoteric knowledge providing a conduit to wealth and prosperity. Who can question their integrity when the very nature of investment is based upon an unpredictable market open to interpretation? The corner shop vendor will tell you of his trading profits with an anecdote regarding earlier failures, adding realism to the events. The bus driver, professor, tailor, surgeon, and refuse collector are all market wizards.

The dream of easy success has been sold to people throughout the ages, and the current boom in sales of software and investment courses holds disquieting historical parallels. In Amsterdam during the sixteenth century, there was an accredited course in alchemy from a respected center of education. Dr. John Dee—mystic, astrologer, and advisor to Queen Elizabeth I—is reputed to have researched alchemy there. Of course, no one ever did turn lead into gold, and we now know that turning lead into gold does not fit the principles of chemistry.

Regardless of the lack of evidence, it did not change the fact that people believed it could be done for almost a thousand years. Great halls were filled with people, and if you could convince somebody that you had done it once, people would pay large amounts to learn the secrets of alchemy.

Investors believe in the authority of expertise, and stockbrokers and financial advisors are trusted with the money of hardworking people. Numerous studies show that advisors on equities consistently do worse than the markets in which they are involved, even before making allowance for any fee. The same applies to the managers of pension funds, unit trusts, and of the portfolios of insurance companies. Some investors are targeted by brokerages as potential clients to exploit. I have been subject to numerous cold calls and recently recorded an attempt by a broker to sell me a "great market opportunity." The broker was unable to answer the most basic questions about how he and his market analyst arrived at their conclusions.

But It Can Be Done

Having discussed the downside of market investment, there is also

The Eight Standards and Criteria

1. Market Analysis

A mastery of one system or methodology based on observable outcomes. My personal preference incorporates trading volume in relation to price spread using Wyckoff methodology and related tools such as tradeguider.com.

2. Stress Management

To identify external stressors, understand its effect on performance, and apply a method of stress reduction on a daily basis. My personal preference is walking, cycling, and using deep-breathing techniques effectively.

3. The Trading Business Plan

To place in writing a plan that reflects decision processes, financial and risk management strategies, and rules of market engagement. Successful investors, without exception, have written rules of discipline and market engagement and review progress regularly at designated periods, often marked on a calendar.

4. Perceptual Biases

To bring into conscious awareness the negative influence of predispositions, beliefs, and common errors of judgment. For example, investors are afflicted by the common error of giving a greater value to information supporting a position than information against it.

5. Emotional Biases

To understand the value of emotions, identify negative emotions, and learn techniques to control moods and emotional states. Some investors may need outside assistance to identify recurring negative emotional states during active investment. The use of modeling and cognitive behavioral therapy has had tremendous success.

6. Financial and Risk Management

The ability to perceive, define, and manage risk. Investors need to keep written records in the form of a trading diary, decision diary, and equity chart. A statement on how the written diaries and charts will be created and then utilized can be added to the business plan.

7. Data Management

Developing personal strategies to manage information. Having a general understanding of hardware and software, being at ease with basic arithmetic, and identifying the difference between relevant and irrelevant information.

8. Continuing Education

Creating a personal training plan using information about strengths and weaknesses learned through using these standards and criteria or something similar. Identifying target dates for completion of learning tasks, and assess outcome. Continuing education is a lifetime pursuit, and setting higher goals in a structured manner will facilitate learning and keep investors in touch with their aspirations.

an optimistic and rewarding element. There are many investors who make regular profits from their homes and brokers who are highly skilled and committed to providing a quality service.

A common attribute of successful investors is their belief in the paramouncy principle—whether they call it by this name or not—and the personal responsibility they take for all investment decisions. Investment success requires a set of skills that enables investors to think clearly under stressful conditions, to make intelligent decisions devoid of perceptual and emotional biases, and to keep control of money in their account. The paramouncy principle makes explicit the requirement of self-awareness and self-management, two important (yet neglected) domains of emotional intelligence.

The journey to investment competence is a challenging yet potentially rewarding path, and we may see things of beauty along the way. It is inevitable that investors will experience loss and fear, frustration and self-doubt; but it is how these events are perceived and managed that determines a place among the ninety-percent majority or ten percent of profitable investors. Are you ready to accept Aristotle's challenge?

Mike Elvin, PhD, resides in London and is author of *Financial Risk Taking: An Introduction to the Psychology of Trading and Behavioral Finance* (Wiley, 2004). He was a research psychologist and managed mental health services in the UK prior to his current employment at a futures exchange. He offers individual tuition and seminars. Further enquiries can be made to m.elvin@blueyonder.co.uk. This article originally appeared in *SFO* in February 2005.

18

WHAT'S THE CROWD THINKING

BY BERNIE SCHAEFFER

An edge. That's what every trader looks for. But, there's no Holy Grail in trading and investing, at least not yet. So for now, we'll just have to settle for that unique edge that gives us a leg up on the competition.

However, some traders have found an edge in an area that until recently generally was considered nothing more than hocus pocus—sentiment. When combined with fundamental and technical factors (a methodology we at Schaeffer's call "expectational analysis"), sentiment can be a powerful tool for analyzing stocks, sectors, or the market overall.

So what is sentiment and why do we consider it so important? Investor sentiment is simply the collective feelings, moods, beliefs, and, in some cases, actions of investors. The most accurate sentiment indicators generally reflect what a group of investors actually is doing as opposed to what they're feeling and saying, although the latter have a degree of validity.

There's no such thing as an infallible indicator, and sentiment is no exception. But, without a feel for the expectational environment surrounding a stock, a trader's analysis is not firing on all cylinders. He or she very well may have a handle on the fundamentals and technicals, but very often it's expectations—or sentiment—that makes the difference. For example, have you ever been at a loss to explain why a stock goes down despite an earnings report that meets or even beats expectations? This is especially frustrating when other stocks that meet expectations rally furiously. What's going on?

The answer often is contained in the differing expectations surrounding the two stocks prior to the event. In one case, the sentiment may have been excessively bullish heading into the report. There could have been a buildup of call options or a lot of anticipatory buying of the stock, which then becomes exhausted by the time earnings are reported. Such a high expectation environment creates a heavy burden on the stock to issue a blowout earnings report. On the other hand, there could have been a general concern about a company's fiscal health and some expectations that earnings might be missed. The result? Increased put buying and shorting activity, which eventually is unwound should the company exceed lowered expectations.

Go Against the Crowd

Just why are expectations so important? Because the price of a stock represents investors' perceptions of reality, and often these perceptions are excellent contrary indicators. If a stock with relatively low expectations stands a good chance of rallying, the price may rise from this artificially low level to one that reflects the real world. Conversely, high expectations can put downward pressure on a stock as the price adjusts itself lower from its unrealistic heights to better match reality.

Put another way, low expectations translate into potential buying power, as skeptical investors (and their money) wait on the sidelines, ready to bolster a stock's appreciation by buying up the supply from profit-takers. This excess demand drives the price even higher. On the other hand, high expectations usually mean that most of the sideline money already has been committed to a stock. Buyers are now scarce, and selling will predominate on any perceived negative news, leaving the stock more vulnerable to a significant decline.

One of the most important tenets of expectational analysis is that the power of a contrarian indicator is much greater when the underlying sentiment runs counter to the direction of the stock. For example, pessimism would be an expected reaction to a down-trending market and, thus, would not be a valuable contrary indicator. On the other hand, skepticism in a rising market is a powerfully bullish combination, as market tops are not seen until optimism reaches extreme levels.

Investors normally are quite bullish during bull markets and quite complacent and relatively lacking in fear on pullbacks in bull markets. It then becomes an art for the sentiment analyst to determine when this bullish sentiment has reached an extreme, at which point buying power will have become dissipated to such an extent that the market will top out. But when negative sentiment accompanies a bull market, the task of the "sentimentician" becomes much easier, as it is then clear that buying power has not yet dissipated and the bull market has further to run before a top.

Sentiment Adds Value to Traditional Technicals

Objectively gauging sentiment can add substantial value to traditional technical analysis, because sentiment extremes are not visible on the charts and can only be viewed and measured by a separate class of sentiment indicators. A trend that is about to end cannot be distinguished on a chart from a trend that has a long way to go in price and time. In fact, there is an old saying in technical analysis to the effect that "the chart looks prettiest just ahead of a top." But, sentiment indicators can help traders distinguish the pretty chart that is going to remain pretty from the pretty chart that is about to turn ugly. Let's examine some of these sentiment indicators and how you can use them to improve your trading results.

Magazine Cover Sentiment

One of the easiest ways to gauge sentiment is with magazine covers. We've found that when a particular stock or industry group makes it to the cover of a business magazine with a bullish feature article, this generally means that the situation is widely known, universally accepted, and has been in place for a long time. These often are the ingredients for a top in a stock. So the stock featured on the magazine cover may be at or near a major top despite all of the bullish buzz from the article. While business magazine covers can be excellent contrarian indicators, business stories appearing on general mainstream magazine covers have even stronger contrarian implications. Why is this so? Quite simply, once a story is noticeable enough to be picked up in the general press, the underlying trend is even more likely to have played itself out.

It is important to note that these publications are not lacking in quality content. In fact, they generally communicate important facts. However, the world of periodicals is in the business of reporting news, not necessarily forecasting. Given that the market tends to discount future events, much of what is being reported has already been factored into the stock by the bigger market players. This sets up a potential reversal in the direction, as the last buyers (or sellers) finally react to the information that was driving the current trend.

Put/Call Ratios

We've found that using option data is an excellent way to measure sentiment. To analyze stocks, we often use option open interest as a means of gauging the relative levels of investor optimism and pessimism. Open interest represents the number of open contracts on an option at the end of each day. Using option open interest data in the form of put/call ratios is one of the better ways to quantify sentiment. Each stock's put/call ratio behaves differently and has its own particular timing implications. The analysis can be taken a step further by combining the open interest of all the stocks in a sector to form a composite put/call ratio for that group.

We use put/call ratio analysis to gauge whether a stock or sector is poised for a rally based upon large amounts of potential buying strength, or vulnerable to stalling out due to a lack of cash available to push it higher. High put/call ratios often are indicative of excessive pessimism and, thus, of large amounts of money on the sidelines. Conversely, low put/call ratios indicate a point at which there is so much optimism that very little money is left to push the stock or index higher, leaving it especially vulnerable to disappointing news.

When gauging sentiment, we're primarily interested in the convictions displayed by the speculative public. Our research has shown that a contrarian view of public (rather than institutional) sentiment often proves to be a more reliable predictor of market movement. To collect options information that is more likely attributable to these speculators, we focus on the front three months of options data, which is where the small speculators tend to gravitate. By comparing the current put/call open interest ratio to previous readings for that stock, we can accurately gauge relative levels of investor optimism and pessimism. This is extremely important because we have found that the absolute ratio readings can vary substantially from stock to stock. Thus, comparing a stock's ratio to previous ratios sets up an apples-to-apples comparison that provides a truer picture of relative sentiment.

The manifestation of this analysis is an indicator we call the Schaeffer's put/call open interest ratio, or "SOIR." It represents a ratio of open puts to open calls on only those options due to expire over the following three months. Each daily SOIR reading then is compared to all other readings over the past year to develop a percentile rank. Higher percentiles indicate relatively more pessimism, while lower percentiles suggest optimism. Thus, a rank in the ninetieth percentile would mean that only ten percent of all SOIR readings over the past year were higher, or more pessimistic. This suggests a relatively high level of negative sentiment, which can have bullish implications for a stock displaying strong fundamentals and technicals. The opposite argument can be made for a low percentile ranking, which can suggest a stock is potentially overextended and vulnerable to a sell-off.

Short Interest

Once a month, brokerage firms are required to report the number of shares that have been shorted in their client accounts. This information is compiled for each security and is then released to the public. Monitoring a stock's monthly short-interest figures provides a glimpse of the public's level of pessimism toward the stock. In most instances, large amounts of short interest indicate that the general outlook for the company is negative (sometimes heavy short interest is created out of arbitrage situations, such as mergers).

From a contrarian viewpoint, we see this pessimism as very bullish for a stock that has benefited from an event such as an earnings surprise. That is, significant short interest on a stock that gaps higher due to a particular event can cause a short squeeze (the shorts buying back their shares) that makes the up-trend persist longer than most would anticipate, based solely on the event itself.

We especially like heavy short interest on a stock displaying strong price action with pullbacks contained at key support levels. This is where market participants will potentially see quick, significant moves, caused by the shorts rushing to buy back shares in order to limit their losses as the stock moves higher from support. This short covering adds another source of buying power for an equity already in a strong up-trend.

Analyst Ratings

Another sentiment measure that is easily tracked and quantifiable is the composite analyst rating, which is available from many major

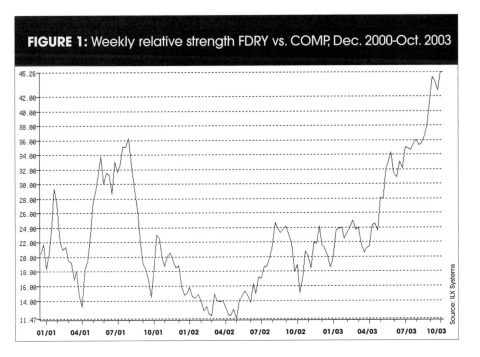

FIGURE 1: Weekly relative strength FDRY vs. COMP, Dec. 2000-Oct. 2003

Source: ILX Systems

financial websites. These ratings simply track the total number of analysts who designate a particular stock as a buy, hold, or sell. While such ratings have come under fire as being too effusive and perhaps somewhat self-serving, they still contain valuable sentiment data that reflect the potential buying power underlying a stock.

There's little doubt that the preponderance of ratings fall on the buy side and that a hold is tantamount to a negative rating. But, we'll often see a smattering of sells that typically reflect a fairly strong degree of negative sentiment toward a stock. On the other hand, a heavy weighting of buys means that optimism is at a peak and that there is much more room for downgrades than upgrades. In other words, the ratings are as optimistic as they are likely to ever be. This can be a warning sign, especially for a stock showing technical weakness.

We also look at the number of ratings. A stock or sector with fewer ratings often means the street hasn't yet jumped on a stock's band-wagon. Because most ratings are buys, additional coverage likely will benefit such lightly regarded stocks. Until recently, for example, gold stocks were largely ignored despite the out-performance they've en-joyed for the past three years.

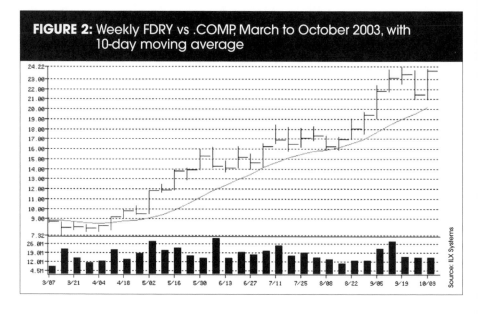

FIGURE 2: Weekly FDRY vs .COMP, March to October 2003, with 10-day moving average

Source: ILX Systems

Putting Sentiment to Work

Let's now see how to combine sentiment with technical measures to create a powerful—and profitable—trading opportunity. The following example is from an option trade recommended in one of our real-time recommendation services. In October 2003, we had our eye on Foundry Networks (FDRY), a stock displaying strong price action. The equity had been steadily outperforming the Nasdaq Composite (COMP) for nearly eighteen months, and its relative-strength measure versus the COMP was near a three-year high, as seen in *Figure 1.*

Elsewhere on the technical front, the shares had been enjoying a monster rally thanks to the steady support of their ascending ten-week moving average. In fact, FDRY had tripled from early April to mid-September before it took a breather and consolidated into its ten-week trend line. We noticed a similar pattern in June and July—consolidation followed by a resumption of the up-trend. The ten-week had been flawless since early April, containing every weekly close and drawdown in the shares, seen in *Figure 2.* Given the stock's technical history, we anticipated the pattern repeating in October.

While the technicals provided a solid entry point—a pullback to a supportive trend line within an intermediate-term up-trend—the key to the trade and the fuel needed to propel the shares higher were provided by a wave of skeptical sentiment. Much of this pessimism was

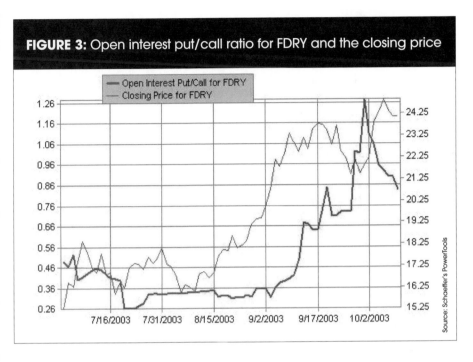

FIGURE 3: Open interest put/call ratio for FDRY and the closing price

seen in the options market, as FDRY's put/call ratio (SOIR) was in the midst of a huge surge, as puts were added at a much faster rate than calls (see *Figure 3*). In fact, the ratio was at a yearly high when we put on the trade, an indication of extreme pessimism among options players. We also knew from our research that huge spikes in put activity typically were followed by strong moves higher by FDRY shares.

Wall Street analysts, who were anything but enthusiastic toward the stock, provided the final piece of the puzzle. Despite the equity's huge ascent, analysts had not bought into the rally, which suggested that sufficient buying power remained on the sidelines ready to flow into the stock and boost its price. In fact, sixty-five percent of the brokerages covering the shares rated them a hold, which left more than ample room for future upgrades compared to downgrades. In short then, FDRY presented us with an ideal bullish play within the context of our expectational framework—negative sentiment on a strong stock that was clearly outperforming the broader market. We thus recommended a call option on FDRY to leverage the expected stock price increase.

The stock behaved as we expected by successfully rebounding off the support of its ten-week moving average. At the same time, some of the pessimism contained in the put/call ratio began to unwind into optimism (note the decline in the SOIR line in *Figure 3*), which translated into buying pressure. The stock vaulted higher by nearly fourteen percent over the next four trading days, while our option garnered a 108-percent profit.

Putting It All Together

Adding sentiment to an arsenal of analytical tools can greatly enhance trading performance. While we have a number of sentiment-based indicators at our disposal, there are four major principles market participants should understand:

- The strongest contrarian implications by far are when there is bearish sentiment during rallies and bullish sentiment during declines.
- Bullish sentiment during rallies and bearish sentiment during declines have the weakest contrarian implications.
- If you are going to trade counter-trend based on sentiment that is in line with your trend, you will be most successful during declines when sentiment becomes very bearish and will be least successful during rallies when sentiment becomes very bullish.
- The crowd can always become more bullish or bearish, even when sentiment seems to be at extreme levels.

Bernie Schaeffer is chairman of Schaeffer's Investment Research. His website, www.schaeffersResearch.com, has been cited by Forbes and Barron's as a top options website. Schaeffer's contrarian approach focuses on stocks with technical and fundamental trends that run counter to investor expectations. This article originally appeared in *SFO* in March 2004.

SECTION FOUR
The Trading Brain

We all like to think of ourselves as totally in control. But in truth, our physiology inherently affects everything we do, including our trading practice. Getting a basic understanding of the way our trading brains work can help us become better traders.

Finding your zone means finding a state of mind where cognitive function and action flow seamlessly, without effort or interference. The process of self-actualization leads to a flow in activities, meaning you've found your zone. Trading psychologist Brett N. Steenbarger walks you through highlights of the prevailing studies, ranging from Maslow's groundbreaking research on human needs to more recent applications to the practice of trading.

Taming and training the brain can have big rewards for the aware trader. We now understand which parts of our brains are working when we process different activities. Learning how the brain anatomically processes information—the difference between neocortex and amygdala-related actions—can help you master your emotions and take a fresh look at your trading habits.

Any modern book on trading psychology must include a chapter on iconic trader George Soros. Soros' curious investment strategy entails paying attention to his aching back. Learn how you can let your gut feelings work together with your analysis in informing your trading decisions. Soros' chief operating principle is a belief in fallibility. He intuitively detects profit opportunities where the prevailing bias creates self-reinforcing trends that reverse when the flaw becomes apparent. It leads him to look for a flaw in every investment thesis. Learn how Soros got where he is by finding the flaw before it becomes apparent to everyone else.

FINDING THE ZONE: New Perspectives on the Mental Game of Trading

BY BRETT N. STEENBARGER, PhD

A number of recent books have emphasized trading as a performance activity, in which mental state is a key element in success or failure. So prevalent is this view that two separate books with the same title—*Trading in the Zone*—have recently appeared. What is this "zone," and how can traders reach it with consistency? In this chapter, I will review ideas about the zone from a variety of sources, including new research in cognitive neuroscience, and spell out the implications for futures and options traders looking to improve their mindsets—and their profits.

Understanding the Zone

The idea of a performance-enhancing zone originated neither in athletics or trading, but in the philosophy of Zen Buddhism. In the 1930s, Eugen Herrigel traveled to Japan to learn Zen through, of all things, the practice of archery. Nearly two decades later, his book, *Zen in the Art of Archery* (Pantheon, 1953), popularized the notion of achieving excellence through mental discipline. His book was the inspiration for the popular novel, *Zen and the Art of Motorcycle Maintenance* (William Morrow & Co., 1974), written by Robert Pirsig. Interwoven in Pirsig's story of a father and son rediscovering each other on a motorcycle journey is a serious exploration of the experience of quality. Traveling on a cycle, Pirsig explains, possesses a different quality from driving a car. In the latter, you are always watching reality through a frame, shut inside a compartment. On a cycle, he writes, you are "in the scene, not just watching it any more, and the sense of presence is overwhelming." This fusion of actor and act, performer and performance, is experienced as "the zone."

Crucial to the philosophy of Zen—and to the accounts of Herrigel and Pirsig—is the idea that our normal state of consciousness ruins the quality of the Zen experience. As soon as we consciously think about our performance, we are no longer one with it. Trying harder at a task only compounds this separation. The discipline of the Zen archer can be found in the performer's ability to still the mind, to remove mental interference, and to allow instinctively honed skills to manifest themselves naturally.

In their books, *Trading in the Zone*, authors Mark Douglas (Prentice Hall Press, 2001) and Ari Kiev (Wiley, 2001) both emphasize the importance of focus and concentration in reaching a state where trading flows without seeming effort. Both authors view the zone as an outgrowth of trading discipline and a positive mindset. Once the trader lapses into patterns of fear, greed, and frustration, the zone is lost and instincts born of long hours of observing market patterns cannot emerge. For the trader, as for the Zen archer, turning off the mind is a crucial element in success.

But how valid is this notion of the zone? Do elite performers in archery, trading, and other fields of endeavor truly find their success in Pirsig's state of quality? This is where research provides surprising answers.

Creativity and the Zone

Abraham Maslow was one of the first psychologists to study healthy, high-functioning individuals rather than mentally ill ones. His investigation of self-actualizing people—those who were unusually creative, productive, happy, and fulfilled—led to several important discoveries. Foremost among these, he found that self-actualizing people report a significantly greater number of peak experiences than the average individual. These peak experiences, he explained, have an almost mystical quality, in which the person feels suddenly at peace, at one with the universe. Invariably these experiences arrive during moments when the self-actualizing person is immersed in an activity of personal significance. Interestingly, they emerge naturally and spontaneously, not by conscious design.

FIGURE 1: Characteristics of work experiences associated with the zone.

1. There are clear goals every step of the way.
2. There is immediate feedback to one's actions.
3. There is a balance between challenge and skills.
4. Action and awareness are merged.
5. Distractions are excluded from consciousness.
6. There is no worry of failure.
7. Self-consciousness disappears.
8. The sense of time becomes distorted.
9. The activity becomes autotelic (pleasurable in its own right).

Source: Adapted from Creativity: Flow and the Psychology of Discovery of Invention, by Csikszentmihalyi

---

Could Maslow's peak experiences refer to the same mind state noted by Herrigel in Zen archery, by Pirsig in his exploration of quality, and by traders who have experienced the zone?

Research by University of Chicago psychologist Mihaly Csikszentmihalyi would answer in the affirmative. Studying unusually creative, successful individuals across a variety of disciplines, Csikszentmihalyi found that their work activity is accompanied by a state of flow. This flow state is experienced as inherently enjoyable, in which workers are so immersed in their tasks that time seems to melt away. They lose awareness of themselves and their settings, becoming one with their labors.

In his book, *Creativity: Flow and the Psychology of Discovery of Invention* (HarperCollins, 1996), Csikszentmihalyi identified nine characteristics of work activities that yield the flow experience (see *Figure 1*). He found that challenging tasks with clear goals and immediate feedback provide the greatest intrinsic pleasure. Summarizing these studies, Csikszentmihalyi writes, "Every person we interviewed said that it was equally true that they had worked every minute of their careers, and that they had never worked a day in all their lives. They experienced even the most focused immersion in extremely difficult tasks as a lark, an exhilarating and playful adventure." He describes performers in the zone as "programmed for creativity" because their pleasure-pain mechanism leads them to seek ever-greater productive challenges.

What makes the creative, successful, self-actualizing person unique, then, is not just the presence of peak experiences, flow, or the zone, but the ability to access and sustain this state with regularity. This is only possible, Csikszentmihalyi asserts, when people intrinsically love what they are doing. The trader who is primarily motivated by factors extrinsic to the markets themselves—by a need to prove himself, a desire to avoid failure, or urges for fame or fortune—is less likely to find the zone than the trader who finds the markets fascinating in their own right. From the Maslow-Csikszentmihalyi perspective, it is the trader who is programmed for creativity—who finds intrinsic enjoyment in the rigors of studying and trading market patterns—that is most likely to develop unique, winning trading strategies.

Exemplary Achievement and the Zone

Persistence of effort fueled by intrinsic love for one's work seems to be a formula for success across a variety of disciplines, not just trading. Studies supporting this conclusion date back to Francis Galton's 1869 work on hereditary genius. Investigating eminent creators, Galton found that these high-functioning individuals were capable of performing large amounts of highly laborious work, as if they were "urged by an inherent stimulus." This "laboring instinct," Galton believed, was a major factor in determining success or failure.

Subsequent research has confirmed Galton's early conclusions. Psychologist Dean Keith Simonton of the University of California at Davis, in his book *Greatness: Who Makes History and Why* (The Guildford Press, 1994), explains of highly productive creators, "These individuals are driven by huge motivational forces that far eclipse the impetus behind less accomplished colleagues...Geniuses cannot spend so many hours without an inherent passion for what they do." The reason successful people are successful, Simonton found, is that they produce more than their colleagues: more works of art, more scientific experiments, and more political initiatives. Because of this productivity, they are more likely than the average person to hit the jackpot and stumble across a truly meaningful contribution.

These findings have significant implications for traders of futures and options. A trader's productivity might be measured, not just by his or her equity curve, but in the number of unique and viable trading strategies that can be generated. The trader motivated by an intrinsic fascination with the markets is constantly working on the markets, seeking a tradable edge. A developer of one hundred mechanical systems, on average, is more likely to come up with a robust trading method than a trader tinkering with the canned systems that accompany many charting software programs. Similarly, the discretionary trader who has observed and paper traded over thousands of days of market action is more likely to internalize tradable patterns than the part-time trader. The zone is important, not just because it blocks negative emotions from trading, but because it provides the motivational fuel for achieving market mastery.

The hypothesis worthy of consideration is that the factors underlying trading success are similar to those underlying success in other fields of endeavor. The successful trader, like the scientific genius or great artist, attains a state in which effortful activity is experienced as inherently pleasurable. This state of flow—what traders know as the zone—blurs the distinction between work and play, fueling an extraordinary level of creative effort.

This hypothesis fits well with the research of K. Anders Ericsson, who has found that successful performers in sports, the arts, and sciences are distinguished by the amount of intensive, deliberative practice they devote to their disciplines. As Ericsson reports in his book, *The Road to Excellence* (Lawrence Ehrlbaum, 1996), there appears to be a lawful, linear relationship between the amount of time spent in high-quality practice and the performer's ultimate level of achievement. Significantly, many of the characteristics of high quality practice, as observed by Ericsson, overlap the factors that generate the flow state including challenge, clear goals, and rapid feedback. It appears that exemplary performers structure their practice in such a way as to maximize flow-zone states, thereby sustaining their motivation for hard work.

Ericsson observes that effort alone is not enough to generate the zone. Physical exertion by itself, for example, does not ensure a pleasurable experience. Rather, it is the specific effort of mental concentration that generates an altered state of consciousness and heightens learning and performance. When a musician is immersed in her craft, Ericsson notes, she can generate a flow experience. When that immersion is interrupted by coaching, the zone is lost. As Herrigel discovered in his investigation of Zen archery, it is not possible to be at one with an activity and simultaneously concerned with the activity's outcome. If traders are to find the zone, it can only be through the highly focused concentration that occurs during trading itself. While positive thinking and trading discipline are necessary for reaching the zone, they are not sufficient. Sustained mental effort appears to be the key.

Cognitive Neuroscience and the Zone

What is happening in the brain when traders are in their zones? While studies have yet to be conducted measuring brain activity during actual trading, we do know quite a bit about the brain activity associated with sustained mental effort thanks to imaging studies and investigations of patients with localized brain injuries.

This research suggests that attention, concentration, and sustained mental effort are associated with a high level of activity in the brain's frontal lobes. In his book of the same title, neurologist Elkhonon Goldberg refers to the frontal lobes as *The Executive Brain* (Oxford University Press, U.S.A., 2001). When people need to coordinate complex activities, such as generating and executing a trading plan, the frontal lobes receive a disproportionate share of cerebral blood flow. The frontal lobes, neurologist Oliver Sacks writes in the foreword to Goldberg's book, "are crucial for all higher-order purposeful behavior...The intentionality of the individual is invested in the frontal lobes."

When there is injury to the frontal lobes, the result is a decline in the ability to carry out purposeful behavior. Neurologists refer to this as the "dysexecutive syndrome," and it is typified by emotional interruptions of intentional activity, impulsivity, and distractability—qualities not unlike those seen in attention-deficit hyperactivity disorder (ADHD).

Figure 2 summarizes characteristics of successful and unsuccessful traders derived from various writings on trading psychology. These include my own investigations with Linda Raschke, in which we surveyed the traits of sixty-four active traders. Notice how the parallels between the successful and unsuccessful traders

FIGURE 2: Characteristics of successful and unsuccessful traders

Successful Trader	Unsuccessful Trader
Trades with a plan	Trades impulsively
Trades in a rule-governed fashion	Trades on hunches and urges
Trades in a clear mental state	Trades emotionally
Trades when focused on the markets	Trades when focused on self
Becomes problem-focused after a loss	Becomes emotion focused after a loss
Trades with tested strategies for trade management	Trades with little or no risk management
Trades selectively, based on risk and reward	Trades inconsistently; over-trades and under-trades

mirror the differences between individuals who have intact versus impaired frontal lobes. Could it be that the conditions associated with frontal lobe activation—the intensive concentration and mental effort of the zone—are also the stuff of which good trading is made?

Research supports such a conclusion. Arthur Shimamura at the University of California at Berkeley summarizes a series of studies that identify the role of the prefrontal cortex as one of "dynamic filtering." The frontal lobes allow us to carry out intentional, complex tasks by filtering out extraneous stimuli. This permits us to keep plans firmly in working memory while we carry out the specific tasks associated with those plans. Among the stimuli that are filtered out by frontal activity are emotional experiences. Activation of the frontal lobes by remaining focused on planned, intentional trading—i.e., trading in the zone—turns out to be among the most effective strategies for eliminating emotional interference with decision making.

Interestingly, the frontal lobes tend to be more involved in novel tasks than routine ones. When a skill is first learned, blood flow to the frontal lobes is at its greatest and is centered in the right brain hemisphere. As the skill becomes automatic, the flow shifts to other brain regions, particularly in the left hemisphere. This makes sense, since the greatest attention and mental effort are needed to process new stimuli. Once a task is routine, such as driving a car, it no longer requires the participation of the brain's executive center.

Experienced futures and options traders know that patterns in the markets are never static. The patterns one finds in a low volatility, bracketing market are different from those observed in a trending, volatile environment. In his book *The Education of a Speculator* (John Wiley & Sons, 1996), well-known trader Victor Niederhoffer refers to this phenomenon as "ever-changing cycles." To the extent that market patterns shift over time, traders are confronted with ongoing novelty. Trading can never become a wholly automatic task, as the identification of new patterns requires the involvement of the brain's frontal lobes. This conclusion suggests that the capacity to sustain mental effort is a necessary ingredient in ongoing trading success, allowing traders to recognize and exploit ever-changing cycles before they melt away. It also helps explain the common understanding among traders that one must filter out emotions to be successful. To the extent that one is immersed in greed, fear, or frustration, the zone is lost and novel patterns cannot be identified and exploited. Temporarily, it is as if the trader functions with a dysexecutive syndrome or ADHD, reducing the capacity for intentional behavior.

This brings us to a second, important hypothesis: the experience we call the zone is an altered state of consciousness that accompanies ongoing activation of the brain's frontal cortex. It facilitates accelerated learning by enabling us to sustain focused attention. The zone can be thought of as the second wind of consciousness. It is a byproduct of sustained, high-quality effort that becomes a motivational state in its own right. Recognition of that fact opens the door to new and promising strategies for trading psychology.

Finding the Zone

How can traders improve their ability to operate within the performance-enhancing zone? Several strategies can be derived from the research covered to this point:

Deliberative Practice The trader can structure practice sessions in such a way as to mirror the conditions needed to produce flow experiences. This means that practice sessions should have clear goals, be sufficiently challenging to require a high degree of mental effort, offer prompt and accurate feedback, and proceed with a minimum of distractions. Such practice sessions are not merely teaching exercises; they also serve as training in reaching and sustaining the zone. Simulated trading exercises using historical data are particularly helpful as tools for deliberative practice. By advancing data bar by bar, constructing trading plans, placing trades, managing and exiting positions, traders can rehearse essential trading skills in a challenging fashion, receiving immediate feedback about their efforts.

Progressive Resistance The development of one's executive capacities—the hallmark of operating within the zone—is very similar to one's physical development. Just as weightlifters must challenge themselves with sufficient resistance to build muscle strength, progressively increasing the resistance over time, traders can improve their focus by tackling increasingly complex trading challenges. For example, deliberative practice involving simulated trading of a single market position could be followed by rehearsal requiring the management of multiple positions. Simulations could also be initiated under conditions of increasing distraction to require greater mental efforts.

Frequent Breaks from Trading and Deliberative Practice One of the interesting findings from research with expert performers is that they rehearse their skills in bursts. Episodes of high-quality concentration lasting no more than a few hours are followed by frequent breaks, often in the form of brief naps. A number of successful traders note that they stop trading when they are tired and stop trading at points in the day when volatility diminishes. This gives them time to recover their concentration and stay in the zone when they are trading. In a recent interview with Mark Etzkorn, for example, well-known trader Mark Cook reported that he finishes most of his trading by 2:00 EST. "At that point," he explains, "I've already been thinking 'market' for seven hours, and that's about my limit." His self-study revealed that his performance diminishes when he trades beyond his fatigue threshold: when he is presumably out of the zone.

Biofeedback Of all the strategies for developing trading expertise, this may have the greatest potential. Biofeedback systems that measure skin conductivity, heart rate, muscle tension, and brain waves are becoming increasingly affordable, allowing individuals to monitor their own levels of calm and arousal. While a calm biofeedback profile does not guarantee that one is in the zone, an aroused profile almost certainly ensures that the wrong brain regions are being activated for optimal performance. By combining biofeedback with deliberative practice, traders can track when their emotional patterns are taking them out of the flow state and threatening to disrupt their trading. In my own research, I have been working with forehead skin temperature biofeedback, which is highly sensitive to enhanced blood flow to the brain's frontal cortex. By tracking rises and declines in forehead temperature during practice sessions, traders can objectively measure the degree to which they are in the zone and discover strategies that maintain the state.

Cognitive Exercises Elkhonon Goldberg raises the intriguing notion of creating gymnasiums for the mind, in which cognitive exercises raise the level of frontal lobe functioning. Such exercises are already utilized with success among patients who have experienced brain injury or dysfunction. Goldberg believes that normal individuals can similarly enhance their brain functioning by exercising their frontal lobes with tasks that require sustained concentration across progressively challenging tasks. For example, in my own research, I measure forehead skin temperature while performing mental sums on the stock prices moving by on the ticker tape. Because the tape moves relatively quickly, the task requires intense concentration. Interestingly, forehead skin temperature tends to stay highly elevated throughout the task (suggesting frontal lobe activation), resulting in a state of quiet focus akin to the zone. Through these and other exercises, such as those found in Zen, it may be possible to create flow experiences on demand, placing traders more consistently in a high performance zone.

Robert Pirsig's *Zen and the Art of Motorcycle Maintenance* offers the interesting observation that the real motorcycle the rider works on is the cycle called the self. Whether it is cycling, Zen archery, or trading, working on one's craft and working on oneself are one and the same. Through disciplined and intensive training, we literally shape the brain and create the motivational states necessary to sustain exemplary performance. I would suggest that traders can greatly accelerate this process. "What I do every day is a mental exercise that increases my mental dexterity..." trader Mark Cook observes. "I always say, 'I am not a trader, I am trading.' Trading has engulfed my being." The real market we are trading, he has found, is the market called the self.

Brett N. Steenbarger, PhD, is associate clinical professor of psychiatry and behavioral sciences at SUNY Upstate Medical University in Syracuse, NY. As director of trader development for Kingstree Trading, LLC, in Chicago, he mentors professional traders and coordinates a trader training program. An active trader of the stock indexes, Steenbarger uses statistically based pattern recognition for intra-day trading. The author of *Enhancing Trader Performance: Proven Strategies from the Cutting Edge of Trading Psychology* (Wiley Trading, 2006) and *The Psychology of Trading: Tools and Techniques for Minding the Markets* (Wiley, 2002), Steenbarger maintains a trading archive and blog at www.brettsteenbarger.com and a blog of market analytics at www.traderfeed.blogspot.com. This article originally appeared in *SFO* in December 2002.

WHAT WOULD FREUD SAY: Stroll Down Freud's Mental Path to Profits

BY DENISE SHULL

I seem to be stuck in a rut. I have good days, and they are usually followed up with bad days. The good days are not good enough or often enough because far too often I hesitate on my trades. The bad days are usually a result of impulse trades. They are trades I make that I know I shouldn't, but I make them on complete impulse and usually end up with a nasty reversal. I've tried a lot of things, and I'm probably more frustrated now than ever.

I realize that dealing with my trading emotions seems much more difficult than the mechanics of trading, albeit more important. How do I break these patterns of what seem to be automatic preprogrammed responses from somewhere inside? Is there a way to interrupt the pattern? It clearly takes more than sheer will power." [An index trader, message board post, February 2004, used with permission]

Every experienced trader knows that success requires developing a plausible strategy for entries and exits—first there's the plan, and then there's the actual trading with that plan. There's no question that this part of the job draws on fairly intense intellectual analysis and decision making.

Realistically, however, as the index trader says, success demands more than logic. Even black box systems subtly involve fear and greed in that emotions color the decisions to go live or keep testing. At a minimum, egos and biases alter the development and implementation of any system. In discretionary strategies, rational analysis and deliberate action theoretically drive trades, but in practice both suffer from the influences of mood and attitude.

Everyone says, "Keep your discipline." Yet despite varying degrees, all traders sooner or later confront the reality that their feelings can derail that discipline. One of the more shocking examples comes from traders who make money, lose it, make it back, lose it again, and never stop the cycle. A lot has been written about this; yet traders of all skill levels still struggle to fully solve the problem.

What Would Freud Say?

Yes, the much maligned field of psychoanalysis offers a powerful perspective. In short, the answer comes from figuring out the pattern to conscious, preconscious, and unconscious feelings. With an idea of the scenarios, a trader can identify the "template experiences" behind them and then disassociate the feelings from the trades.

Essentially, this is because the solution resides not in barricading the feelings of fear, elation, stupidity, or whatever, but in sending them an invitation—rather like the adage, "keep your friends close and your enemies closer." The steps of modern psychoanalysis—sorting out unconscious perceptions and learning to express any emotion—can provide a mental edge.

This works because of the uncanny nature of hidden feelings. Take, for example, the tendency to hesitate when entering a market position. Usually the general feelings are nervousness, uncertainty, or just plain fear. The more valuable insight lies in actually decoding the underlying emotions and associations. Is it anxiety over losing money, being wrong, getting in trouble with oneself, being criticized, or feeling stupid? What actually ends up happening when a good trade isn't taken? Ironically, the exact results occur anyway. A trader still loses the money he might have made, feels bad about being wrong, gets in trouble with himself, criticizes himself, and feels stupid—the exact same list as the reasons for not taking the trade in the first place. It's easy to see the circular drama here.

If one looks hard enough, it's not too difficult to find scenarios of thoughts, feelings, and actions that happen over and over again. The order might be mixed up—action, thought, feeling or feeling, action, thought—but a pattern will indeed emerge. It might occur over minutes or it might occur over years, as in the case of a terrific trader experiencing a stunning loss. Yet a pattern always exists.

Sigmund Freud first discussed "the repetition compulsion" in 1920. He described how some people act not according to what would most likely bring the greatest pleasure or success, but instead, in response to a compulsion to repeat. LaPlanche and Pontalis (*The Language of Psychoanalysis*, W.W. Norton & Company, 1974) defined this phenomenon as "... an ungovernable process originating in the unconscious. As a result of action, the subject deliberately places himself in distressing situations, thereby repeating an old experience, but he does not recall this prototype; on the contrary, he has the strong impression that the situation is fully determined by the circumstances of the moment."

In trading terms, the phrase "he has the strong impression that the situation..." translates to "if I could just find the right strategy," or "if that unexpected news event didn't again cause the fast market to blow through my stop," or "if I could just eliminate the spontaneous trades" or ... or ...or.

Neuroscience Says

How can this be? The brain and how it develops give us some clues. In very basic terms, the brain has three major sections: the brainstem, which controls things like heartbeat and digestion; the sub-cortex, which lies above the brainstem and in the middle of the head; and the cortex, which processes what we think of as complex thought and perception. Development starts with the brainstem and progresses through the highest areas in early childhood and beyond. Two primary structures, neurons and the spaces between them, called synapses, form networks that extend throughout the brain and provide the core infrastructure.

During growth, each area greatly influences the development of the next higher one. Therefore, functions learned and managed primarily by sub-cortical structures, like the amygdala or the hypothalamus, become enveloped within the tasks processed primarily by the higher cortical subsections. The process, however, does not negate the power of the lower structures. By virtue of their earlier development and resulting influence on subsequent growth of the brain, the sub-cortical areas from which emotions appear to emanate hold great sway over the higher thinking centers.

If it is hard to believe that intellect can be controlled by a more primitive part of the brain, think of handwriting. When a child first learns to write in cursive, it requires a very deliberate moving of the hand. Later, however, the entire effort to sign one's name operates well below the level of awareness. Likewise, feelings often operate outside of consciousness, but that doesn't take away their power. In fact, the opposite is true.

Contrary to popular thinking, the sub-cortex actually is more powerful because the critical period for how a person perceives himself happens at the same time as the growth of the neuronal networks supporting his emotional processing. Critical periods, well known in biology, refer to the times when certain conditions are necessary for the brain to develop properly or for when a given function or skill will be acquired.

Allan Schore, UCLA neuroscientist, notes that the orbital cortex, a specific subsection of the highest brain, matures in the middle of the second year when average children know less than seventy words. The core self, he says, is nonverbal and unconscious, and it resides in emotional patterns. Schore also says that the bonding between mother and child specifically changes a baby's right brain.

One example of how this could happen comes from another group of neuroscientists led by Hiroki Yamada. The scientists showed how an infant's vision improves at around eight weeks old and creates the possibility for eye contact between mother and child. As in adults, emotional messages, crucial to the infant's development of its understanding of itself, get communicated through the eyes. For example, if a crying baby irritates his mom, and in her exhausted state she looks at the baby with disgust, the child will absorb that response into his own emerging picture of himself.

Later these early ideas echo in the choices we make for ourselves. The perceptions that originated before we had words for them reflect a baby's interpretation of external events that have no actual relationship to our true worth or intelligence. Yet the reverberations remain because they originate within the networks of neurons and synapses that develop before rational thought.

The constant feedback germane to trading offers up a particularly potent reflection of these unconscious feelings. Every tick can serve as an amplifier of a subtle and unheard refrain singing about our right to be successful. Consequently, the cure for irrational or impulsive trading choices lies not in a different system or in another resolution to control the uncontrollable, but rather in shining a light into the hidden decisions regarding our success.

It's Not Personal: The Challenge of Being Human

Realize that no matter how many mistakes have been made, their root cause means nothing in relationship to one's capacity to ultimately be more successful. Almost all traders have or have had emotional stumbling blocks, so it's nothing personal; it simply is part of the challenge of being human in an environment where one's success or failure virtually flashes across the screen in milliseconds.

Second, traders need to ignore the voices, inside or outside, that say "you must control your emotions, or you must do this or that"—things that one finds difficult to do. Listening to them only causes the trader to feel worse about himself. It accomplishes nothing except—maybe—making more impulsive trades or not trading at all. Ultimately, the root feelings generating the problem always fall into the category of "I'm not good enough," and supposed solutions that join that chorus won't stand the test of time.

Ask questions. What were the important events of your childhood? What are your most vivid memories? What happened to you during these times? What stories does your family tell about you? Taking it to the next level, ask how your father treated you when you were little. What did your mother say about your performance in school? What did your sisters and brothers do to you? It is important in this exercise to look outside of yourself for the behaviors of others to whom you were close. Just take note of their behaviors and how it might have affected your life and your feelings back then.

The story line in dreams provides another source of information. Don't worry about interpreting the meaning—just think about the scenario of the dream and the typical emotion associated with it. It doesn't matter if you are the central character in the dream or not. The players in a dream can be anyone; the feelings involved often reflect your own unconscious.

If, by chance, you were separated from your mother early in life, through adoption or illness or divorce, take that into account, as well as the likely behavior of whoever took care of you. Despite the reason for separation, an infant knows that his mother is gone and blames himself. This creates a particular challenge in retaining profits for two reasons—the inherent supposition of unworthiness that occurs ("My mother isn't here—therefore, she must not love me—therefore, I really must be awful.") and the completely unacceptable feelings of hatred over being rejected that simply must be denied in order to function ("I am so lucky these nice, wealthier, smarter people adopted me that, of course, I have nothing but thankfulness for what happened to me.").

Seek and Ye Shall Find

Regardless of what you find, search for a match with your emotions in trading. Look both at specific trades and the overall endeavor. Think of today's trading choices and the feelings they bring up as an analogy to the emotions and thoughts of an earlier time. Look particularly at the recurring scenarios. It could be how the neighbor kids treated you or what your teachers usually said about you, but these memories provide the bridge between our adult experiences and emotional outlines formed in infancy. The insight will begin to unravel the labyrinth of hidden thoughts and feelings behind unprofitable trading.

Here's how it works. One day, after a string of good day trades in Merrill Lynch (MER), I let a short go too far against me. Anyone who trades MER knows that the bid-ask spread gets wide and can jump around in a matter of seconds. Hence, I rationalized. During the trade, I didn't feel bad or even very worried. I did manage not to talk myself into taking the trade overnight and covered for a rather large loss. Afterwards, I felt terrible—not just annoyed, not just bad—but awful.

Putting what I preach into practice, I focused on the substance of what I felt. Beating myself up, I realized the basic emotion was shame over being so stupid. "You idiot, you know better," resounded in my head.

Then it hit me! What had actually happened from a psychoanalytic point of view is that as I let the stock trade through my stop, I unconsciously felt stupid. I wasn't aware of this in real time. I was counting on MER's erratic pattern to save the trade. In not being aware of it, I "acted it out." In other words, I indeed acted stupid by letting it get worse. If during the trade I had known about the underlying feelings, I would have been able to separate the trade from the feeling and implement the right exit.

Not for the Faint of Heart

Of course, do-it-yourself psychoanalysis isn't exactly easy. Going it alone, you can certainly make progress—particularly if these ideas strike you as mumbo jumbo—but like everything, it is easier with a guide. On your own, you can find a pattern to the PRE-conscious "voices in your head." Finding the UN-conscious, by definition, gets more than a bit tricky. Psychoanalysis hasn't marketed itself, so finding a good teacher might require a bit more work, but it falls in the category, "you get what you pay for."

Furthermore, Hyman Spotnitz, founder of modern analysis, extended Freud's work to the point where he cured cases of psychological disturbance that many believed incurable. One of his best tools revolves around the reality of anger and frustration. By helping clients deal with these shunned feelings, he achieved remarkable results. Therefore, the ultimate clue to solving self-defeat lies in working with negative emotions that usually meet with criticism and punishment.

Once you become friendly with the chorus singing about your lack of worthiness to make or keep money, the more difficult but powerful step involves learning to get mad. This works because as we grow up we are taught that getting angry is bad. We don't actually stop getting angry, though. What really happens is that we take those feelings and turn them onto ourselves. This inversion, if you will, then gets played out in the actions that limit our successes.

If there is one thing that distinguishes "moderns," it is the techniques used to turn unconscious rage into energy for success. We actually like it when our clients get angry at us. Invariably the patient becomes more successful when he starts to tell his analyst how much he doesn't like that analyst, that the analyst has let him down, isn't doing his job, or any other version of expressing dissatisfaction. This contrasts with what happens if you tell your parents, spouse, or boss this stuff. In one form or another, you get punished, right? Or at least you expect to.

A talented therapist, on the other hand, will react much differently. The atypical response paves the way for more primitive and unconscious anger to come to the surface. As it does, it can then be put into words. The process of expressing it—without punishment or retribution—unblocks unconscious emotional doors to success.

Short of hiring a coach trained in modern analysis, try writing out whatever feelings of anger—at whomever—you can come up with. Just allow them to be. No one has to know, and nothing has to be done. Another idea—instead of reading or listening to music while working out—focus on the feeling in your gut. List out in your head who or what you feel mad at. Expect to find excuses and rationalizations that prevent the process. The admonitions to "be a good boy (or girl)" or to "be positive" hold enormous power over us.

Ultimately, the objective is to be able to put any and all unconscious feelings into words. Look for two themes: first, how you beat yourself up, and second, who or what you wish you could beat up. If you can find those feelings and accept and put words to them, your trading results will improve. It will become easier to take the next step—whatever that is in your particular situation.

Conceptually, the strategy mirrors the idea in some martial arts— using an enemy's strength to your advantage. We think that we have to control our emotions when, in reality, they are not controllable. They consistently rear their ugly heads in the things we do that aren't according to our plan. The act of being able to say anything destroys their power to covertly influence decisions. As insidious powers weaken, the impulses go away, and clear-headed thinking takes charge.

Then, finally, as the hidden emotions lose their power, the enormous preparation you have done for profitable trading can be implemented with consistent discipline.

Denise K. Shull, MA, a member of the Chicago Board of Trade and a short-term trader since 1994, combines her trading experience and her training in psychology to assist traders in the consistent execution of their trading plans. She founded Trader Psyches Inc., which operates TALKING TRADERS, to offer lectures, workshops, discussion groups, and individual coaching focused on understanding and managing the relationship between intellect, emotion, and trading action. Shull holds a Master's degree from The University of Chicago, where she studied how neuroscience supports the theories of the unconscious. She continues her studies at The Mid-Manhattan Institute, with a focus on modern psychoanalytic techniques. Shull can be reached at denise@traderpsyches.net. This article originally appeared in *SFO* in December 2004.

21

LOVE THE LIZARD BRAIN AND PROSPER

BY TERRY BURNHAM, PhD

"Brain-damaged people make better traders" was the headline summary of a recent academic paper. In the study, patients with brain lesions in the emotional centers of the brain outperformed normal participants in an investment setting. Other recent advances in behavioral finance and neuroeconomics point to our own brain as the source of money-losing decisions.

Sigmund Freud invented the most famous model of internal brain warfare, in which the id, ego, and superego fight for control of incestuous sexual desires, scatological susceptibilities, chocolate fantasies, and other less titillating tensions. Other scholars, from Plato to Professor Marvin Minsky at MIT, model the brain as multiple competing entities with a varying number of parts.

I divide the human brain into just two entities—the prefrontal cortex and the "lizard brain." The prefrontal cortex coolly analyzes the world, while the lizard brain wants to buy flashy cars, eat fatty foods, break marital vows and generally act like a teenager on steroids. This lizard brain classification captures the most important fact about self-control—the brain is not a single, cohesive entity. Stare at a big pile of french fries or some other tasty junk food and you'll immediately feel a competition between doing what feels good and what is right.

My research suggests that the lizard brain is a major culprit in trading losses. "We have met the enemy and he is us." So wrote Walt Kelly in the comic strip Pogo. Similarly, while we are pushed around by the Fed, oil prices, and corrupt CEOs, our toughest financial battles often are with ourselves. The good news is that we control our own trading destinies. Because our challenges come from inside, we have the ability to improve regardless of the environment in which we exist. Those who learn to understand, love, and outsmart the lizard brain can prosper amidst market chaos.

The Lizard Brain: A Set-Up for Financial Failure

Before we get inside the brain, let's remind ourselves of the opportunity. People are naturally terrible at navigating financial markets. Our instinctual, untrained response is to buy high and sell low, exactly the opposite of our goals. While this inherent craziness is bad for some, it creates opportunity for others.

The tendency to be out of sync with opportunity is apparent in many different aspects of trading and investing. In 1982, for example, the average P/E of stocks in the S&P was seven. The Dow sat below one thousand, and the biggest bull market in the history of the world was about to begin. Did most people recognize the opportunity? Absolutely not. Stocks were scorned; they represented miniscule allocations in people's portfolios. *Business Week* published its infamous cover story with a paper airplane made of a stock certificate crashing with a warning that, "the old attitude of buying solid stocks as a cornerstone for one's life savings and retirement has simply disappeared." When stocks were dirt cheap in the early 1980s, they were hated. Investors missed most of bull market and only began piling into stocks in the late 1990s, just in time for the subsequent decline.

In recent years, this uncanny ability to be precisely wrong in financial markets has been analyzed in detail and with better data. In one study, Professor Terrance Odean examined thousands of investors' decisions to switch horses—that is, to dump a particular stock and scoop up another. What happened? The stocks that people bought underperformed those that they sold by 330 basis points in the following twelve months.

Everyone seems built to lose money. Even the great Sir Isaac Newton, who brought us scientific marvels ranging from apples on the head to calculus, got sucked into the bubble of his day. Newton participated and lost big in the South Sea Bubble. He exited early with a profit, but after watching the market continue to soar, Newton bought back in, at which point the market promptly disintegrated.

Experience may be the best teacher, but in financial markets there is no simple performance improvement over time. Even veterans tend to make the wrong moves. For example, it is well known that cash levels in mutual funds are contrarian indicators of market moves. When managers fear market declines they build up a safe cushion of cash. Such moves tend to systematically predict market rallies—exactly the opposite of the managers' expectations.

Novices, pros, and geniuses all share an amazing ability to be out of sync with financial opportunity. We start the trading game with a natural ability to lose money. Why? A major source of our trading woes sits in our own lizard brain, as demonstrated in the study of brain-damaged patients. The investment task in the study was extremely simple. Subjects were asked to pay $1 for a fifty-fifty chance to win $2.50. They had to make this decision twenty times in a row. The expected payoff for taking a risk is $1.25 for each payoff, twenty-five percent more than not taking the risk. Furthermore, because the same gamble is repeated twenty times, those investors who took a risk every period faced only a thirteen-percent chance of earning less than taking the sure route.

To make the most money in this experiment, the correct decision is to take the gamble in every period. What happened? The brain-damaged patients took the money-maximizing route, choosing to gamble more than eighty percent of the time. Normal participants only made the right choice about fifty percent of the time. Consequently, the brain-damaged investors made more money. Furthermore, the normal participants exhibited all sorts of costly quirks in their behavior—they were, for example, more likely to play it safe after a series of wins, an irrational behavior in this setup.

Can we be sure that it was the back of the brain that messed up our normal investors? Yes. The scientists included two sorts of patients with brain lesions. Only those with brain damage in the emotional centers made the correct investments moves. Lesions in other parts of brain did not remove the trading errors. So we have direct evidence, in this study, that the lizard brain causes money-losing moves.

The brain damage study is intriguing, but it is in an artificial setting. Do real traders also lose money because of their emotions? Yes. Professor Andrew Lo and Dmitry Repin of MIT went right to a trading floor to wire up a group of professional traders to measure body temperature, skin conductance, and other variables. Lo and Repin report that more profitable traders had less-powerful emotional involvement in their decisions. All the traders had measurable physiological responses to news events. However, the more experienced and profitable traders had less extreme emotional responses than their less-experienced colleagues.

While the Lo and Repin results suggest the back of the brain as the source of our trading struggles, recent neuroeconomics studies provide direct, scientific evidence of the lizard brain's role in costly behavior. For example, a recent study put people into a brain scanning MRI machine and gave them a choice between money today and money in the future. The amounts were set so that the rate of return for waiting was extremely high, up to one hundred percent per year. To make the most money, the correct decision was to wait.

What happened to the brain of our subjects? The front of the brain coolly calculated the rate of return and counseled for delay. The lizard brain acted more like a teenager, saying "I want the money now; I want it now, and I don't care about the future." Those subjects with stronger activation in the back of the brain were more likely to take the impulsive step that had lower returns. The message is the same from a variety of neuroeconomic studies—when we make stupid decisions that cost us money, the lizard brain is the cause.

The Logic of the Lizard Brain

Why is the back of the brain built to miss market opportunities? The human brain is built to eat, survive, and reproduce; it is not built to trade. In most non-market settings, the past is a good predictor of the future. Accordingly, our lizard brains are backward-looking, pattern-recognition machines. This design works almost magically in natural tasks, even those that are very complex.

Our ancestors lived in small groups and earned their food the old-fashioned way—by hunting animals and gathering plants. The lizard brain is fantastically good at performing tasks that were important to our ancestors. Enter a room with twenty strangers, and see how long it takes you to find the most important person, the strongest person, the most handsome or attractive. The answer is just seconds, and these analyses are done in the back of the brain.

In social settings, the relationship between information and success tends to be invariant. Precisely that which led to good decisions in the past is most likely to work in the future. Accordingly, the lizard brain is built to look for patterns that worked in the past. There are no similar rules in investing. Should we, for example, buy stocks that have positive earnings surprises? Perhaps, unless too many other investors are making the same decision. If so, then the stock prices of these companies will become overvalued, and we'd be better off selling them.

Investing is fundamentally different from many ancestral tasks. Rather than do what worked best in the past, investing requires staying a step ahead of others. Thus, there can be no stable relationship between information and the correct course of action. For investing, the only rule is to predict what everyone else is doing and move to profit from their behavior. Investors who do what comes naturally—or who use a fixed rule based on fundamental data—tend to become prey. The lizard brain is great for many activities, but it causes us to be optimistic at market peaks (after rises) and to be pessimistic at market bottoms (after falls).

We've learned some disturbing news: we are influenced by our lizard brains, our lizard brains cost us money, and even the fact that our lizard brains helped our ancestors is small consolation to those us who want to make money today.

Is there any good news? Yes. The good news comes in two forms. First, it is precisely other people's irrationality that provides us with opportunity. When someone is willing to buy a tulip for the price of a house, as they were in the tulip mania, the tulip seller can make a fortune. If the world were filled with emotionless robots, there would be no way to make money. Second, while it is not possible to kill the lizard brain, it is possible to shackle the impulsive beast that lives within and improve our performance. In order to make money, I suggest at three-part process with the acronym of W.I.N.:

- **Wake up** to the fact that your emotional responses are the enemy. Stop blaming others for losses, and look to your own brain.
- **Investigate** the internal source of losses. Become a student of your own trading; identify how your own patterns cost you money.
- **Neutralize** the lizard brain. Set up systems to prevent your impulsive side from taking control. This is not a one-size-fits-all

solution, but comes directly from the self-investigation of the patterns of mistakes.

The lizard brain is part of human nature. It can never be defeated. The road to success requires understanding and respecting the crazy part of us that lives in the back of our heads. To paraphrase Commander Spock, love the lizard brain and prosper!

Terry Burnham, PhD, is the director of economics at Acadian Asset Management and the author of *Mean Markets and Lizard Brains: How to Profit from the New Science of Irrationality* (Wiley, 2005). Before his tenure at Acadian, he was an economics professor at the Harvard Business School. He can be reached at tburnham@acadian-asset.com. This article originally appeared in *SFO* in October 2005.

TRAIN YOUR BRAIN: How to Trade Using Instinct and Reason

BY RICHARD W. FRIESEN

He leaned forward. His eyes strained beneath the brow that covered most of his sloped forehead. His hairy hand slowly brushed a large leaf aside. His eyes widened as he saw his prey, a megaloceros, the gigantic ancestor of the deer family with antlers ten feet wide. He paused.

He smelled a familiar aroma so faint that his descendents fifty thousand years later wouldn't even notice it. His brain started an automatic chain reaction. He froze as his limbic system sent a shot of adrenaline through his body while non-critical functions shut down. His heart rate skyrocketed, and his muscles received a surge of glucose. An instantaneous release of hormones in his brain gave him heightened alertness. A twig cracked. Automatically calculating distance, danger and timing, he whirled with his spear, catching the tiger mid-leap in the shoulder and throwing it off-course just enough to send it into the brush inches from the Neanderthal.

Fast forward fifty thousand years. Opening the door to his trading room, he sets the latte beside the keyboard and hits the escape key. The screen shows his tick chart of the E-mini futures contract and the stocks he is long. He smiles when he sees the S&P index up three percent. His eyes widen when he sees that his most leveraged long position has dropped a buck fifty.

The same limbic system that had taken control of the Neanderthal hunter gives this modern-day trader the same physiologic reaction. He does a quick scan of the news and finds nothing. He grabs the mouse, clicks on the stock symbol, and hits the sell button. The confirmation window seems to appear in slow motion. "Sell ten thousand XCOM market long." He hits the "yes" button, and the fill price is ugly. Ten minutes later, stock trading is halted pending news.

The primitive reactions that saved the life of the Neanderthal hunter have survived in the form of the limbic brain that we all still have today. Does this mean our brains are wired wrong for trading? Can the lightening-fast, adrenaline-pumping limbic system be used to achieve a trading advantage like the latte-drinking trader did? Or, is the goal to tame the emotional "amygdala brain" and trade with the rational neocortex? What brain process produces the best trading results? How does brain wiring affect a trader's success?

A Quick Lesson in Neural Anthropology

The human brain has adapted over many centuries by providing processes that improve survival of the individual and the species. The bulk of the brain's adaptation has taken place in a world of hunting, gathering, and tribal culture. The modern brain is a pretty remarkable machine. However, there are still vestigial parts of the brain that haven't changed much since our Neanderthal ancestors were hunting and gathering across the plains of Europe, Asia, and Northern Africa.

The amygdala sits within the more primitive limbic brain. It is an almond-shaped mass of gray matter that is the oldest part of the cerebral cortex dating back sixty million years. It can instinctually operate at lightening speed with very little information; no symbols or language are necessary. In a heightened state, it acts like memory glue, conferring the ability to retain emotional experiences including traumas and fears. It makes judgments about likes and dislikes instantaneously and passes its prejudices to the outer brain, coloring more rational thought with feelings.

Wrapped around the limbic system is the neocortex, which makes up the bulk of the brain and is the center of reason. It processes all sensations and puts them into context giving the individual a good idea of what is happening. The neocortex controls such high-level processes as logic, creative thought, language, and the integration of sensory information. The prefrontal cortex section is like a control center. It has a high concentration of nerve fibers and dopamine, a neurotransmitter. The prefrontal cortex knows what the amygdala is up to and can stabilize instant reactions with longer-term memory. It can look at a wide set of data to draw conclusions and make forecasts, but it is much slower than the "twig-snap" reactions of the amygdala.

It is obvious to any visitor to the floor of a futures exchange on a busy day that the scalpers in the pit are, by and large, operating primarily from their amygdala. They are screaming, swearing, and reacting, often with red faces and veins standing out on foreheads. The modern scalper's version of the "twig-snap" is the quote board and the behavior of other people in the pit. These red-faced folks aren't long-term traders and, therefore, don't need a big draw on their neocortex.

However, if we move to an options pit, the demands of complex options valuations go beyond what the amygdala can deliver. An options or futures floor trader who walks into the pit is also walking into a jungle. Although he still needs to react quickly using animal responses driven by the amygdala, he also needs to use his neocortex to correctly evaluate the worth of different strike prices of options. He can manage this split by bringing his neocortex to the floor in the form of sheets or option values. The neocortex has already calculated these values (with a little help from the computer). The instructions to the animal on the floor can be, "Buy options under these values, and sell them over these values." The amygdala then can take over and go crazy, reacting instinctively to the broker's call.

For upstairs traders, the computer screen isn't as much like the jungle environment as the trading floor. However, the same principle applies. An active twitch trader can use his neocortex to create a game plan and set up rules; but when actively trading, it is the amygdala that is executing.

In the final extreme, a visit to the offices of a high-technology commodity trading advisor (CTA) won't reveal any yelling or cursing. There is not a red face or throbbing facial vein to be found in the room. These men and women have tamed their amygdala and are in full-blown use of the neocortex. In fact, to make sure that a stray emotional bullet from the amygdala doesn't interfere with reasoned response, these people have taken their rational process and dumped it into coded software. The software drives computers (notoriously short on primitive, emotional reactions) that generate trades.

Processing Input

How does one manage such a range of reactions from the same brain? Here is the process. Sensory input hits the thalamus, which relays the

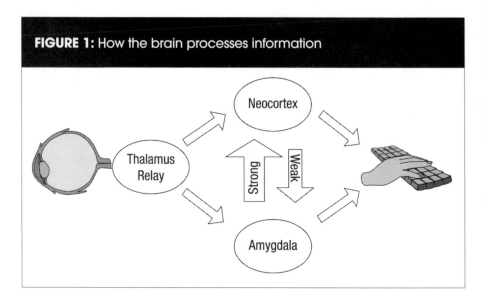

FIGURE 1: How the brain processes information

data to both the amygdala and the neocortex. The amygdala does a quick scan of a small portion of data with a twelve-millisecond response rate. The neocortex takes in the full information but it takes twice as long to process. The amygdala then outputs the information to the neocortex, along with an emotional wrapper that includes a glue to cement memories of a threatening event. It also prepares the body for instant reaction should it judge the data as a risk. The amygdala is quick and, when triggered, it overwhelms the controls provided by the neocortex (see *Figure 1*).

Human responses to information can range from boredom to panic. The key to the response is whether or not the amygdala has been triggered. Recall that the amygdala has the ability to cement memories, such as traumas, to events. The amygdala can deliver a temporary sense of heightened awareness and reaction, but it can also trigger panic. The question for the trader is how to manage these alternatives.

The floor trader on a futures exchange who scalps the nearby futures month and goes home flat each night needs the amygdala. Traders who come from urban streets are often more comfortable in this environment than some of the book-smart Harvard MBAs. This is because the MBA-type wants to rationalize each trade and takes too long making a decision—also known as paralysis by analysis.

Many traders who have left the floors to engage in screen trading from an office look and feel lost. All the "twig snapping" cues they are accustomed to on the floor are no longer available. The traders that make the transition successfully have to go through the discipline of starting to use a different brain process. It feels like slow torture and is not a trivial task.

To move from one brain process to another requires the building of new dendrites and neural pathways. The experience of doing this is that it just feels hard and requires discipline to push through. The process is similar to that of learning to drive a car with a stick shift. The trader, like the new driver, must consciously think of every movement until the neural pathways are built and shifting becomes automatic. However, once brain processes and trading styles are correctly mapped, trading output should improve.

Separating Instinct and Reason

An active day trader executing from a keyboard will need both the functions of the amygdala and the neocortex. However, it is difficult to use the neocortex when the amygdala is in preemptive mode. Not only does the amygdala react faster, it also has a direct conduit to the neocortex which colors the activity of the neocortex. Separating the functions with time and place is helpful. For example, an options trader on the floor will not be able to execute a trade if he or she has to calculate the risk of the trade before screaming the bid to the broker. That calculation should be handled prior to the trade with pre-calculated option values for each price of the stock.

Once a position is on, that position has risk. The management of this risk requires the separate function of a risk manager. Larger firms solve this problem by having these very different tasks covered by different people. When a single trader must do all these tasks, it is helpful to break the neocortical reasoning functions into time segments before and after the amygdala functions that require instant response. The neocortical functions can not only be done at different times but at different places, or even with different physical objects to signify the shift in brain function. For starters, actually put on a blue cap when calculating position risk (or any other analytical trading function), and wear a red cap when trading an active market. The act of wearing different hats while using different brain functions can produce a Pavlovian response to help the trader attach the correct brain function to the appropriate task.

On the other extreme, a systems trader will want to save the use of his amygdala for more important tasks, such as bar fights or skydiving. Every trader needs to recognize when the amygdala has been triggered because decisions made from an emotional state will most likely create losses for the system that took so long to create. Awareness of tell-tale symptoms, like accelerated heart rate and sweaty palms, should alert the trader to an amygdala takeover and be a reminder to take a moment to calm down and put on the "blue hat."

Controlling the Amygdala

Recall that the amygdala can wrap data in an emotional container and send it to the neocortex. Once this process happens, it becomes difficult to know if the information the neocortex is receiving is straight from the source or distorted by the amygdala. Every trader can pay attention to the symptoms that occur when the amygdala has been triggered. Even more important is knowing how to not set it off.

It is possible to avoid giving control of the brain to the amygdala by not giving it a message it can interpret as a threat. The amygdala can be set off by external sensory input, but it can just as easily be set off by imagining threatening or negative situations. Everyone can recall a fearful or threatening event in their lives such as a mugging or a jealous reaction. Simply recalling these events in memory can cause the brain to stimulate the same physiologic reaction. A trader can do the same thing by reliving threatening trading events that speed the heartbeat and dampen the palms.

A trader who puts himself in fearful or stressful positions over a long period of time can produce a response similar to battle fatigue. The fears can develop a life of their own and remain long after the threat is gone, causing loss of sleep and paranoia.

Consider two traders with the same position, the same risk, and the same capital as they watch the same trade go against them. One of them will start thinking dark thoughts, bringing up old memories of failure glued to the memory cells by the amygdala during previous negative emotional experiences. The other will think, "Well, is this interesting!" as he concentrates on the unexpected event and what can be salvaged from it. The successful trader will consciously stop thinking dark thoughts to avoid triggering the amygdala and manufacturing fear.

Changing mental processes is just plain hard. It is hard because it takes so much conscious effort to grow the millions of new dendrites that form newly forged neural pathways that change how the brain responds. Like learning to drive a stick shift, it takes time on the road to build the new neural processes. For those who persist, there is a light at the end of the tunnel. It is possible to manage your brain functions more efficiently for better trading results.

Five steps to efficient brain use:
1. Know what part of the brain to use with what type of trading;
2. Always be aware which brain function is dominant at any given time;
3. Actually change time/place/hats when changing use of the brain;
4. Avoid trading activity, positions, or risks that produce fear and trigger an amygdala brain reaction;
5. Think happy thoughts when trading.

Think happy thoughts? Yes. Everyone does better when they enjoy what they are doing. So, cultivate a fascination with market activity, accept the surprises it offers, and appreciate the markets for what they are. Taming and training the brain can have big rewards for the aware trader.

Richard W. Friesen is a corporate trainer and the founder of Trade Management LLC, and ePIT Systems, a software company for financial institutions. Combining his experiences as a therapist and businessman, he developed the Alpha Presence training program to teach leaders the power of absolute engagement and hone their public speaking tools. Friesen is an award-winning speaker on politics, business, and personal development. Friesen formerly built a trading desk for Chicago Research and Trading on the Pacific Stock Exchange and was a futures broker for Merrill Lynch. He holds a Master's in clinical psychology and completed his training at the San Francisco Gestalt Institute. He currently lives in Fairfax, California, with his wife. His hobby is finding back roads in the Sierras for his motorcycle. This article originally appeared in *SFO* in July 2004.

REASON AND PASSION

BY PHILIPPA HUCKLE

In 400 BC Plato described human behavior as a chariot driven by two horses: reason and passion. Decisions based on reason are cognitive, involving logic and careful thought, the deliberate weighing of pros and cons, or logically working through a problem like when solving trigonometry problems.

Decisions based on passion have a psychological basis and are the result of a mix of instincts and emotions. For instance, we jump when we are startled. Our everyday human behavior combined with our psychological makeup means that sometimes we respond carefully and deliberately, and at other times our response is far more primal.

The cognitive methodologies for successful investing have been conclusively formalized and proven over the past three hundred years. They are logical and straightforward. Simply put, these involve the construction of a formulated asset allocation plan, multiple asset class diversification, and systematic rebalancing.

While investors can understand these methodologies intellectually, DALBAR's Quantitative Analysis of Investor Behavior, a comprehensive United States-based annual study, conclusively demonstrates that average investors substantially under-perform the markets they invest in. This under-performance is not due to a lack of intelligence, but because investment decisions are also the result of our human psychology.

Using second-by-second magnetic-resonance imaging (MRI) techniques to film the brain in action, neuroscientists have identified two separate types of brain activity which are, in fact, Plato's "reason and passion" happening live. Neuroscience reveals that particular parts of our brain are active when we respond analytically and other parts are active when we respond emotionally.

Neuroeconomics and behavioral finance explain the impact of our emotional psychology on our investment decisions. Neuroeconomics is the physical study of decision processes in the brain at the chemical level of cells and synapses while we are making investment decisions. Behavioral finance looks at economics through the eyes of a psychologist to explain why people often inadvertently make irrational investment decisions that cause investors to buy high and sell low, even while intending to do the opposite. So, while cognitive investing methodologies explain what investors should do, behavioral finance explains what investors really do, and neuroeconomics explains why.

Primal Instincts

Emotions are a significant part of our psychological makeup. There is biological reason for emotions—they essentially serve a survival-based purpose, providing an important internal behavior gauge as to whether what we are doing is good or bad for us (for example, feeling guilt when we are doing something that we know is wrong).

Intended as primal calls to actions in response to perceived opportunities and threats, emotional processes are ignited by sensory or conceptual triggers in our environment: a particular sight or sound, the way someone behaves toward us, and, for traders and investors, by market movements.

The overriding investment objectives are to buy when markets are low, in order to sell for a profit when they rise. Because investments move in cycles, the rational way to accumulate assets is to take advantage of these cyclical movements by accumulating cheap assets in the lower part of their cycle, and sell them in the higher part of the cycle. Cognitively, every investor understands that the overriding investment objective is to continuously buy low and sell high.

Yet there is a conflict between our cognitive and psychological responses to market cycles, because market movements ignite our emotions counterintuitively. Being human, investors experience the emotions of excitement and euphoria when markets are rising, and are despondent, anxious, and panicked when they are low or falling.

Psychologically, it is human nature to feel euphorically compelled to buy more at the top of a market (the point of greatest risk), while at the bottom of a market (the time of greatest opportunity) to despairingly want to exit, escape, and sell, sell, sell. When triggered, these emotions can all too easily override investors' cognitive thought processes.

Natural Highs and Lows

Neuroscience has shown that the emotions we experience are caused by chemical releases in our brain. Dopamine is a reward-related chemical which is designed to keep us doing things that have previously worked well. A dopamine rush creates a natural high that feels wonderful. And because dopamine feels so delicious, it spurs us on to repeat the actions that caused the dopamine release, in order to experience that feeling again.

But dopamine is a poor decision driver in the cyclical investment world of recurring peaks and troughs, because a rising market will sooner or later subsequently turn downward. Dopamine triggers rush-hungry investors to unwittingly buy high into rising markets.

Adrenaline is a chemical designed to help us survive. A part of our brain called the amygdala fires off adrenaline when it thinks we are in danger. It is triggered by sudden change in our physical environment, and sparks our most primal protective fight or flight response.

In situations of danger, the time saved by an emotional rather than a cognitive response can be the difference between life and death. From the point of view of survival it is far better to respond to potentially dangerous events as if they were real, rather than to fail to react at all. But investment decisions are not a matter of short-term survival.

To survive financially we need to consistently make long-range investment decisions in a cyclical environment, yet falling market prices spark an instinctive and compelling urge to get out, get away, to sell, sell, sell. The more vivid and dramatic the trigger, the more explosive the amygdala's response—a situation only exacerbated by sensational financial headlines and dramatic real-time market commentary. This is why it is so difficult to buy when markets are low.

Instead of calmly and deliberately buying low and selling high, these chemically triggered emotions incite investors to respond defensively and emotionally to perceived loss by fleeing from things that make us feel bad (such as low or falling markets), and to chase after those that make us feel good (like high or rising markets). So while emotions are important guides for making decision in some aspects of our lives, they are a terrible barometer for investment decisions. While we can't turn these chemicals off, we can take steps to minimize their impact.

The Cognitive Approach

Implementing a reliable investment methodology which consistently buys low and sells high requires cool, calm, cognitive thought. By better understanding the complex relations between mind and action we can acknowledge the powerful pull of our human psychology, and instead choose to neutralize their impact by reframing the investment decision into a cognitive structure: constructing formal mathematical asset allocation weightings, and adhering to this formulated allocation by religiously executing a clearly defined, thoroughly disciplined rebalancing policy.

In investing, the more calm and cognitive these decisions, the better. Essentially, investing is a never-ending stream of decisions to buy, sell, or hold. By understanding what is happening in our minds when we are making decisions we have more control over how we choose to respond, which ultimately leads to more cognitive decisions—and better results.

Clear, long-term objectives, supported by a clearly formulated methodology, support the cool, calm, calculated responses required for a lifetime of successful investing.

Philippa Huckle is the founder and CEO of The Philippa Huckle Group, a leading investment advisory firm headquartered in Hong Kong. Huckle is regularly quoted and published in regional and international media including, the *Sunday Times UK*, CNBC, and *Asian Wall Street Journal*. She is the author of *Perspective*, an online publication read by more than five thousand people in forty countries. By successfully integrating classical economic methodologies with the discipline of behavioral finance, the group's highly personalized service guides each high-net-worth client to robust, sustained returns. This chapter is an original work for this publication.

GEORGE SOROS: How He Knows What He Knows

BY FLAVIA CYMBALISTA, PhD, AND DESMOND MAC RAE

To many who worship at the altar of the icons of Wall Street, billionaire George Soros is considered the 20th century's greatest trader. His lifetime record as a speculator who made massive wagers on market direction at numerous opportune times is unparalleled—even though he inevitably made some expensive mistakes along the way. Anyone who had invested $1,000 in his Quantum Fund when it jumped out of the box in 1969 would have realized a cumulative thirty-plus-percent annual return—or about $4 million—by the turn of the new century. How did he achieve his incredible performance? He attributes his success to a combination of theory and instinct.

In Soros's theory of how markets operate, participants' perceptions help create their own reality. This leads to self-reinforcing processes that are eventually self-defeating. According to Soros, his body gives him the signals that inform his trading decisions. The making of a self-reinforcing trend makes his mouth water. The need for a portfolio shift makes his back hurt. His body "knows" he needs to take action, or to take careful note of a situation before his intellect can grasp it.

The way in which Soros's theory and his body work together remains a mystery for most people. Not having understood his theory, they wrongly take the now famous quote by his son, Robert, as evidence that Soros trades using nothing more than instinct:

"My father will sit down and give you theories to explain why he does this or that. But I remember seeing it as a kid and thinking...at least half of this is bull_ _ _ _. I mean, you know the reason he changes his position on the market or whatever is because his back starts killing him. It has nothing to do with reason. He literally goes into a spasm, and it's this early warning sign." [1]

Relating economics and gut feeling is, admittedly, no easy task. Most economists' idea of the market is an information processor, a machine. They appear to believe that rational economic man is a computer that obviously does not have instincts.

Computers follow rules rigidly. But rigidly following rules can only be rational in a world devoid of uncertainty, where things change in the future in the same ways that they changed in the past. Most economic models assume uncertainty away. They leave it out of the picture because, unlike probabilistic risk, uncertainty can't be quantified. But for Soros, uncertainty is the nature of the game.

Fallibility

The single belief that traders hold most dear is that the market is always right. George Soros takes the opposite position and assumes that markets are always wrong. For Soros, it is impossible to form a mental picture of the world in which we live without distortion. All mental constructs—models, theories, hypotheses, and systems—are potentially and often actually flawed. Even when they contain significant elements of truth, they are distortions of reality.

Market reality is an intricate web of interlocking, interdependent processes or systems so complex that it cannot be captured by any single market model. Any market hypothesis is based on a "cut" or a small slice of reality.

No single cut of reality is unique, nor is it permanent. This is why all hypotheses are flawed for two reasons. First, one's mental map does not describe the real territory. Second, reality doesn't stay put, so that a useful cut today doesn't necessarily remain useful tomorrow. The territory itself keeps changing.

When we open a trading position, we are testing a hypothesis. It can be as simple as "prices are going up or down," or as complex as relationships between macro-global economic forces. But the market itself can be viewed as constantly adapting and testing hypotheses. When one hypothesis fails, the market takes on another. The market's hypotheses are based on cuts that make up the current collective view of reality. Markets are always wrong in the sense that they are always biased.

Not only does Soros assume that the markets are always wrong; he also assumes that his own hypotheses are always flawed. Most people are invested in being right and don't like to admit that they are wrong. Soros thinks the other way around. In his book *The Crisis of Global Capitalism: Open Society Endangered* (Public Affairs, 1998), he wrote: "I derived actual pleasure from discovering a mistake."

In *Soros on Soros* (John Wiley & Sons, Inc., 1995), he explained further, "Once we realize that imperfect understanding is the human condition, there's no shame in being wrong, only in failing to correct our mistakes."

The belief in fallibility is a psychologically sound principle. It allows Soros to avoid holding himself to standards that no human being can possibly meet. This protects him from crises of confidence. For most people, the possibility of being wrong is threatening. It gives rise to anxiety. Soros, on the other hand, is anxious as long as he hasn't found a flaw in his investment hypothesis. He actively looks for it—and his back hurts as long as he hasn't found it. Once he knows the flaw, he's at ease. He's got his edge. The discovery of a flaw, an error in his thinking, allows him to take whatever profits he had made from his flawed insight—or cut losses. The difference between Soros and most other traders is that he accepts fallibility, so he starts out by assuming his hypothesis is wrong.

While markets are always wrong, it doesn't follow that one should trade against a prevailing trend. Finding a flaw in an investment or trading thesis doesn't make Soros discard it. Rather, it helps him play it with greater confidence because he knows what is wrong with it while the market doesn't. Finding a flaw puts him ahead of the curve.

Finding Flaws

"It pays to look for the flaws," Soros writes in *The Alchemy of Finance* (Simon & Schuster, 1987). The fact that a trading hypothesis is flawed doesn't mean that Soros won't commit money to it—as long as he thinks some other people believe in it and that there is a larger group of people who are likely to be convinced of the validity of this thesis. The billion-dollar question is: How do we find them?

Soros finds the flaw by combining theory and instinct. This is puzzling because theory and instinct are usually considered mutually exclusive. This might be one of the few matters on which economists and traders agree. Economists think that gut feelings are irrational. And for most traders, instinct and method contradict each other. When traders do use their instincts, they're overriding their methodology. But in Soros' method, theory and instinct are inextricably linked. Soros himself, however, could not explain how.

Reflexivity Revealed

Traditional economists view markets as efficient. In efficient markets, prices are unbiased estimates of fundamental values. A small deviation from rationally expected fundamentals creates a self-correcting movement in another direction. But Soros disagrees. Instead, he sees that there is a feedback loop between market participants' thinking and the reality they observe. He calls this circular relationship "reflexivity."

In this theory of reflexivity, markets are always biased. Prices cannot be unbiased estimates because they actually help shape the fundamentals they are supposed to reflect.

Reflexivity introduces uncertainty into the system. As a result, Soros says, market behavior cannot be predicted by the same methods used in the natural sciences. This is why he chose the word "alchemy" for the title of his book.

In his theory of reflexivity, Soros tries to explain how trends form and what makes them reverse. It doesn't give him rules and indicators for catching those trends or reversals, but it does tell him where to look. In essence, then, it tells him to look at how the market is constructing the reality that the participants are seeing. Case in point, take the example of the collapse of Long Term Capital Management. Nobel Prize winners Robert Merton and Myron Scholes, who owned the fund, thought they could scientifically measure their risk—and could not see how their own trades were actually shaping reality in ways that their models could not anticipate.

Profit Opportunities

Soros found his greatest profit opportunities in situations in which a market trend at first supports the prevailing bias. The conglomerate boom of the 1960s is a classic example in which the prevailing bias emphasized earnings growth over other fundamentals. The market favored companies that showed above-average growth. Rising stock prices allowed these companies to increase their earnings by using their increasing stock value to buy other companies. This in turn strengthened the prevailing bias, which led to further stock price increases, and so it went. The trend gained momentum until corporate results could no longer sustain investors' expectations.

The flaw here was that growth was only sustainable as long as acquisitions would continue to advance at an ever-accelerating pace. The turning point was reached when Leasco Corporation failed to take over Chemical Bank. This brought the flaw to public attention.

The flaw varies from case to case, as each situation is unique. What the flaw turns out to be depends on the nature of the prevailing bias, the market involved, and many other variables. There are no rules for finding the flaw, but I can tell you where Soros finds it. It is always in the wider picture.

Organic Thinking

Market action, of course, takes place within an intricate web of interlocking economic processes, not within a vacuum. Any market hypothesis is based only on a cut or a piece of a multi-layered web that is continuously developing.

There's no question that market action has a visible side—certainly, the trend is there for everyone to see. Like the conglomerate boom and recent technology boom, the prevailing bias at first is confirmed. But, at the same time, the market is in interaction with a larger and more intricate economic web, causing changes in the broader picture that are not yet visible. The not-yet-visible underlying level is where Soros finds the flaw.

Soros had difficulty showing how this theory played out because once new facts in the wider picture actually emerged publicly, it appeared as if they had been there all along. In hindsight, it simply looked as if the public had disregarded or overlooked them. In fact, however, at the point where Soros looked for these new facts, they were still in the making. They weren't overlooked at all; they just weren't there yet.

In reality, the evolution of the wider picture is never fully captured by any market model. There's always that gap between our particular cuts of the "real" market and the wider picture. It is in the gap between these developing changes and the prevailing bias that Soros looks for the flaw.

Empathizing with the Mind of the Market

Most approaches to trading emphasize the importance of a detached stance. Detachment, however, is far from the approach of George Soros. "As a money manager, I was emotionally engaged in managing my fund," Soros writes in the introduction to *The Alchemy of Finance* (Simon & Schuster, 1987). "I managed it as if my existence depended on it, as it indeed did. I relied on my instincts and intuition as well as my conceptual framework to guide me through uncertainty."

Empathy builds on emotional resonance, which is a biological ability. Babies, for example, will cry when they see another baby falling. When we are emphasizing with another person, our bodies track what's happening inside the other person and mimic it.

Although most traders don't know how to turn it to their advantage, the capacity to track market sentiment and the patterns that it creates is instinctive. This capacity is a mechanism that allows us to handle complex and uncertain situations. When a trader resonates with the mind of the market, his physiology mimics market sentiment. For most traders, this results in getting carried away by the herd. To learn how to turn bodily reactions into sources of information, as Soros does, one must first learn how to listen.

Listening

Most people are terrible listeners. Say your partner tells you about a situation he or she is currently facing. You respond with your opinion and your best advice. But your partner gets irritated and says, "You're not listening." Assume for a moment that you really don't know what your partner is saying. Many people can't. They jump to conclusions. Their biases interfere with what they actually hear.

Good listeners are naturally empathetic. They suspend judgment and immediate interpretation and, instead, build a sense of what they are hearing. This doesn't mean that they do not have their own opinion, only that they can suspend it for a while so they can absorb what they might not yet know.

If you're truly empathizing, your biological software–your body– will resonate with the meaning of what you're hearing. Resonance comes before thought, interpretation, or analysis. Assume that there is more to what you're hearing than you originally thought – even though you don't yet know what that "more" is. At first, it's just an uncomfortable nothing. Your body will construct a meaning that includes the situation as a whole, not only what you knew before, but also what you did not yet know.

Listening to the market requires the same capacity to suspend judgment and stay with a puzzling feeling. It's easier when you're not invested in the outcome. The first step in learning how to empathize with the mind of the market is to practice listening separately from decision making.

Most traders don't know how their bodily sense of the market situation differs from emotions. This bodily sense of the market is not itself an emotion. An emotion is often sharp and clearly felt, while the bodily sense is more complex and at first murky. This bodily sense that contains subliminal knowledge is difficult to access because what we first feel is emotion. When we sense ourselves, emotions spring out. We have to pass through them in order to access deeper layers of bodily knowledge.

Confidence Biases

For traders, access to deeper layers of bodily knowledge is hindered by habitual responses triggered when a lack of certain knowledge makes them anxious. When we cannot tolerate uncertainty, we exhibit two basic tendencies. The first is denial. We are overconfident and minimize the fact that we don't know for sure. The second tendency is withdrawal. In this case, traders remain aware of uncertainty as they, in fact, need to. But, this makes them afraid to act and prone to premature disengagement. Their confidence collapses. These confidence biases distort a trader's sense of a market situation. They prevent him from seeing the way in which the future might turn out differently from what he hopes or fears. They do not let him think beyond what he already knows.

Normally, these opposing tendencies that push one forward and pull one back are present in any trader's psyche. It's as if each trader has an overconfident, greedy, or hopeful sub-identity and a fearful one. The first feels energetic, without doubts, and eager to act. The second is apprehensive, scared to make decisions, and worried about outcomes.

A biased participant is in the grip of either one of these tendencies. He alternatively identifies with one and dissociates from the other. There's an inner war going on, and the process is not under his control. He is pushed and pulled in different directions until one of the tendencies takes over and determines his decision. The way out is to set oneself outside of the process.

Many people need guidance before they can fully separate intuition from emotional biases. Like any learning process, you need to know what to pay attention to. If your ski instructor tells you inside the lodge how to perform a particular technique and you go out by yourself to do it, it's hard to know if you're applying the technique correctly or not. It's hard to make the necessary adjustments. Of course, there are many details and ways of overcoming difficulties, which can't be covered here. But, if you manage to feel both tendencies at once, you're on the right track! Instead of projecting your own fears and hopes into what you're sensing, you'll then truly be empathizing with the mind of the market.

Using Reflexivity in Trading

By now, most pros on Wall Street consider themselves "reflexivists" in the sense that they understand the course of markets and economic events by looking at how other participants' views create their own reality. Market participants base their actions on their own expectations, which are based on their views, models, or theories. Their decisions affect price behavior. The market, in turn, influences the variables that the participants are looking at—both the variables related to price action and the fundamental variables. Both shape participants' new expectations.

Reflexivity was not accepted quickly. Soros' use of instinct was one reason. Another reason was that reflexivity contradicts the different ways of looking at markets that most traders use. These conventional approaches fall into three main groups. First is an approach derived from modern portfolio theory, which is based on equilibrium economics. This is the basis of the widespread use of indexed funds that make up a high percentage of market volume. The second approach is fundamental analysis. Third is technical analysis. Understanding Soros' critique of each of these methods will help you grasp reflexivity more easily.

The Irrelevance of Equilibrium Economics

Both modern portfolio theory and fundamental analysis are based on traditional economic equilibrium theory. Soros went to great lengths—

both in the original Alchemy and in his new introduction to the book—to explain why equilibrium theory gives a misleading picture of financial markets.

Equilibrium theory applies to financial markets the same type of thinking used by classical physicists to model physical phenomena such as the behavior of the planets. The theory assumes that financial assets have a fundamental value that is objective; it is determined by the conditions of supply and demand in the real economy. Just like the orbit of the planets, which is not affected by astronomers' theories, the fundamental value supposedly does not depend on what financial market participants think about it. In equilibrium, market prices are a passive reflection of the underlying fundamental reality. In other words, market valuation mirrors fundamentals without affecting them.

But market reality doesn't work like orbits of planets that stay put regardless of our expectations. Situations involving thinking participants have a different structure. Financial market participants try to discount a future that doesn't yet exist. What the future will turn out to be will depend on how the market discounts it at present. Current perceptions help shape the future. When market participants change their views, they can create a very different future.

Reflexivity introduces an element of uncertainty into the system. The fact that traditional economics assumes this uncertainty away is the reason it fails to help us understand the real world.

Market Efficiency and Indexation

Do economists really believe that equilibrium theory applies to the real world? The answer, surprising as it might seem to anyone who has ever actually traded, is that the majority do. According to advocates of efficient markets theory, market prices are unbiased estimates of fundamental value. A small deviation from rationally expected fundamentals creates a self-correcting movement in another direction.

This is the reasoning behind modern portfolio theory. If prices always reflected fundamentals, it would be impossible to beat the market, so everyone should invest in index funds. According to this view, Soros's superior performance and the performances of other noted traders and investors like Sir John Templeton, Warren Buffett, and Paul Tudor Jones would be attributed to luck.

Financial economists have spent a lot of time, effort, and research money trying to collect evidence supporting the notion of market efficiency. They have tested the profitability of a great number of both fundamental and technical rule-based strategies extensively. For the most part, they have interpreted the results as evidence that the market, indeed, is efficient. However, the failure of rule-based strategies to outperform the market averages does not mean that prices reflect fundamentals, nor that you can only beat the markets by chance. It only means that markets can't be beaten by the methods that they have tested. Soros agrees.

Fundamental Analysis

Fundamental analysis is an outgrowth of equilibrium theory. It assumes that stocks have a true or fundamental value distinct from their current market price. The market price is supposed to tend toward the fundamental value, not necessarily immediately, as efficient markets theory asserts, but over a period of time. The analysis of fundamental values should tell you which stocks are overvalued or undervalued and, thus, provide a guide to investment decisions.

Fundamental analysis assumes the connection between prices and companies to be in one direction. The fortune of the companies determines—sooner or later—the value of their stock traded in the market. The possibility that stock market developments may affect the fortunes of the companies is left out of the account.

But stock market valuations do influence underlying values directly through the issue and repurchase of shares and options and through corporate transactions like mergers, acquisitions, new stock offerings, and the like. Valuations are influenced indirectly by credit ratings, consumer acceptance, and credibility of management. Fundamental analysis accepts the influence of these factors on stock prices, but it doesn't recognize the influence of stock prices on those factors. This conceptual flaw impairs its ability to help you make money. Traditional fundamental analysts missed the opportunity to make money during the bubble, for example.

The same is true for currencies and other financial markets. The connection between market prices and fundamentals is always two way. Participants' expectations are active factors in a process in which both market prices and non-market economic events are determined.

Technical Analysis

Technical analysis tries to anticipate price fluctuations by studying the dynamics of price movement and patterns of market behavior. It estimates probabilities by comparing different instances of similar patterns of behavior. Unlike fundamental analysis, it is not encumbered by the shortcomings of economic equilibrium theory.

Trend following is an important element of Soros's strategy. He views up-ticks and down-ticks as important predictors of price trends, because they provide information about the strength of supply and demand.

However, technical analysis is limited by the fact that financial markets are not closed systems. The market is always interacting with the much wider economic system and constantly receives input from the outside world. This means that a trader cannot assume he or she can predict the future with a mechanistic reworking of past data, even in the probabilistic sense!

Technical approaches that calculate probabilities on the basis of past experience lose the context in which each particular instance occurs. This is why traders always need to use their bodily sense of the current situation. Bodily knowledge is needed to complement whichever trading system a trader uses.

Trend Formation and Reversal

Soros's method, on the one hand, involves reading the mind of the market, which is what technical analysis tries to do. On the other hand, it also pays attention to economic relationships, which is what fundamental analysis does. However, his method is not constrained by the shortcomings of either method.

The starting point in Soros's approach is the participants' bias. The participants' bias gives rise to trends, which Soros at first follows. He then looks for the flaw in the prevailing rationale behind the trend. Of course, market participants have different views and base their decisions on different approaches. It must be remembered, however, that for a strong trend to form, there must be some consensus among different groups of participants—for instance between fundamentally oriented participants and technical trend followers. Finding the flaw in the market's hypothesis puts him ahead of the curve—he still follows the trend, but he is on the lookout for what would make it reverse.

In reflexive situations, the market trend at first supports the bias. Bias and trend reinforce one another. But the trend also has unintended consequences that affect economic relationships the conventional view does not take into account. At this underlying level, the market's action is creating an effect that eventually makes the trend unsustainable.

Boom and Bust

Boom-and-bust sequences are the most dramatic examples of reflexivity at work. Soros's archetypal boom-bust sequence has seven stages:

1. The prevailing bias is present, but a trend is not yet recognized.
2. The period of acceleration, when the trend is recognized and reinforced by the prevailing bias.
3. The period of testing. Prices suffer a setback. If the bias and the trend hold, prices emerge stronger than before and become more exaggerated.
4. The moment of truth when reality can no longer sustain these exaggerated price expectations.
5. The twilight period. People continue to play the game, but they no longer believe in it. They hope to be bailed out by greater fools.
6. The crossover point at which the trend turns down. Even the last fools give up hope.
7. The rapid, catastrophic price acceleration in the opposite direction, in short, a crash.

In the Internet boom, this sequence started almost unnoticed when a few e-commerce companies went public. Their stocks were highly valued by the public, and the popularity of the stocks helped to promote the companies. The prevailing bias and the prevailing trend reinforced each other, accelerating the boom.

As Internet services spread, online trading increased exponentially. Valuations reached outlandish levels. Few companies were really profitable, but investors didn't care. They counted only the number of customers or subscribers as the basis for valuing these stocks. Then companies began to give away services, because by increasing their customer base, they could raise capital on more advantageous terms. Raising capital, rather than making profit, became the game.

The trend was tested in July 1999 when the *Wall Street Journal* exposed this game. At the same time, the holding periods for many of these

IPOs expired, so investors unloaded their shares. Internet stocks fell by more than fifty percent, but many recovered, and some rose to new highs. Expectations again were inflated until the Internet bubble burst in March 2000. E-commerce companies could no longer finance their growth by selling stock at ever-higher prices. The market's attention then turned to other tech sectors like telecoms until they, too, finally crashed.

Reflexivity is not the exception but the rule. It's at work not only in extreme cases like bubbles, but all the time. Reflexivists look for opportunities in situations where the prevailing bias, via price action, is affecting the variables that enter into the participants' decisions in ways that are not anticipated and in ways that at first are not visible.

Let's look at a recent example of reflexive profit opportunities.

Risk-Management Models

In a new edition of *The Alchemy* (Wiley, 2003), Soros hints at the existence of reflexive profit opportunities in relationship to risk-management systems—but doesn't tell us more about it. Here's how it works.

Every time a major Wall Street firm blows up, new "improved" risk management theories and algorithms are created to guard against future losses. Because Wall Street is a pretty small community, it's a safe bet that if one major firm employs a program, other firms are running the same program. Because most major firms are always on the same side of a big move, the fact that they have similar risk management systems can be exploited by reflexivists.

Say everyone is long a security that has been trending up gradually with very low volatility. Assume institutions have acquired big positions. Suddenly, an unanticipated event pushes up implied volatility. Risk models suddenly tell these firms at the same time to sell the same security to reduce exposure. They do, and prices fall. The clever reflexivist, who anticipates that these firms' risk models are likely to trigger sales, establishes shorts and covers when prices do fall, making a handsome profit. The basic lesson for trading success is to understand the big picture. Reflexivity gives us critical insight into the path of the big moves, and that can give you more confidence in your trades.

Soros is a macro-investor. This, in and of itself, gives him an edge. Most market participants have neither the resources nor the expertise across many product lines, industries, or markets that Soros has. However, you don't have to be a macro-investor or a fundamental trader to use reflexivity to improve your trading. For that, you need to watch not just the market but also the thinking of market participants who affect that market.

You can gain an edge if you can identify the major players that are moving prices now (in the markets you trade), and if you can learn that on which they are basing their decisions. Look for situations where everybody is doing the same thing for the same reason. Then, look for the flaw in this reasoning.

It would be wonderful if there were some hard and fast rule for determining situations in which everyone indeed was doing the same thing for the same reason, but there really isn't. You have to be intimate with the market, and then you can sometimes tell by both looking at price and volume data as well as at the news where the liquidity is emanating.

For example, a fund manager that closely follows a stock often knows whether prices are going up on news or simply because day traders have moved them to the point where hedge funds have to cover their shorts. And, in some markets it's easier than in others. Perhaps it's a bit easier in commodities where, on the one hand, you have the participants that need to hedge, and on the other hand, technical traders that tend to be trend followers. It's occasionally possible in bonds markets, too. A reflexivist knows that Fannie Mae and Freddie Mac have to sell bonds because they have a duration problem, and so the reflexivist will short bonds, too. In currency markets, central banks are major players, and so on.

Another possible way to find situations where everybody is doing the same thing for the same reason is to look for consensus in the media. People watch the same news—that is, their ideas of why this and that are happening and are likely to continue tends to be the same. There are times when this is particularly strong. For instance, sometimes a stock is strongly recommended by a number of analysts. This then will create demand that will, in turn, be reinforced by trend followers, and so on.

When everybody sees only the upside, look for the downside. When everybody sees the only the downside, look for the upside. Ask yourself what is it that the average opinion is not taking into account and what news would make the average market participant change his mind.

No matter how well you understand its theoretical principles, reflexivity won't help you until you know how to work with your body to access the knowledge it contains. Reflexivity is all about recognizing changes in the rules of the game, and there's no formula for capturing that.

Market opportunities are context-dependent. This means that you have to rely on your bodily sense of the market situation to complement your analysis. The focusing methodology here will help you come to understand how George Soros—who time and time again has told us he uses his instincts—knows what he knows.

Flavia Cymbalista, PhD, is an uncertainty specialist: a financial economist specialized in market psychology and the psychology of uncertainty, who helps fund managers, traders, investors, and other businesspeople make better decisions. Using the work of Eugene Gendlin, PhD, a world-renowned philosopher and psychologist, she developed a methodology called MarketFocusing, which combines gut feeling and logic to improve decision making in markets. This chapter is based on her academic paper, *How George Soros Knows What He Knows*, which can be found on her website: www.marketfocusing.com. Cymbalista holds a doctorate in economic sciences from the Berlin Free University and was a post-doctoral research fellow at University of California, Berkeley. Her publications include the book, *On the Impossibility of Rational Valuation under Uncertainty*, published in Germany. Cymbalista can be reached at flavia@marketfocusing.com.

Desmond MacRae is a New York-based business writer specializing in banking, finance, and investments. He can be reached at desmondmacrae@nyc.rr.com. Versions of this article appeared in *SFO* between July and November 2003.

[1] George Soros: The Life and Times of a Messianic Billionaire , by Michael T. Kaufman (Knopf, 2002, 140).

SECTION FIVE
Creating a Healthy Balance

Achieving life-balance is an important goal for everyone, but it is critical for those who make their living in a high-intensity field like trading. When is enough enough? Everything in your life shows up in your trading practice in the end. Learning how to take your life back from the screen can help your bottom line, in addition to improving your health, relationships, and family life.

We'll help you explore what trading time frame is right for you. While most people in the working world are used to clocking in on a 9-to-5 schedule, your best trades may not be found by sitting in front of the screen for eight hours. Finding your best time of day to trade (and reducing your hours) may actually improve your results.

It's easy to think that the top trading gurus have some special brand of psychological magic that propels them to success. But, frankly, they all put their pants on one leg at a time. It takes the same mental wherewithal—and discipline—to keep from melting down and dropping out for even the most seasoned trader. In this section we'll learn life-balancing words of wisdom from top traders, including Linda Bradford Raschke, John F. Carter, and Adrienne Laris Toghraie.

Contrary to popular belief, life and trading can coexist amicably. We'll share some tips that can help you take the time to find balance, including the remarkable power of positive thinking, voicing and eliminating your fears, and developing effective routines and rituals. Regaining your life balance can help you manage your trading practice more effectively, while appreciating the small things in life that make it worth living.

FULL-TIME TRADING:
Is There Life Away
From the Screen?

BY ADRIENNE LARIS TOGHRAIE, MNLP, MCH

With virtually twenty-four-hour markets a part of the investment landscape, trading full time can translate to anything from grueling sixteen-hour workdays to a scant one hour per day or any combination of time in between. It is important to discover what time frame is right for you in order to get the greatest results from your trading while maintaining a balanced life. Too many traders get trapped into thinking that they should put a certain amount of time into their trading day. Consequently, the amount of time that they choose can be either too much or too little for fostering the best results.

Being a consistently profitable trader takes just as much time and energy as any profession where rewards can be exceptional. The problem for many traders is that the pattern of long hours becomes an addictive behavior that is difficult to overcome. Traders begin to think that if they do not keep up with long hours, their trading results will suffer. It is highly advisable for traders to put a considerable amount of time into study while they are in the process of becoming a trader. But, if a trader continuously pressures himself, the imbalance in his life will have an adverse effect on his trading results. For a trader to maintain a consistent top performance level, he must be physically, emotionally, spiritually, and socially in balance. In short, this means that he must also have a life beyond trading.

It Ain't Necessarily So

The old work ethic would have you believe that in order to earn a living from your work, you must work at least eight hours per day. By observing the patterns of clients, I have found that many of them would earn considerably more money if they did not put as many hours into their trading.

When I restate to a client what he has verbalized to me about the activities of his trading day, he becomes aware of the obvious solution, which is to use his time more effectively. For example, Ron traded on the floor of an exchange for years. He has been diligent about being there at the opening and closing of almost every day for the last ten years. Though he has consistently made money, working in the pits has taken its toll on his body to the point where trading has stopped being fun.

He said to me, "Yeah, sometimes I think it's just a waste of my time to come in the afternoons. I lose a lot of the money that I made in the mornings because I've never been good with handling volatility when I'm tired." I asked him, "What do you imagine your results would be if you hadn't traded in the afternoons for the last five years?" He said, "Hell, I'd be ahead by twice the amount, or more."

Now Ron is trading only in the mornings, enjoying the rest of the day at the gym, and feeding the ducks by the lake. He is also earning considerably more money than he was and is enjoying trading once again.

The best way to improve your system or methodology is to be consistent in following your trading rules over a period of time. Patterns will emerge showing when and where you earn the most profits. Sometimes, a trader is too close to notice it himself. In Tom's case, he simply did not want to notice the obvious.

Tom was trading two time frames. Trading the long-term time frame was supporting the short-term trading and his lifestyle. After I held a mirror up to Tom so that he would admit to his day trading gambling addiction, he decided to choose computer war games as a substitute for his compulsions. Now, he is earning a full-time salary working one hour per day on his long term position trading.

Less Is More

Traders get models of what is an appropriate amount of working time from their parents, their teachers, their peers, and other traders. Most of them don't get to know the many fine traders who work a shorter day and earn good profits doing so. They are more likely to believe someone like me, a trader's coach, because of the experience I have had working with many traders, than people in their family who tell them the same thing. For example:

When Marty first started trading, he made mistakes that cost him a great deal of money. Since he made these mistakes, he felt that he had to rethink his trading decisions over and over before he made a final decision. I asked him how many times he had to look at a chart before he recognized an opportunity. "Only once," was his response. Marty finally understood that he did not have to recheck himself, and that it was okay to spend less time analyzing the markets. In fact, he is making more money now, feels less stressed, and has more time for his family and friends.

Watching a trading screen for some traders is more exciting than other activities in their lives. For people who love this intensity, trading is hard to walk away from unless there is something equally compelling to anticipate. For example:

Tim once had a wife, children, community activities, and hobbies to keep him balanced and happy. His wife, who was his activities director, passed away and his children went out on their own, but Tim did not know how to do things on his own. He started spending more and more time behind the computer screen until it consumed all of his time. He missed his old life but did not know how to get himself interested in other things beyond trading. When I worked with him, I gave him weekly assignments of activities that he had to accomplish. At first, he was reluctant and told me that all of my suggestions were not as interesting as sitting and watching the screen. One week some old friends asked him to a party. Normally, he would have refused, but I insisted that he attend the party as his weekly assignment. At the party, he met a woman who was like his wife and had a very active social life. She took over as his social director, and he is back to a balanced life, working on trading six hours per day instead of sixteen and is earning just as much, if not more, money.

When one member of a family is working ten to twelve hours per day and making perhaps half as much money as the trader in the family, it sometimes becomes an issue that their spouse is not at least "putting in his time" for the hard stuff in the relationship. Many traders waste time at the screen because they do not want to become the errand boy or the Mr. Mom that would be expected of them if they did not sit behind the screen all day. Here is an example:

Linda was always complaining that her trader husband, Harry, failed to get chores done around the house. I suggested that Harry ask Linda for a list of the chores to be completed and agree that if the chores got done, he could do what he wanted with his time. Harry found people to handle most of the handyman stuff. As a result, he spent less time at the screen and easily handled the added expense with the increase in income from working fewer stressed hours.

Every trader has a war story of the big trade that they missed when their attention was diverted from the screen. For this reason, traders glue themselves to the screen through countless hours waiting for the big one to hit. Most of the best traders that I know do not look for killings, but consistently pull profits out of everyday trading experiences. These traders at the top pace themselves to have a life while enjoying the time they do spend trading. This strategy prevents the build up of tension that most traders develop by not allowing themselves time away from the screens. For example:

Yes, there was that time that Joe missed that big trade when his wife dragged him away on vacation. And yes, there was that time when he was sick that afternoon and missed another big trade. He still talks about the big trades that got away. He was spending so much time watching the screen that he over-traded and missed opportunities that were smaller fortunes. I asked Joe to give up fifty percent of his trades and work a four-hour day for one month and check the results. While he reluctantly committed to my suggestions, he accomplished giving up twenty percent of his normal trades and worked a six-hour day. He made more money in that month than ever before. He was still uncomfortable, but the profits were strong evidence that he was missing larger profits by gluing himself to the screen in his effort to catch the next big one.

Albert was in the habit of watching his stops very closely. Often, he would lower his stop, thinking that it would get hit and the market would immediately bounce back. It was not okay for him to be wrong and lose money on a position. He forced himself to watch the screen for most of his waking day and sometimes through the night. Albert was exhausted and a nervous wreck. I pointed out the obvious when he told me his problem. In order for him to trust himself, he was going to have to commit to his stops and feel that he could walk away from the screen. I suggested that he go back to his trading plan. He needed to work on contingencies for his rules and back-test all of the positions that he had taken to see what the results would have been if he had kept to his original stops. What he found was that he would have made more money if he had consistently stayed with his original stops. We worked on his issues of the fear of being wrong. We also worked on mentally rehearsing feeling comfortable trading his rules and staying with his initial stop loss. Now, he is able to leave the screen with confidence that his rules for stop placement are the best for his method. Albert works a four-hour day and is well rested because he's making better choices.

Here are some questions you can use to coach yourself. They will help you recognize if you are using the right amount of time to produce the best results.

- Why do you work the hours that you work?
- What would happen if you worked fewer hours?
- When do you make most of your money?
- How much of your day do you waste?
- During what part of the day do you make most of your money?
- During what part of the day do you make the least amount of money?
- Who expects you to put in a certain amount of hours to be considered full time?
- Would you make more money if you worked less or more hours?

Successful trading initially demands many hours of studying and planning. One of the challenges of being a professional trader is that the traditional eight-hour work day is not necessarily the rule for getting the most in monetary reward. While some traders need those extra hours to produce great profits in the markets, I have found that many traders who reduce the hours they spend in the markets produce better results.

Adrienne Laris Toghraie, MNLP, MCH, is a trader's coach and internationally recognized authority in the field of human development for the financial community. She is founder and president of Trading on Target (www.TradingOnTarget.com). Toghraie's eight books on the psychology of trading, including, *Winning Edge 4* (Traders Press, 2002), have been highly praised by financial magazines. Her public seminars and private counseling, as well as her television appearances and keynote addresses at major industry conferences, have achieved a wide level of recognition and popularity. This article originally appeared in *SFO* in November 2002.

MAINTAIN YOUR MINDSET: Using the Three Rs and Positive Thinking

BY LINDA BRADFORD RASCHKE

I have been a professional trader for more than twenty-five years and am quite sure that my experiences in this business parallel those of many, if not most professional traders. I experience both successes and failures and periods of both satisfaction and frustration. Like others, I have had to stretch and grow as markets and products have changed over the years. The markets continually cause me to reaffirm my values and reflect on my own self-identity, and even after all these years, I keep vigil against fear and doubt. Thankfully, I am blessed with the knowledge of how powerful a tool positive thinking can be and with the ability to implement this tool on a daily basis.

When the markets are closed, I divide my time equally between preparing for the next day, performing market research, and working on my own mindset. Part of this includes reading a paragraph from a motivational book each night, studying sports psychology, or working on the physical elements, such as exercise, nutrition, and diet that support my ability to concentrate and focus during the day.

I wish I could say there was a point where I felt like I had "arrived." More often than not, however, I feel as though I am not even close to reaching that point. I have come to accept the fact that this business is nothing more then a continual process to be taken one day at a time, like so many other endeavors in life. For me, the term "trader" has become synonymous with "lifestyle."

I have learned that everything I do with my lifestyle to support the trader function equally supports a separate self. Much of it has to do with eliminating stress, anxiety, and burnout. I have experienced all three many times in my career, and each time it affects my trading performance. My more stressful life experiences are not so different from those of many people: death, divorce, and taxes. I juggle many balls at once. I trade, run a business, have a responsibility for ten employees, and am a single mom. I shoulder responsibilities as head of my household, and I maintain a large property. In addition, I strive to excel at outside interests and hobbies.

Stay in the Game by Beating Stress

I wish I could say that I was an extremely efficient person, but I am not. I dilly-dally and procrastinate with the best of them. However, I have become a master at beating stress and anxiety and dealing with the mental side of trading. I figure that if I can take care of this one particular area, the numbers will take care of themselves. This has worked for me each year and has kept me in the game.

So, allow me to share some of my personal experiences, routines, and rituals for handling some of the more challenging psychological aspects of trading. Sometimes traders can feel alone in their experiences—particularly when stupid errors and large losses occur and during long, flat periods. Believe me, I have made every mistake in the book, have suffered through many sleepless nights, and have had conversations with the higher powers that be. Through it all, I have never wanted to leave the trading business. I don't love trading and I don't hate it; it is just what I do. I love working.

Some people are lucky in knowing their game right away, and I am one of those people. I know the style of trading with which I feel comfortable. I will never be a long-term trend-follower and will never be one of those who will easily interpret fundamentals or long-term major trend changes on a macro level. I would never feel comfortable running a strictly mechanical system. And I do not want to trade in a way that depends totally on my reflexes. Remember, a trader can't begin to improve his game until he defines exactly which game he is playing. At this stage in my career, I know my abilities, my strengths, and my weaknesses. I try and exploit my strengths instead of becoming something I am not nor ever will be. This is what you should be trying to develop as well. Know thyself.

Positive Brainwashing

OK, knowing my game is helpful, but just because I know my game does not mean that I will be successful at it. There are numerous steps that must be taken outside of market hours in order to do well during the trading day. I can go through the motions of preparation, organization, and outside research. But, I still do not think these are the things that guarantee success. The great equalizer for me is that I believe I will succeed. I have brainwashed myself on a daily basis into believing I will succeed, especially during periods when inevitable doubts have crept in. A positive mental attitude is a form of religion to me.

If a trader has a positive attitude, it allows him to believe that by focusing on the process, the results will take care of themselves. This involves an element of trust. Sometimes it is like diving off a high dive and knowing that if you follow correct form, you will hit the water just right and have a beautifully executed dive. Some people find it hard to accept that occasionally their form will be off, and it is going to hurt when hitting the water. If doubt or negative thoughts creep into my mind when I dive off that platform, I am doomed. I have so many tricks for eliminating the negative self-talk that the positive thinking has become purely habit.

Self-talk is the way that we speak to ourselves, and sometimes negative thoughts are very subtle. For example, if a trader says to him or herself, "I have to do well" or "I need to make X amount of dollars this month," this type of thinking automatically creates stress and anxiety. Anxiety causes emotional decision making during the trading day. Emotions invariably lead to losing trades.

The First Step Is Awareness

Eliminating negative thoughts is a process. First, become aware of when you are thinking negatively, and recognize that you can choose to refocus your thinking pattern. Simply rephrasing "I have to do well" into "I can do well" is a step in the right direction. The first phrase places demands upon performance, while the second phrase emphasizes confidence in your abilities.

Second, interrupt mental thoughts by changing your physical state. Clap your hands, snap your fingers, or stand up out of your chair.

Third, refocus your thoughts on the process at hand in order to replace worry, doubt, or anxiety. "I can trust myself to make the right decisions today." "I can take advantage of the opportunities as they unfold throughout the trading week." These processes seem simple enough, maybe even intuitive, yet they are probably not as intuitive as one might believe. Positive thinking is something that takes practice.

I cannot emphasize strongly enough how important the power of positive thinking has been in my own trading career. It has allowed me to convert every fiasco that has happened in the marketplace into a learning experience. I tell myself that what has happened occurred for a reason; then, I must find a way to convert, just as in a sport.

Consider the tennis player who goes on a losing streak during a match and drops six games in a row. Things are looking rather bleak to the spectators. However, the player manages to pull off a winning shot or a killer serve. And sometimes the other player makes an unforced error. Top athletes will seize one small victory and convert that momentum to their favor. This happens in team sports as well, such as football, where a turnover provides a new burst of momentum that carries the formerly losing team to a win.

It is no different in trading. Reframe the negative experiences into positive ones, and find a way to learn from them. For every mistake I make, I tell myself that it is a good thing that it happened now so I could learn from it, instead of when I am trading an even larger size in the future. I thank the market for bringing any of my weaknesses to my attention so I can learn and improve. If market conditions change or the environment stops favoring my game, I tell myself that this is a great opportunity to do research and find new techniques. All of my best research has come following a drawdown.

There is a fine line between working hard and burnout. I have learned the hard way about setting boundaries and defining my limits. In the past, I chose not to acknowledge that I had any limits, and the result was a major compromise of my immune system. It is better to recognize when it is time to step back a bit, instead of waiting for deteriorating health to take its toll or being faced with a major trading loss. Most traders know when they are making mistakes. But, when a trader is burned out, he or she is not able to react properly to correct mistakes. It is almost as if the subconscious is saying, "This loss is going to get so big that it is going to force you to take a break from the markets."

Aside from the physical symptoms that can indicate burnout, other signs include increased irritability and anxiety, forgetfulness, and inability to concentrate. A trader is more likely to take greater risks when burned out. Procrastination, fatigue, neglecting to do the proper preparation the night before, or basically turning a blind eye toward a current position is often the next stage. When someone is burned out, they are likely to increase their consumption of coffee, cola, or alcohol. Ultimately, burnout can lead to thoughts of throwing in the towel—quitting the business altogether or chronic depression.

The main strategy for avoiding burnout is to lead a healthy and balanced lifestyle. This can include daily exercise, proper nutrition, outside hobbies or activities, periodic vacations, or even taking just one day on the weekend to go on a field trip and enjoy a change of scenery. Educational strategies include attending workshops or seminars, joining a professional organization, reading trade journals or books on sports psychology or motivational subjects.

Sometimes changes to the work environment—something as simple as rearranging the office—can make a difference. Finally, some type of support system is important—a close friend, fellow trader, or counselor in whom you can confide. Each time I have had a particularly challenging period, I feel better after confiding my situation to a friend or fellow trader. After all, we all have similar experiences at one time or another. Losses and errors are part of the game. Talking about them with others helps us put our normal human weaknesses in their proper perspective and allows us to move on.

The Three Rs

Let me leave you with the three Rs I use as a way of maintaining a mindset and keeping focused: record keeping, rituals, and research.

Record keeping is the departure point that carries an endeavor beyond just being a hobby to taking the next step towards professional status. At the end of each day, I log statistics such as breadth, volume, trin, and put/call ratios to name just a few. I have been doing this since the first day I started trading. Once upon a time, I updated charts by hand each night because the charting software we have now did not exist. For the past fifteen years, I have logged by hand the closing price of twenty-five different markets, in addition to momentum readings and a few other notations. If I do not log my numbers at night, I do not trade as well the next day.

During the day, each trade is written down with the ticket number, times executed, and fill prices, along with the name of the executing broker. This is essential for reconciling any out-trades the next day and ultimately can save a great deal of time when an error does occur. I also write down my available trading capital each day along with current open positions.

When using electronic platforms, never take it for granted that the trades will hit up correctly the next day. The platform that I use keeps an accurate log of all trades I make, so I do not actually write these down, but save the log files instead.

Compared with many other businesses, trading and markets can seem a somewhat abstract arena. Activities such as record keeping help me feel more productive and in control of my business. As much record keeping as I do, I do not keep statistics on my trading performance, such as win/loss ratios, average-win, and average-loss. I find that this will become a source of anxiety or stress to me. Instead, I monitor my equity curve and how I am doing on a month-to-month basis instead of on a day-to-day basis. Why? Sometimes it's easy to get too excited about looking at the net profit after a large winning day. Large wins can do just as much to tamper with an even mindset as large losses.

Routines and rituals are excellent tools for eliminating emotions—especially those in the doubt, fear, and anxiety category. Though I personally do not have any particularly titillating rituals to share, I find that writing things down is particularly helpful for me. I write out my trading plan for the next day after the close each day. During the trading day, I will jot down swing highs and lows as they are made throughout the day. Years ago when I started out on the trading floor, I watched many of the better traders sketch out point-and-figure charts or swing charts by hand during the trading day.

Physical and mental routines are the key to building both confidence and consistency. I can't say enough about the importance of this area in my own business. It is not just the ability to concentrate, but also the focus of our concentration. It does no good to concentrate on the wrong things. Much of what I am doing during the day is simple observation. But I have a very specific routine and ritual for what and how I observe things during the day.

First, I concentrate on monitoring just a few relationships. Though I have built up my ability to process a large amount of information, I am still subject to brain-fry like everyone else. If I try to do too much or trade too many markets at one time, I am asking for trouble. I have specific times of the day when I note certain relationships. I have a limited universe of stocks that I watch. I have three main patterns that I watch for in the cash commodity markets. So, in this regard, I am a classic tape reader, lying in wait for my particular technical conditions or market cues. This is my market routine; you may have another that suits you better.

Outside of market routines, there are personal life routines. For example, I try to wake up at the same time every morning, take my nutritional supplements, and eat the same breakfast. This helps me get into the zone or on autopilot before the markets open. These mental and physical routines help me maintain my concentration and keep my mind from wandering. If they are broken during the day, it's easy to become vulnerable. I continually guard against outside distractions and subscribe to the philosophy that anything that can be handled at the end of the day has to wait until then.

Still, unforeseen things will always happen during the day to any trader, no matter how dedicated he or she is to keeping the noise out. One day, a neighbor decided to transplant some huge fica trees in front of his house. A giant digging machine with a ten-foot claw sunk deep into the ground and pulled up all the neighborhood phone lines, including our T1s. It took twenty-four hours to fix. These things are guaranteed to happen whenever you have your largest positions on, and it happens to each of us.

By the way, at the end of each day, I consider my number logging to be just one more essential ritual to help me forget about any unfavorable events that occurred during the day, whether it's the fica transplant disruption or an unforeseen family emergency.

Research is an integral part of my business, and as a trader it should be an important part of yours, too. Research is a process that never ends. I strongly believe that if I do my own research, I will always have an edge over someone who does not.

Research is important, even if a trader already has a successful method of trading. Anyone who has been in the markets for a while will attest to the fact that market relationships can and very often do change. Thus, research gives me confidence that there is an edge to my approach to trading. I continuously update my research to keep that confidence level high. Research constantly reminds me that trading is a game of probabilities and averages and shows all of the ways that a signal or pattern can fail.

Please remember, research should never be done to validate a personal bias. This type of research too often draws conclusions based on a limited sample size and will usually break down over time. I place very little value on research results generated on a sample size of less than two hundred occurrences.

Each day that I trade, I constantly remind myself of how far I have come. It would be so easy for me to pick apart my own performance each day. Instead, I go out of my way to make note of the areas where I have improved.

Yes, old dogs have to learn new tricks. I look at how my skills in using electronic trading platforms have improved. For so many years, I simply picked up the phone and called down to the pits. The first two years that we started using an electronic platform, I simply could not execute profitably with them. My brain would short circuit with the extra steps required for placing an order. The only way I could trade was to have someone else in my office do the execution while I called out the orders. I felt pretty silly not being able to execute my own orders. I tried a number of different trading platforms before I found one with which I felt comfortable. There was definitely an educational process involved in figuring this out.

Keep Your Mind in the Game

Trading is really no different than most sports. I just try to stay in the game mentally. I know that my unforced errors decrease as my market preparation and experience level increases. I convert emotions or frustrations into research or better market preparation. I know my game and work on eliminating more marginal trades. I know that focusing on the process will help the outcome take care of itself. In the end, though—no matter if I work forty hours a week or seventy hours or one hundred—I will not be successful unless I believe in my ability to be successful. The power of positive thinking, teamed with hard work and proven routines, will always win out over doubts, fears, self-imposed pressures, and marginal disciplines.

Linda Bradford Raschke has been a full-time, professional trader since 1981. She began as a floor trader and later started LBR Group, a professional money management firm. In addition to running successful programs as a CTA, she has been principal trader for several hedge funds and has run commercial hedging programs. Raschke was recognized in Jack Schwager's book, *The New Market Wizards* (Wiley, 1995), and is well known for her book, *Street Smarts* (M. Gordon Publishing Group, 1996). She is a frequent contributor to SFO and other publications. Numerous educational articles are available at her website at www.lbrgroup.com. This article originally appeared in *SFO* in July 2004.

KICKING LIFE UP A NOTCH: Managing the Stretch Between Trading and Living

BY ADRIENNE LARIS TOGHRAIE, MNLP, MCH

Recently, a trader named Jack came to me for private consulting. Clearly he needed help, not necessarily solely with his trading, but in his life balance. In his own words, he expressed the problem: "I'm doing okay in my trading, although I could be doing a lot better, but my personal life is not working." Based on my findings from taking him through my trader's evaluation, I told him that he needed to "kick his life up a notch" if he wanted to get his trading and his personal life to succeed.

What does it mean to kick life up a notch? And more importantly, why is it important to a trader? Yes, I borrowed the expression "kicking life up a notch" from the famous television chef and restauranteur Emeril Lagasse. He uses this expression on his show as he adds spices to his dishes to make them more appealing. Kicking life up a notch to a trader, however, means making choices and taking actions that are beyond the ordinary. These actions and choices are the ones that force you to stretch. They require that you look beyond the obvious solutions, challenge conventional wisdom, and take the more difficult path when the easy path is comfortable, safe, convenient, and well traveled. The great American poet, Robert Frost, said it best:

> *Two roads diverged in a wood, and I—*
> *I took the one less traveled by,*
> *And that has made all the difference.*

If you are a trader, you have already made the decision to kick life up a notch by taking the road less traveled. Trading is not an ordinary profession, and traders do not lead ordinary lives. It is possible to survive as a trader, but you cannot thrive as a trader if you are not willing to stretch. This, of course, was the situation in which Jack found himself. He was merely surviving, not flourishing.

So, how effective is your life as a trader? Do you wake up each morning enthusiastic and excited about the day's activities, or do you live your life simply because you are scheduled to do so? The schedule is your list of responsibilities. To live responsibly to others is to keep your commitments. But, to live responsibly to yourself, you must not only keep your commitments...you must also make the effort to enjoy the process. This commitment to enjoying the process requires you to take the road less traveled, add spice to the stew, stretch and grow, try something new and, as a result, to feel more alive.

Short Circuiting Aliveness

Every moment of the day is an opportunity to enjoy the experience of life. However, most of us deny ourselves these opportunities to kick life up a notch by taking short-cuts.

- Instead of sitting down with our family in the morning to have a nutritious breakfast, we eat a Pop-Tart on the go and forget to acknowledge the people that we love.
- We deny our bodies the healthy nutrition that we need to sustain an energetic, positive day.
- We time-manage our day so closely that we forget to include the simple joys of interaction with our colleagues.
- We forget that trading was a choice we made to live our passion.
- Workday routines become so mechanical that we fail to notice the nuances that make each day a special experience.
- Exercise becomes a chore or a sentence instead of an experience.
- Dinner digresses to an opened can here and a frozen dinner there instead of an opportunity to enjoy the tastes and smells of great food and the art of preparation.
- And, finally, we spend time with the family in front of the television instead of a time of closeness, playfulness, intimacy, communication, and exploration.

Does any of this sound familiar? Consider the fact that each choice of non-aliveness creates more of the same until you are left with no valuable moments. Then, you have nothing from which to draw when you need inspiration, motivation, and support. Every area of life affects every other area of life. So, when you look to improve the bottom line in your trading, you must also look to improve the bottom line of all of the other areas of your life.

Savoring Value

Valued moments come from kicking life up a notch. Some of the widows of the September 11 terrorist attacks have expressed regret about the last moments they spent with their spouses on that morning when they left for work. These grieving wives and husbands are wishing that those final goodbyes could have been different. Even with the horrible outcome they have to face, they keep thinking about the importance of those last few moments together with their spouses. If only they had taken more time for breakfast, then the memory of those last spoken words would give them more of a sense of peace.

Today, most people only savor the intense moments of life that mark the significant beginnings and endings. These moments are the extreme high times of celebration and the extreme low times of devastation. These powerful moments tend to completely overshadow the seemingly endless succession of ordinary, forgettable moments that make up the large majority of life. Auntie Mame, the outrageous and larger-than-life character from the play bearing her own name, said it this way, "Life is a banquet, but most poor bastards are starving to death." Without minimizing the deprivation experienced by those in the midst of hard times, it is important to remember that most of us have a great deal for which to be thankful. Each time you recognize the blessings that you do have and express gratitude for them, you are ratcheting up your experience of life.

A prime example of the way that placing value on the blessings in your life can kick up your life a notch came from a young trader who was deeply depressed about a lack of money. I asked him if he would sell his right arm for one million dollars. Naturally, he declined the offer. I kept raising the price offered for his arm and he continued to decline the offer. I pointed out to him that while he valued his right arm at millions of dollars, he placed no value on his entire body, which he was slowly destroying chemically and mentally. This young trader had failed to see the value of his own life and as a result, was willing to give it up when things were difficult to handle. It requires a willingness to take the road less traveled to continually appreciate the simple, ordinary things that life offers that are so easy to take for granted.

Choice of Focus

You cannot do the extraordinary if you are focused on the negative, the limited, or the impossible. These negative thoughts drain the energy from your life and prevent you from being exceptional. We tend to focus only on the things that justify our feelings about life and, thus, support our position, proving that we are right. Imagine what you could be right about by focusing on the following negative thoughts:

- The markets are a disaster and there is no way to survive in market conditions like this;
- The people on this planet are the constant victims of weather, fire, and terrorist attacks as shown on the nightly news;
- Your wife is a constant nag;
- Your children look and act like the cast of a circus freak show.

Because you have chosen to focus only on the parts of the picture that support these negative positions, you conclude that you are right about all of it. However, what does being right about the negative part of this picture give you? It certainly does not kick life up a notch. However, it does take you down the well-trodden path that leads to complacency and insignificance.

Consider being right about focusing on what you do have, but turning the negatives into positives:

- There are always opportunities in the markets. Someone is always on the positive side of a trade, and I am going to enjoy the process of being the trader who finds that opportunity;
- I live in a free country, in a beautiful neighborhood, with a good family and I am going to continue to celebrate each day that I have this fortunate life;

- My husband or wife is an incredible partner and loving parent. Actively listening and letting him or her know how important he or she is to me enhances both of our lives;
- My children are healthy, creative, and amusing with the choices that they make. I see myself in them when I was their age.

Living an Artful Life

Imagine that you are about to play a board game where you play a character making choices about how he will live his life. Wouldn't you choose to be a character living a dynamic life with lots of adventure, fame, fortune, and exciting challenges? Wouldn't you take more calculated risks, visit more places, and risk more special moments than you do presently in your own life? I think you would.

Well, guess what? You are playing a character in your life and you do get to make choices! What are the choices that you are making? Do any of these things stop you from living your life as dynamically as you would like it to be?

- Fear of failure or success;
- Fear of being wrong and losing what you have;
- Routine and bad habits;
- Negative interaction and negative influence from those around you;
- Living life from the position of "I can't afford to!"

There are lots of good excuses for not living life artfully. Do you want to excuse your way out of living the best you can with what you have?

A trader named Greg told me the story of his life, demonstrating the importance of enjoying what you have while you possess it. While his parents struggled to put meals on the table and a roof over their family's head, they failed to fulfill their family's most basic need for adequate loving and nurturing in the process.

Through hard work and dedication, the family developed a local candy store into a small chain of supermarkets. Greg told me that he could not remember when each step in the process did not come out of sacrifice, worry, and pain. Then, Greg's father had a stroke. The stress of his being in a wheel chair without hiring needed assistance eventually killed both of his parents. Greg's parents lived their lives in the same neighborhood with the same hand-me-down furniture, never taking vacations until the day that they died. The only significant money that his family ever spent was on Greg's education, his wedding, and on a trust fund that was established for the grandchildren's education.

When his parents died, Greg inherited three times the amount of money that he had been told to expect. Now, you would think that money and the ability to spend frivolously after his parent's death would bring Greg some form of pleasure, but it didn't. No matter how much he has had, it has never been enough. Greg could not rid his consciousness of the struggling, poverty-ridden mentality of his youth. No matter how many people he has brought into his life, he has still felt starved for love and attention.

Because Greg was programmed to struggle, he was attracted to trading and the markets. The adage, "you attract what you want out of the markets" applied to Greg. His need to struggle was satisfied in his trading. He wanted to prove himself and to be successful in his own right without his family's money. He thought that if he earned his own money he would not feel guilty about spending the money that came from their struggle and sacrifice.

In his struggles, Greg managed to make the wrong choices. As a result, he lost a great deal of his fortune along with his wife and children. Before he was able to ask for help, he also became very depressed. He could not give himself permission to appreciate and nurture anything or anyone, especially himself. Greg had to learn the importance of giving before he could learn to live successfully and prosper as a professional trader. The one saving grace for Greg was a resource that he received from his education, and that was his willingness to seek out and pay for help.

Now, Greg lives a much simpler life with a new family. He is happy with an average to good trading career. He has much less monetarily than he had before, but he has said that his life is good. He has learned to savor each moment and does not find it necessary to prove anything. He has also found it unnecessary to continue in his family tradition of struggle and sacrifice. Greg now lives a rich life.

What if you were to spice up the flavor of your life by simply intending to do so?

Recipe for Kicking Life up a Notch with Intention:

- Recognize what you are thinking and what your actions are when you are depressed. Listen to what you are saying to yourself. Write it down in a notebook and read it aloud so that you can hear yourself talk.
- Take a specific pre-determined time to be as miserable as possible until there is nothing left to think about except a repeat of the same self-talk.
- Take a vacation from your negative thinking. Do only what you want to do for a day or two.
- Decide how you would like your life to be. Take into account your present situation.
- Write down what is in the realm of your control and what specific tasks you can take that would make your situation better. Take action on these tasks.
- Check off from your list what you have accomplished at the end of the day.
- Now, think outside of the box of possibilities and consider what you could do if you had the resources and the right frame of mind to accomplish something beyond what is in the realm of possibilities.
- Ask others for help and ideas.
- Decide what you are willing and capable of doing without the resources that you feel you need. Add these tasks to your list of actions.
- Now state your intention out loud. Proceed to stretch yourself just beyond what you thought your limitations were.
- Each day, kick your life up a notch.

Each day, you make choices that affect how you play the part of your character in the board game of life. If you are presently in a blessed situation, you can appreciate it more by acknowledging your good fortune and by celebrating each moment. It is important to appreciate each good moment because you never know when life will throw you difficult times.

When you are handed difficulties instead of the bouquet of roses that you were expecting, realize that you still have choices. Sometimes, it is necessary to wallow in depression and worry for a time in order to be able to move on. However, you can either add to the problems by remaining stuck in your misery for too long or you can pick up the pieces as soon as you are able and make the best of the bad situation. By intentionally making better choices, you can free yourself from the role of victim to your need to be right. In good times and in all the other times, always remember to ask yourself, "How can I kick my life up a notch?" Once you ask the question, you will have already taken the first step. The next step is up to you.

Adrienne Laris Toghraie, MNLP, MCH, is a trader's coach and internationally recognized authority in the field of human development for the financial community. She is founder and president of Trading on Target (www.TradingOnTarget.com). Toghraie's eight books on the psychology of trading, including, *Winning Edge 4* (Traders Press, 2002), have been highly praised by financial magazines. Her public seminars and private counseling, as well as her television appearances and keynote addresses at major industry conferences, have achieved a wide level of recognition and popularity. This article originally appeared in *SFO* in December 2002.

STRIKING A BALANCE:
Trading and Having a Life

BY JOHN F. CARTER

What do a lawsuit, disgruntled employee who quits, computer crash, mini-sized Dow (YM) trade gone bad, and a poopy diaper all have in common? No, this isn't a riddle with a door prize. These are all events from my life during the week I took notes for this article.

As a new father, work-at-home trader with hired assistants, and head of a business that runs a few trading-related websites, there is always, always, always a challenge. My days mimic ocean waves rolling on a beach, a constant ebb and flow, shifting between moments when I'm merely busy to moments when I feel I'm beating off the headwinds of an approaching hurricane. Why not just blow my brains out and get it over with? It's all about learning how to manage life and not let life manage me—especially the trading life. To do this, I follow the four Fs: focus, fuel, facts, and fun.

The Day Begins

The week began auspiciously enough. Monday was a quiet day with quiet markets. I made a few grain trades. I bought some gold. The peace and solitude ended abruptly with a phone call from my darling wife. She is pregnant with our second child and recently started getting nauseous at the smell of eighteen-month-old James' poopy diapers. Normally we have a nanny on hand, but this week she had the nerve to take a vacation. "Hi, Hon," she says on the phone. "James pooped."

Sigh. "OK, I'll be right down."

I check my orders. Stops and targets are in place and every-thing looks fine. It doesn't escape me that I'm in a trade that could mean tens of thousands of dollars in profits or losses … and I'm about to go run downstairs and wipe an ass. I could ask one of my employees to do it, but I'm fairly certain they would point out that their job descriptions do not include it. Resigned, I run down and change the diaper. It's actually a fun bonding time with my son. He laughs at me while I struggle to hold up his legs and clean up his mess, rub on butt paste, and put on a fresh Pamper. (If you aren't a parent, you'll think that's the stupidest thing you've ever heard. Just wait.)

On Tuesday the trading day is humming along. I wait for set-ups, and take them when they occur. I get stopped out on my first YM play and I move my stop to breakeven on a CBOT gold futures play (ZG). As these trades unfold, I monitor my orders accordingly. Then, just as I short a thirty-minute breakdown on soybeans, I get a call from an attorney threatening my company with a trademark lawsuit due to a new Fibonacci-related website we had just launched. I talk to the lawyer. He focuses on intimidation tactics instead of partici-pating in an adult conversation. I watch my soybean trade and miss half the stuff he says. I yawn, which seems to offend him as this is "serious business." That is one thing that is good about spending your life as a trader—there really isn't much that can happen to you that stresses you out because you have already experienced every range of extreme emotion that a human being can tolerate. The at-torney wraps up the conversation by saying, "You have to take the site down right now."

"We're not taking down the site," I reply.

Yells. Threats. When he stops, I say, "Relax, we're going to change the name. We just need a day or so to implement the changes. When do we have to have the new name up and running?"

"This must be done immediately. We will fight to protect our inter-ests. We …"

"Yeah, yeah I got it. How about by tomorrow?"

"Immediately. We must protect our …"

"Well, it's going to be tomorrow, because we have to find a new name and obviously make sure it's not already trademarked. We aren't being malicious. This isn't IBM versus Microsoft. It was an error. We're fixing it. If you want to proceed with the lawsuit and waste your client's money, that's fine." Click.

Focus

Although I don't get sued every week, there is always something going on around me. The two examples above, poopy diapers and lawsuits, show the importance of focus. Part of being a trader is being able to have a game plan and keep that game plan on the forefront of my mind throughout the trading day, no matter what is going on around me. If I planned to buy gold on a pullback to the eight-period exponential moving average with a ten-point stop, then nothing should distract me from that. The computer next to me can ignite and burst into flames, but if gold prices hit my buy zone, then I'm buying, and I won't even try to put out the fire until my stop is in place. Once my orders are in place, however, then my job is done and I can turn my attention to the fire.

Once in a trade—a well thought-out and planned trade—I don't need to stare at every tick. My orders are like my employees, and they are now doing the work for me. Nothing that happens around me is going to change that.

In my experience, a trader without a specific plan can get hammered during interruptions. They become unfocused, prone to impulse trades. They start blaming losses on factors outside of their control. "I lost money on the trade because my wife took me to lunch." Dig a little deeper and the trader may find that he or she left the office without a stop or a target in place. Whose fault is that? Not the wife's. Stay focused.

On Wednesday, as I'm in an CME E-mini S&P (ES) trade, one of my employees (who is also my sister-in-law) grabs her purse, storms out the door, and drives off. I ask another employee (who also happens to be my sister-in-law) what happened. Apparently she's extremely upset with me, because I'm keeping her out of the loop on new and upcoming projects. This is true. I gave her a few big projects, and she fumbled the ball. I feel it's time to give her a break from major responsibility until she can gain more confidence in our procedures and gradually become more self-sufficient in handling major responsibility on her own.

At this point, she is 24 years old and earning $80,000 a year to essentially answer the phone and check e-mails. I want to say,

"Girl, enjoy the down time while you have it!" I find it semi-rewarding to work with people in a tough-love situation and push them to think bigger and shove them through their comfort zones. In my experience, this is what a person needs to do constantly to lead a more rich and rewarding life—do the thing that scares him or her the most.

In this case, however, tough love equals no love. After the markets close she calls me and tells me she is giving her two-weeks notice because, essentially, "management sucks." That would be me, since I'm management.

"That's fine," I say. "Come in tomorrow, and we'll work out the details."

Although I think she is making a hasty decision and a mistake, I also admire her for putting a stake in the ground and saying, "I'm not going to stand for this." I don't pretend to understand the individual torments of the human soul. Reality is merely a reflection of what we are thinking about all day long. In her mind, she hit her stop loss. I call the paper and place an ad for a new employee—sisters-in-law need not apply.

Fuel

A trader needs stamina to get through the trading day and balance the multiple demands on his or her time. The best way to get that stamina for both the body and mind is through specific types of fuel. There are two types: physical and mental. Physical fuel has to do with keeping the body fine-tuned and optimized for performance. The easiest way to do this is to drink a gallon of clean water a day, replace refined sugars and flour with whole, unprocessed grains, and remember your fruits and veggies. Sodas and fast food eat away at a trader's body and result in poor sleep, nervous ticks, and a continually weakening ability to handle day-to-day challenges effectively. If you find yourself screaming at the bank teller or shaking your fist at a fellow driver, it's you who are running on empty.

Mental fuel has to do with choosing the best thoughts on which to dwell throughout the day. It is impossible to control all thoughts, but focusing on certain ones will help strengthen the mind instead of weakening it. This may sound trite to realists out there, but this is based on the theory that external circumstances are not very important, that all of the events of one's life, whether they are emotional, social, or professional, are just a mirror image of one's thoughts.

Life is exactly how we picture it to be. Everything that happens to us is brought on by our thoughts. Do I believe that a person gets into a car wreck because of what they were thinking? No, that's why it's called an accident. But I do believe a person can calm his or her mind and attract the things they want around them by thinking calming thoughts throughout the day. Repeating ideas such as, "every day, in every way, I'm getting better and better" has a better effect on the mind than repeating, "I'm a stupid idiot, I hate my life, and the market is out to get me."

So if you want to change your life, balance your life, then you must start by changing your thoughts, balancing your thoughts. Besides, being rational is such a boring way to live.

On Thursday I'm in a YM trade, contemplating yet another interesting week in the life of a trader. My wife comes into the office to check on me, which is fine. She knows not to come in around key times like market opens and closes. We've established the fact that I have zero interest in household chores like changing light bulbs. She's resigned herself to this and hires a handyman service to come in whenever we need tasks done around the house. However, there are still times when she will come up and ask if I can do something for her. She knows that sometimes the answer will be no. This week so far has already been trying, plus the nanny is gone. She asks if I can watch James while she goes to get a pedicure. Just as she asks this, my platform locks up.

That's part of the joy of working at home and having kids—you get to spend more time with them, and I truly enjoy playing with James. However, there are times during the trading day when I just can't drop everything and do that. Having my platform lock up when a YM trade is going against me qualifies as one of those times. I tell my wife I can't watch James. She gets a little peeved that she can't go get a "manny and peddy." As she stalks out of the office, I call my broker to tell him to flatten me out.

By the way, my wife read a late draft of this article that I left open on my computer. After telling her mother about what I'd said, she decided to add the following: "You know you are a trader's wife when the phrase 'the markets are closed' is as exciting as 'Honey, we're going to Hawaii,' because it means that your husband is now ready to interact with you with more than a grunt and a nod."

Facts

In a situation like this, it is important for a trader to dwell on the facts. The facts in this case were: 1) I was in a highly leveraged trade; 2) the markets were open and moving; and 3) my platform locked up. As a trader dealing with facts, this overrode the pedicure. It's not about emotions or who is right and who is wrong. Just the facts.

Finally, one of my employees who didn't quit this week (and who is not related to me), forwards me an e-mail from a client who is disputing a $99 charge on his credit card for one of our services. It reads, "Dear Sir or Madam, I did not authorize this charge. You are crooks. You will hear from my lawyer today, and he will take you and your organization down." This e-mail makes it to our bulletin board. We have a "Freak of the Week" contest for customers who send e-mails that reveal they are, in fact, freaks. This one is a winner, and we take down the one from the prior week and replace it with this one. We call him and work it out but neglect to tell him about the award he has just won.

Fun

Trading, life, and business can all be stressful at times, and that's why it is important to have fun. It's not worth going through the ups and downs if you can't at least smile and be thankful that you have an interesting way to make a living. One of my favorite quotes is from Felix Dennis, billionaire publisher of a variety of computer magazines among other things. He says, "If you cannot treat your quest to get rich as a game, you will never be rich." This reminds me not to take things too seriously, no matter what the quest.

By following the four Fs traders can stay in tune on what is going on around them without getting distracted. They can stay balanced and avoid getting the fifth "f." The fifth "f"? Ah, that's the one we don't want. And if James says it anytime soon, he will wind up with a mouthful of soap!

The market is a stern mistress whose greatest tool is in teaching human beings an appreciation for humility—a unique trait for a group of people who spend their days waiting patiently for an opportunity to kill. As a trader, I've learned to understand and accept the fact that the market is always right, no matter what else is going on around me. That is the basis for the four Fs—a realization that the market will never make a mistake, will never be wrong, and to use that knowledge to bring balance to the swirling activity around me.

John F. Carter grew up the son of a Morgan Stanley stockbroker and was introduced to trading as a sophomore in high school. He has been actively trading for the past nineteen years. Carter studied international finance at the University of Cambridge in England before graduating from the University of Texas at Austin. He has been a full time trader since 1996. In 1999, he launched www.tradethemarkets.com to post his trading ideas for the futures, equities, and options markets. In 2005 he launched www.razorforex.com to focus on the forex markets. Today he has a following of more than ten thousand people. Carter is a commodity trading advisor with Razor Trading, manages a futures and a forex fund, and is the recent author of *Mastering the Trade* (McGraw-Hill, 2005). To keep his sanity, he relies on physical activity after the close to deal with the financial swings he and his subscribers encounter. He clears his head running, water skiing, and practicing Tae Kwon Do. This article originally appeared in *SFO* in July 2007.

GLOSSARY OF TERMS

A

Adrenaline: A neurotransmitter, or hormone, that helps the body overcome physical or mental stress.

Algorithm: An advanced mathematical model that can be used in a trading system to make transaction decisions in the financial markets.

American Stock Exchange (AMEX): A stock exchange; a private, not-for-profit corporation, located in New York City and founded in 1842. Also called AMEX and the curb exchange.

Amygdala: Groups of neurons located in the brain that form a primary role in determining emotional reactions.

Arbitrage: The simultaneous purchase of one asset against the sale of the same asset (usually in different exchanges or marketplaces) in an attempt to profit from different prices for the same security, commodity, or financial instrument in different markets.

Ask: The price a seller is willing to accept for a security, futures contract or other financial instrument. Also called the offer.

At or better: (1) In a buy order for securities, futures, or other financial instruments, a purchase at the specified price or under it (2) For a sell order, a sale at the specified price or above it.

At-the-money: An option with a strike price equal to the current price of the instrument, such as a stock, upon which the option was granted.

At-the-opening order: An order that specifies it is to be executed at the opening of the market or of trading or else it is to be canceled. The order does not have to be executed at the opening price, but within the opening range of prices.

B

Bear market (bear, bearish): A market in which prices are declining. A period of generally falling prices and pessimistic attitudes.

Behavioral finance: A field of study that analyzes the impact of psychology on economic decision making, such as trading and investment.

Bid: The price a buyer is willing to pay for a security, futures contract or other financial instrument.

Biofeedback: A process of measuring bodily functions, such as skin conductivity, heart rate, muscle tension and brain waves, to monitor levels of calm and arousal.

Black box system: A software trading program where the inner workings, or algorithms, are unknown, and the variables cannot be modified.

Board of Trade: Any exchange or association of persons engaged in the business of buying or selling a commodity. Usually an exchange where commodity futures and/or options are traded. Sometimes referred to as Contract Market or Exchange.

Bollinger bands: A method used by technical analysts that indicates if a market is overbought or oversold. The bands are comprised of fixed lines above and below a simple moving average. As volatility increases, the bands widen.

Bond: A debt instrument that pays a set amount of interest on a regular basis. The issuer promises to repay the debt on time and in full.

Book value: The value of a financial instrument as shown by accounting records, often not the same as the instrument is valued by the market.

Booked: The point at which a transaction is processed. Though funds may not yet be available, the system has posted it and marked it as having a value date in the future.

Booking date: The date the payment is to be booked and executed. The date the payment will be passed to the automated system to book.

Bookings: A collection of records of financial transactions processed by automated systems. Booking are also called postings.

Brainstem: The lowest part of the brain, which is continuous with the spinal cord.

Break: A rapid and sharp price decline.

Break-even point: (1) The point at which gains equal losses. (2) The price a market must reach for an option buyer to avoid a loss if he or she exercises.

Broker: (1) An individual or firm that charges a fee or commission for executing buy and sell orders placed by another individual or firm. (2) A floor broker in commodities futures trading, a person who actually executes orders on the trading floor of an exchange.

Brokerage: A fee charged by a broker for execution of a transaction.

Bull market (bull, bullish): A market in which prices are rising. A trader who believes prices will move higher is called a bull.

C

Candlestick Chart: A price chart that includes information on the opening price, closing price, and direction of movement during a trading session. Also called a Japanese candlestick chart, since the method was developed to analyze rice markets in 17th century Japan.

Cash market: The underlying commodity, security, currency, or money market in which transactions for the purchase and sale of cash instruments which futures and derivative contracts relate to are carried out.

Charting: The use of graphs and charts in the technical analysis of markets to plot trends of price movements, volume, and open interest.

Chicago Board Options Exchange (CBOE): An exchange at the Chicago Board of Trade to trade stock options. The CBOE has markets in equities, options, and over-the-counter securities.

Chicago Board of Trade (CBOT or CBT): The oldest futures exchange in the United States, established in 1848. The board announced their intention (in late 2006) to merge with the Chicago Mercantile Exchange (and operate under the name of the CME). The exchange lists agricultural commodity futures such as corn, oats, and soybeans, in addition to financial instruments—e.g., Treasury bonds and Treasury notes.

Chicago Mercantile Exchange (CME): The exchange announced their intention (in late 2006) to merge with the Chicago Board of Trade to become the largest futures exchange in the world. The Exchange operates the International Monetary Market (IMM), the Index and Options Market (IOM), and the Growth and Emerging Markets (GEM), and will eventually operate Chicago Board of Trade agricultural commodity futures such as corn, oats, and soybeans, as well as financial instruments such as Treasury bonds and Treasury notes.

Clear: The formal completion of a trade.

Close: The period at the end of a trading session during which all transactions are considered to be made at the close.

Closing balance: The balance of entries posted to the account at the close of the statement period.

Closing price: The price at which transactions are made just before the close on a given day.

Closing range: A range of closely related prices at which transactions took place at the closing of the market; buy and sell orders at the closing might have been filled at any point within such a range.

Coach: A teacher who helps traders (or people in other disciplines) strategically improve their practice by mentoring, setting goals, teaching skills, and talking through challenges.

Commission: (1) A fee charged by a broker to a customer for performance of a specific duty, such as the buying or selling of futures contracts. A commission must be fair and reasonable, considering all the relevant factors of the transaction. (2) Sometimes used to refer to the Commodity Futures Trading Commission (CFTC).

Commodity: An entity of trade or commerce, services, or rights in which contracts for future delivery may be traded. Some of the contracts currently traded are wheat, corn, cotton, livestock, copper, gold, silver, oil, propane, plywood, currencies, Treasury bills, Treasury bonds, and stock indexes.

Commodity Exchange of New York (CMX): A division of the New York Mercantile Exchange.

Commodity Futures Trading Commission (CFTC): The federal agency established by the Commodity Futures Trading Commission Act of 1974 to ensure the open and efficient operation of the futures markets.

Composite analyst rating: A summary of the total number of analysts who designate a particular stock as a buy, hold, or sell.

Congestion: Sideways movement in the market.

Consolidation: A technical analysis term. A pause in trading activity in which price moves sideways, setting the stage for the next move. Traders are said to evaluate their positions during periods of consolidation.

Contract date: Date on which the contract is agreed between the parties.

Contract month: The month in which deliveries are to be made in accordance with a futures contract.

Contract: (1) An agreement between at least two parties to buy or sell, on certain conditions, a certain product, as a result of which a legal status concerning rights and duties of the parties exists. (2) A term of reference describing a unit of trading for a commodity.

Corner: To secure control of a market so that its price can be manipulated.

Correction: A technical analysis term. A price reaction against the prevailing trend of the market. Sometimes referred to as a retracement.

Cover: The action of offsetting a futures securities or other financial instrument transaction with an equal and opposite transaction. Short covering is a purchase to offset an earlier sale of an equal number of the same delivery month. Liquidation is a sale to offset the obligation to take delivery.

Covered: An investment strategy in which the seller owns the underlying security.

D

Day trader: Traders who take positions in the market and then liquidate them prior to the close of the trading day.

Dealer: An individual or company that buys and sells financial instruments for its own account and customer accounts.

Debit spread: The simultaneous purchase of one option, hedged by the sale of another option, when payment comes into an account when the spread is expended.

Delta: A measure of the relationship between an option price and its underlying futures contract or stock price. Measures how rapidly the value of an option moves in relation to the underlying value.

Demand: A consumer's desire and willingness to pay for a good or service.

Dendrite: A slender projection of a nerve cell which conducts nerve impulses from a synapse to the body of the cell.

Derivative: A complex investment whose value is derived from or linked to some underlying financial asset, such as a stock, bond, currency, or mortgage. Derivatives may be listed on exchanges or traded privately over-the-counter. For example, derivatives may be futures, options, or mortgage-backed securities.

Discount brokers: Brokers who charge lower commissions than full-service brokers.

Discount rate: The interest rate charged by the Federal Reserve on loans to member banks. This rate influences the rates these financial institutions then charge to their customers.

Divergence: A situation in which the price of an asset and an indicator, index or other related asset move in opposite directions. Can be positive or negative and is used in technical analysis to make investment decisions.

Dopamine: A neurotransmitter associated with movement, attention, learning, and the brain's pleasure and reward system.

Drawdown: The peak-to-trough decline during a specific record period of a trade, usually quoted as the percentage between the peak and the trough.

E

Earnings per share (EPS): The portion of a company's profit allocated to each outstanding share of common stock. EPS serves as an indicator of a company's profitability and is often considered the single most important variable in determining the price of a share.

Equity curve: A chart that plots the ups and downs of the value of an account.

Elasticity: A characteristic which describes the interaction of supply, demand, and price. A commodity is said to be elastic in demand when a price change creates an increase or decrease in consumption. Inelasticity of supply or demand exists when either supply or demand is relatively unresponsive to changes in price.

Electronic trading: The computerized matching of buyers and sellers of financial instruments. GLOBEX, Project A, and Access are examples.

Equity: The dollar value of a futures account if all open positions were offset at the current market price. In securities markets, it is the part of a company's net worth that belongs to shareholders.

Exchange: An association of persons or entities engaged in the business of buying and selling futures and/or options, usually involving an auction process. Also called a board of trade or contract market.

Execution date: The date on which a trader wishes to exercise an option.

Execution: (1) The completion of an order for a transaction. (2) The carrying out of an instruction.

Exposure: A possible loss of value caused by changes in market value, interest rates, or exchange rates.

F

Fed: The short name for the U.S. Federal Reserve Banks.

Federal Open Market Committee (FOMC): A committee of the Federal Reserve Banks that makes decisions concerning the Fed's operations to control the money supply. Their primary purpose is the purchase and sale of government securities, which increases or decreases the money supply. It also sets key interest rates, such as the discount rate and Fed fund rate.

Federal Reserve: The central bank of the United States that sets monetary policy. The Federal Reserve and FOMC oversee money supply, interest rates, and credit with the goal of keeping the U.S. economy and currency stable. Also called the Fed.

Fill: The act of completing an order (such as buy or sell) for a security or commodity.

Financial instruments: Also known as financial products or simply as instruments; includes bonds, stocks, derivatives, and other financial representations of assets.

Flag: A chart formation that results from the market's tendency to pause between impulse moves.

Floor broker: An individual who executes orders on the trading floor of an exchange for any other person or entity.

Floor traders: Members of an exchange who are personally present, on the trading floors of the exchanges, to make trades for themselves.

Floor: (1) The lowest rate a financial market is allowed to fall. (2) The trading floor of an exchange.

Forward: A rate or the price of a financial instrument or event which is in the future.

Friction: The implicit and explicit costs associated with market transactions.

Fundamental analysis: An approach to the analysis of markets which examines the underlying factors which will affect the supply and demand of the market, overall economy, industry conditions, etc.

Futures contract: A standardized, binding agreement to buy or sell a specified quantity or grade of a commodity at a later date. Futures contracts are freely transferable and can be traded only by public auction on designated exchanges.

Futures option: An option on a futures contract.

G

Globex: A global, after-hours electronic system for trading in derivatives, futures and commodity contracts. A Reuter's system for the Chicago Mercantile Exchange.

H

Head and shoulders: A technical analysis chart pattern that has three peaks resembling a head and two shoulders. A head and shoulders top typically forms after a substantial rise and indicates a market reversal. A head and shoulders bottom (an inverted head and shoulders) indicates a market advance.

Hedge: An investment made in order to reduce the risk of an adverse price movement.

Hedging: A transaction strategy used by dealers and traders in foreign exchange, commodities, and securities, as well as farmers, manufactures, and other producers, to protect against severe fluctuations in exchange rates and market prices. A current sale or purchase is offset by contracting to purchase or sell at a specified future date.

Hypothalamus: A region of the brain located below the thalamus, functioning to regulate body temperature, some metabolic processes, and governing the autonomic nervous system.

I

Implied Volatility (IV): The estimated volatility of a security or commodity's price.

In-the-money: An option having intrinsic value. A call is in-the-money if its strike price is below the current price of the underlying futures contract. A put is in the money if its strike price is above the current price of the underlying futures contract.

Inelasticity: A characteristic that describes the interdependence of supply, demand, and price. A commodity is inelastic when a price change does not create an increase or decrease in consumption; inelasticity exists when supply and demand are relatively unresponsive to changes in price.

Initial margin: Customers' funds required at the time a futures or forex position is established, or an option is sold. Margin in futures or forex markets is not a down payment, as it is in securities.

Insider trading: (1) The legal trading of securities by corporate officers based on information available to the public. (2) The illegal trading of securities by any investor based on information not available to the public.

International Securities Exchange (ISE): The world's largest electronic equity options exchange.

Interest: The charge or cost for using money; expressed as a percentage rate per period.

International Options Market (IOM): A division of the Chicago Mercantile Exchange.

Introducing Broker (IB): A firm or individual that solicits and accepts commodity futures orders from customers but does not accept money, securities, or property from the customer.

L

Leverage: The use of borrowed assets to enhance the return to the owner's equity, allowing an investor to establish a position in the marketplace by depositing funds that are less than the value of the contract.

Liquid market: A market where selling and buying can be accomplished easily due to the presence of many interested buyers and sellers.

Liquidity: The ease of converting an asset to cash

Long hedge: Buying futures contracts to protect against possible increased prices of commodities. See also Hedging.

Long position: An excess of assets (and/or forward purchase contracts) over liabilities (and/or forward sale contracts) in the same currency. A dealer's position when net purchases and sales leave him or her in a net-purchased position.

Long: To own (buy) to a security, currency, futures contract, commodity, or derivative.

Long-term Equity Anticipation Security (LEAPS) options: Options that expire more than nine months from the current date.

M

Margin call: A call from a brokerage firm or clearing house to a customer or clearing member firm to bring margin deposits back up to minimum levels required by exchange regulations.

Margin: (1) In the futures industry, the amount of money deposited by both buyers and sellers of futures contracts to ensure performance against the contract. (2) In the stock market, the amount of cash that must be put up in a purchase of securities.

Market: (1) Any area or condition where buyers and sellers are in contact for doing business together. (2) The generic term for a financial instrument.

Market order: An order to buy or sell securities, futures contracts, or other financial instruments to be filled immediately at the best possible price. A limit order, in contrast, may specify requirements for price or time of execution.

Mechanical system: A method of buying and selling stocks according to a screen based on results from predetermined indicators and other criteria.

Minis or E-Minis: Mini-sized versions of stock index futures traded electronically. Contracts are available on a wide range of indices such as the Nasdaq 100, S&P 500, S&P MidCap 400 and Russell 2000.

Momentum indicator: A line that represents the difference between today's price and the price of a fixed number of days ago. Momentum can be measured as the difference between today's price and the current value of a moving average. Often referred to as momentum oscillators.

Moving average: An average of prices over a fixed period. The value changes over time, eliminating fluctuations in data. Moving averages emphasize the direction of a trend, confirm trend reversals, and smooth out price and volume fluctuations that can confuse interpretation of the market.

Moving Average Convergence Divergence (MACD): A trend-following momentum indicator that shows the difference between two moving averages.

N

Neocortex: The brain's center of reasoning. The neocortex controls logic, creative thought, and language.

New York Stock Exchange (NYSE): The largest stock exchange in the United States. It is a corporation, operated by a board of directors, responsible for administering the Exchange and member activities, listing securities, overseeing the transfer of members' seats on the Exchange, and determining whether an applicant is qualified to be a specialist.

NYFE: New York Futures Exchange.

Nymex: New York Mercantile Exchange.

O

Offer: An indication of willingness to sell at a given price, also referred to as an ask, or asking price. The opposite of bid.

Offset: (1) The liquidation of a purchase of a futures contract, forward, or other financial instrument through the sale of an equal number of the same delivery months; (2) The covering of a short sale of futures forward or other financial instrument through the purchase of an equal number of the same delivery month. Either action transfers the obligation to make or take delivery of the actual financial instrument to someone else.

Online broker: A retail securities, futures or options broker that provides services over the Internet.

Online trading: Using a computer and an Internet connection to place your buy and sell trading orders with an online brokerage firm, without the physical inclusion of a broker. Orders are entered and returned electronically via computer terminals.

Open: The period at the beginning of a trading session during which all transactions are considered made "at the open."

Open interest: The total number of options or futures contracts that have not closed or been delivered.

Opening range: The range of closely related prices at which transactions took place at the opening of the market; buying and selling orders at the opening might be filled at any point within such a range.

Option contract: The right, but not the obligation, to buy or sell a specific quantity of an underlying instrument on or before a specific date in the future. The seller of the option has the obligation to sell the underlying instrument (in a put option) or buy it from the option buyer (in a call option) at the exercise price if the option is exercised.

Option period: The period between the start date and the expiry date of an option contract.

Option premium: The money, securities, or property the buyer pays to the writer (grantor) for granting an option contract.

Option seller/writer: The party who is obligated to perform if an option is exercised by the option buyer.

Option: An agreement that represents the right to buy or sell a specified amount of an underlying security, such as a stock, bond, futures contract, at a specified price within a specified time. The purchaser acquires a right, and the seller assumes an obligation.

Order execution: The handling of an order by a broker, including receiving the order verbally or in writing from the customer, transmitting it to the trading floor of the exchange, and returning confirmation of the completed order to the customer.

Order to buy: An instruction to buy a given quantity of an identified financial instrument under specified conditions.

Order to sell: An instruction to sell a given quantity of an identified financial instrument under specified conditions.

Oscillator: A technical analysis tool that attempts to determine when an asset has become over- or under-priced. As the value of the oscillator approaches the upper extreme value the asset is deemed to be overbought, and as it approaches the lower extreme it is deemed to be oversold.

Out-of-the-money: A call option with a strike price higher, or a put option with a strike price lower, than the current market value of the underlying asset.

Over-The-Counter-Market (OTC): Trading in financial instruments transacted off organized exchanges, including transactions among market-makers and between market-makers and their customers.

Overbought: A technical analysis term that the market price has risen too steeply and too fast in relation to underlying fundamental or other factors.

Oversold: A technical analysis term for a market price that has experienced stronger selling than the fundamentals justify.

P

Parity: Equal standing.

Pip: Unit that expresses differences between exchange rates. The minimum incremental price change in the inter-bank markets.

Pit: A specially constructed arena on the trading floor of some exchanges where trading is conducted by open outcry. On other exchanges, the term "ring" designates the trading area.

Platform: A computer interface that provides the user with information and the means to place trades electronically.

Pledging: The act of putting up security for a loan or other financial transaction.

Point: The minimum fluctuation in prices or options premiums. Also called ticks.

Portfolio: A selection of financial instruments held by a person or institution, often designed to spread investment risk.

Position trader: A trader who buys or sells financial instruments and holds them for an extended period of time, as distinguished from the day trader, who will normally initiate and liquidate positions within a single trading session.

Position: A market commitment. For example, a buyer of futures contracts is said to have a long position, and, conversely, a seller of futures contracts is said to have a short position.

Prefrontal cortex: A section of the brain located in the back part of the frontal lobes which functions as the control center of the brain.

Premium: (1) The amount that an option buyer pays to an option seller. (2) The difference between the higher price paid for a financial instrument and the financial instrument's face amount at issue. (3) The additional payment allowed by exchange regulations for delivery of higher-than-required standards or grades of a commodity against a futures contract.

Price limit: Maximum price advance or decline from the previous day's settlement price, permitted for futures in one trading session by the rules of the exchange.

Price-to-Earnings Ratio (P/E): A measure of comparison of the value of different common stocks that is calculated by dividing the market price of the stock by the earnings per share.

Protective stop: An order to exit a trade if a price reaches a predetermined level, placed to defend against extreme loss.

Pullback: A fall in price from its peak.

Put (option): An option that gives the option buyer the right, but not the obligation, to sell the underlying financial instrument at a particular price on or before a particular date.

Q

Quote: The actual price, or the bid or ask price, of a security, commodity, futures, option, currency, or other financial instrument at a particular time.

R

Rally: An upward movement of prices.

Range: The difference between the high and low price during a given period.

Reaction: A short-term countertrend movement of prices.

Relative Strength Index (RSI) or (RS): A technical momentum indicator that compares the magnitude of recent gains to recent losses in an attempt to determine overbought and oversold conditions of an asset.

Resilience: The mental capacity to cope with and recover quickly from stress, misfortune or catastrophe.

Resistance: The price level where a trend stalls. The market stops rising because sellers start to outnumber buyers. The opposite of a support level.

Retracement: In technical analysis, price movement in the opposite direction of the prevailing trend. Also described as a correction.

Retrenchment: A decline in price.

Return on equity: A calculation of a corporation's profitability, specifically its return on assets, calculated by dividing after-tax income by tangible assets.

Risk management: Management to control and monitor the risks of a bank, financial institution, business entity, or individual.

Risk: The potential to lose money.

S

Securities and Exchange Commission (SEC): The Federal agency created by Congress to regulate the securities markets and protect investors.

Security: A note, stock, bond, investment contract, debenture, certificate of interest in profit-sharing or partnership agreement, certificate of deposit, collateral trust certificate, pre-organization certificate, option on a security, or other instrument of investment.

Self-actualize: To develop or achieve one's full potential.

Sell-off: A period of intensified selling in a market that pushes prices sharply lower.

Settlement price: (1) The closing price, or a price within the range of closing prices, which is used as the official price in determining net gains or losses at the close of each trading session. (2) Payment of any amount of money under a contract.

Short covering: Trades that reverse, or close out, short-sale positions.

Short: One who has sold a cash commodity, a commodity futures contract, or other financial instrument; a long, in contrast, is one who has bought a cash commodity or futures contract.

Slippage: The difference between estimated transaction costs and the amount actually paid, usually attributed to a change in the spread.

Speculator: One who attempts to anticipate price changes and make profits through the sale and/or purchase of financial instruments.

Stochastics: A technical momentum indicator that compares the closing price of a commodity, security or option contract to its price range over a given time period.

Stop limit: An order that becomes a limit order once the specified price is hit.

Stop order or stop: A dormant order that is triggered and becomes active only when a stock or commodity hits a price specified by the customer. A sell stop is placed below the market; a buy stop is placed above the market. Sometimes referred to as a stop loss order.

Strike price: A specified price at which an investor can buy or sell an option's underlying financial instrument. The exchange rate, interest rate, or market price that is guaranteed by an option transaction.

Supply: The total amount of a good or service available for purchase by consumers.

T

Technical analysis: An approach to analysis of markets that anticipates trends of market prices based on mathematical patterns. Technicians normally examine patterns of price range, rates of change, changes in volume of trading, and open interest. Data are charted to show trends and formations which serve as indicators of likely future price movements.

Tick: A minimum upward or downward movement in the price of a securities, futures, or other financial instruments. Also called points.

Traders: Individuals who negotiate prices and execute buy and sell orders, either on behalf of an investor or for their own account.

Trading system: A method of buying and selling stocks according to a screen based on results from predetermined indicators and other criteria.

Trailing stop: An order to exit a trade at a predetermined price level. Trailing stops automatically follow the stock tick-by-tick by a specified amount as the market moves in a trader's favor, ensuring that a winner does not turn into a loser.

Transaction costs: (1) The costs of negotiating, monitoring, and enforcing a contract. (2) The total cost of executing a financial transaction.

Trend line: A line that connects either a series of highs or lows in a trend. The trendline can represent either support (a positive trendline) or resistance (a negative trendline).

V

Volatility: (1) A measure by which an exchange rate is expected to fluctuate over a given period. (2) A measure of a commodity's tendency to move up and down in price based on its daily price history over a period of time.

Volume: The number of contracts, shares, or other financial instruments traded during a specified period of time.

Y

Yield: The annual rate of return on an investment, as paid in dividends or interest. It is expressed as a percentage.

CONTRIBUTORS

Linda Bradford Raschke has been a full-time, professional trader since 1981. She began as a floor trader and later started LBR Group, a professional money management firm (lbrgroup.com). Raschke was recognized in Jack Schwager's book, *The New Market Wizards* (Wiley, 1995).

Eliot Brenner, PhD, is a licensed clinical psychologist who has published articles on emotional intelligence in financial magazines and psychology journals. He has a private practice in Fairfield, Connecticut, where he coaches and consults with traders.

Terry Burnham, PhD, is the director of economics at Acadian Asset Management. Before his tenure at Acadian, he was an economics professor at the Harvard Business School.

John F. Carter has been a full time trader for the past decade and is one of the principals at www.tradethemarkets.com, an online trading and financial markets analysis firm and at www.razorforex.com, which focuses on the forex markets.

Mark D. Cook won the 1992 U.S. Investing Championship and was profiled in Jack Schwager's modern classic, *Stock Market Wizards* (Collins, 2001). He hosts regular seminars at his trading office in East Sparta, Ohio. Cook also issues an advisory service for professional traders.

Flavia Cymbalista, PhD, is an uncertainty specialist, a financial economist specialized in market psychology and the psychology of uncertainty. Cymbalista developed a methodology called MarketFocusing (www.marketfocusing.com). She holds a doctorate in economic sciences from the Berlin Free University.

Mike Elvin, PhD, was a research psychologist and managed mental health services in the UK prior to his current employment at a futures exchange. He offers individual tuition and seminars for traders.

John Forman is a near twenty-year veteran of the markets and author of *The Essentials of Trading: From the Basics to Building a Winning Strategy* (Wiley, 2006). He can be reached through his website, www.TheEssentialsOfTrading.com.

Doug Foster II is an independent consultant in electronic trading and co-owner of Zoo Trading Group in Chicago. He began his career as a fixed income trader at the Chicago Board of Trade. Foster has also worked at EasyScreen, PLC, and at Kingstree Trading.

Richard W. Friesen is a corporate trainer and the founder of Trade Management LLC, and ePIT Systems, a software company for financial institutions. Combining his experiences as a therapist and businessman, he has developed a public speaking training program. Friesen is an award-winning speaker on politics, business, and personal development.

Ned Gandevani, PhD, is a professional trader and the developer of the Winning Edge system, which is based on chaos theory (www.winningedgesystem.com). He has conducted trading psychology seminars throughout the U.S. and Europe and currently teaches MBA courses in New York City.

Kyle Handley is a consultant for McSherry Anderson, LLC, an investment advisory firm (www.maportfolios.com). Handley is a doctoral student in economics at the University of Maryland and holds a master's degree from the London School of Economics.

Philippa Huckle is the founder and CEO of The Philippa Huckle Group, a leading investment advisory firm headquartered in Hong Kong. She is the author of *Perspective*, an online publication read by more than five thousand people in forty countries.

Peter Kaplan is the co-founder of Nexus Capital Management, LLC. He is a securities trader specializing in intermediate and longer-term trading, with a comprehensive approach to the equities market.

Adrienne Laris Toghraie, MNLP, MCH, is a trader's coach and internationally recognized authority in the field of human development for the financial community. She is founder and president of Trading on Target (www.TradingOnTarget.com).

Ilan Levy-Mayer is the vice president of Cannon Trading Co., Inc., E-futures. com, and E-mini.com. He is also the chief investment strategist of LEVEX Capital Management Inc., a commodity trading advisor specializing in short-term, diversified, momentum trading.

Desmond MacRae is a New York-based business writer specializing in banking, finance, and investments.

Gail Osten has been in senior marketing, advertising, and corporate communications in the derivatives and commercial real estate industries for more than thirty years, including positions with Chicago Mercantile Exchange and the Chicago Board of Trade. She is a former executive editor of *SFO* magazine.

Bernie Schaeffer is chairman of Schaeffer's Investment Research (www.schaefferresearch.com). His approach focuses on stocks with technical and fundamental trends that run counter to investor expectations.

Sam Seiden is a trader, research analyst, and instructor with more than a decade of experience. He provides research and guidance to clients through speaking engagements, workshops, magazine articles, and advisory services via www.samseiden.com

Denise Shull, MA, is a member of the Chicago Board of Trade and a short-term trader. She founded Trader Psyches Inc., which offers lectures, workshops, discussion groups, and individual coaching focused on understanding the relationship between intellect, emotions, and trading actions.

Brett N. Steenbarger, PhD, is associate clinical professor of psychiatry and behavioral sciences at SUNY Upstate Medical University in Syracuse, NY. As director of trader development for Kingstree Trading, LLC, in Chicago, he mentors professional traders and coordinates a trader training program.

Christopher Terry is a full-time professional trader with LBR Group, specializing in index futures and equities markets. He speaks regularly at derivatives conferences and has written articles for several publications.

Van K. Tharp, PhD, is the founder of the International Institute of Trading Mastery. He has been coaching traders and investors since 1982 and was featured in Jack Schwager's book *Market Wizards* (Prentice Hall Press, 1989).

Toni Turner is a best-selling author and a popular speaker and educator at financial conferences and forums nationwide. For more information, see www.toniturner.com.

Russell R. Wasendorf, Sr., is chairman and CEO of Peregrine Financial Group, Inc., one of the largest Futures Commissions Merchants in the world. He is publisher of *SFO* and the author of several books on futures trading.

INDEX

Mentoring and coaching, 12, 14, 23, 41-46, 66-67, 113, 132, 168, 182, 247, 259-260

N

Nasdaq (National Association of Securities Dealers Automated Quotations), 33-34, 130, 141, 160, 252
Neocortex, 162, 190-194, 252
Neuroeconomics, 183, 186, 197

O

Options, 118, 155, 157-158, 161-162, 164, 167, 171, 191, 193, 209, 244, 246-249, 251-254
Osten, Gail, 57, 59-67, 69-73, 75-76, 107, 117, 259

P

Performance anxiety, 55, 78, 81-82
Position trading, 10, 25, 94, 217
Prefrontal cortex, 170, 183, 190, 254
Psychoanalysis, 176-177, 181
Put/call ratio analysis, 157-158

R

Repetition compulsion, 177
Resilience, 47, 84-92, 255
Risk, 5, 9, 20, 24-25, 28, 30, 33, 36, 38-40, 44, 47, 52-55, 57, 60, 63, 70-72, 74, 76, 80-81, 94-95, 97-99, 112, 118, 123, 125, 128, 130, 133, 136, 139-140, 142-143, 145, 150, 152-153, 170, 185, 192-194, 198, 201, 203, 212, 225, 234, 250, 254-255

S

Schaeffer, Bernie, 118, 154, 162, 259

Seiden, Sam, 112, 259
Sentiment indicators, 154-162
Shull, Denise, 175, 182, 259
Soros, George, 104, 163, 200-214
Steenbarger, Brett N., 6, 15, 48, 56, 58, 60, 62-68, 70-73, 75-76, 84, 92, 163-164, 174, 259
Subcortex, 178
Swing trading, 26, 29, 34, 94

T

Technical analysis, 35, 40, 105-106, 146, 156, 207, 210, 246-248, 250, 253, 255-256
Terry, Christopher, 31, 40, 260
Tharp, Van K., 16, 23, 260
Turner, Toni, 77, 83, 115, 260

W

Wasendorf, Sr., Russell R., 1, 3, 260

Z

Zen, 164-167, 169, 173